D1528817

Mind, Reason and Imagination

Much recent philosophy of mind has fallen for a mistaken conception of the nature of psychological concepts. It has assumed too much similarity between psychological judgements and those of natural science, and has thus overlooked the centrality of the fact that other people are not just objects we may try to predict and control but fellow creatures with whom we talk and co-operate.

In this collection of essays, Jane Heal argues that central to our ability to arrive at views about others' thoughts is not knowledge of some theory of the mind but rather an ability to imagine alternative worlds and how things appear from another person's point of view. She then considers the implications of this account for such questions as how we represent others' thoughts, the shape of psychological concepts, the nature of rationality and the possibility of first-person authority.

This book should appeal to students and professionals in philosophy of mind and philosophy of language.

Jane Heal is Professor of Philosophy at the University of Cambridge and a Fellow of St. John's College, Cambridge, U.K.

RECENT TITLES:

Mind, Reason and Imagination

Selected Essays in Philosophy of Mind and Language

JANE HEAL

St. John's College, Cambridge

CAMBRIDGE
UNIVERSITY PRESS

PUBLISHED BY THE PRESS SYNDICATE OF THE UNIVERSITY OF CAMBRIDGE
The Pitt Building, Trumpington Street, Cambridge, United Kingdom

CAMBRIDGE UNIVERSITY PRESS
The Edinburgh Building, Cambridge CB2 2RU, UK
40 West 20th Street, New York, NY 10011-4211, USA
477 Williamstown Road, Port Melbourne, VIC 3207, Australia
Ruiz de Alarcón 13, 28014 Madrid, Spain
Dock House, The Waterfront, Cape Town 8001, South Africa

http://www.cambridge.org

First published 2003

Printed in the United States of America

Typeface Bembo 10.5/13 pt.   *System* LaTeX 2_ε [TB]

A catalog record for this book is available from the British Library.

Library of Congress Cataloging in Publication Data
Heal, Jane.
Mind, reason and imagination : selected essays in philosophy of mind and language /
Jane Heal.
p.   cm. − (Cambridge studies in philosophy)
Includes bibliographical references and index.
ISBN 0−521−81697−1 (hdb) − ISBN 0-521-01716-5 (pbk.)
1. Philosophy of mind.   2. Language and languages − Philosophy.   I. Title.   II. Series.
BD418.3 .H44   2003
128′.2−dc21   2002073696

ISBN 0 521 81697 1 hardback
ISBN 0 521 01716 5 paperback

Contents

Preface

This collection assembles a number of papers published over the past fifteen years which deal with interrelated topics in philosophy of mind and philosophy of language. In two cases (4 and 8) it seemed worthwhile to incorporate some second thoughts into the papers themselves, since the revisions were self-contained and not lengthy. Otherwise the papers appear very much in their original form, except for some minor stylistic tidying.

The papers were written to be self-standing but they dovetail in various ways. Themes touched on in earlier pieces reappear for further treatment later. Ideas developed in some detail at one point are, at other places, merely summarised as the basis for further explorations. These overlaps are, I hope, not excessive and I have not tried to remove them. The Introduction sums up the themes of the various pieces and tries to indicate how they fit together.

The papers have benefited in many ways from discussions with colleagues and from their comments. In particular, I would like to thank Martin Davies, whose invitation to contribute to a collection he was assembling got me thinking about "mental simulation" again in 1994. The paper which was the most direct outcome of his suggestion (Heal 1994) is not included here, since doing so would have increased the amount of repetition. But without the spur presented by that initial invitation, and other encouragement and comment, this collection would not exist. Others whom I would like to thank for invitations to talk, comments, criticism, discussion or encouragement include Kent Bach, Peter Carruthers, Jonathan Cohen, Guy Deutscher, Alvin Goldman, Robert Gordon, Chris Hill, Jennifer Hornsby, Denis

McManus, Adam Morton, Barry Smith, Stephen Stich, Tim Williamson and anonymous referees for *Mind*, *Mind and Language* and *Philosophical Quarterly*.

Jane Heal
March 2002

Sources

'Replication and Functionalism.' In J. Butterfield (ed.) *Language, Mind and Logic*, 135–150. Cambridge: Cambridge University Press, 1986. Reprinted by permission of Cambridge University Press.

'Understanding Other Minds from the Inside.' In A. O'Hear (ed.) *Current Issues in the Philosophy of Mind*, 83–99. Cambridge: Cambridge University Press, 1998. Reprinted by permission of the Royal Institute of Philosophy.

'Simulation, Theory and Content.' In P. Carruthers and P. K. Smith (eds.) *Theories of Theories of Mind*, 75–89. Cambridge: Cambridge University Press, 1996. Reprinted by permission of Cambridge University Press.

'Simulation and Cognitive Penetrability.' *Mind and Language* 11 (1996): 44–67. Reprinted by permission of *Mind and Language*.

'Co-Cognition and Off-Line Simulation.' *Mind and Language* 13 (1998): 477–498. Reprinted by permission of *Mind and Language*.

'Other Minds, Rationality and Analogy.' *Aristotelian Society, Supplementary Volume* 74 (2000): 1–19. Reprinted by courtesy of the Editor of the Aristotelian Society: © 2000

'Semantic Holism: Still a Good Buy.' *Proceedings of the Aristotelian Society* 94 (1994): 325–339. Reprinted by courtesy of the Editor of the Aristotelian Society: © 1994

'Indexical Predicates and Their Uses.' *Mind* 106 (1997): 619–640. Reprinted by permission of *Mind*.

'On Speaking Thus: The Semantics of Indirect Discourse.' *Philosophical Quarterly* 51 (2001): 433–454. Reprinted by permission of *Philosophical Quarterly*.

'Lagadonian Kinds and Psychological Concepts.' In C. Hill and H. Kornblith (eds.) *Philosophical Topics* (forthcoming). Reprinted by permission of *Philosophical Topics*.

'What Are Psychological Concepts For.' In D. McManus (ed.) *Wittgenstein and Scepticism*. Routledge (forthcoming). Reprinted by permission of Routledge.

'Moore's Paradox: A Wittgensteinian Approach.' *Mind* 103 (1994): 5–24. Reprinted by permission of *Mind*.

'First Person Authority.' *Proceedings of the Aristotelian Society* 102 (2002): 1–19. Reprinted by courtesy of the Editor of the Aristotelian Society: © 2002

Mind, Reason and Imagination

1

Introduction

Much philosophy of mind in the analytic tradition, as practised in the last few decades, has been in the grip of a mistaken conception of the nature of psychological judgements and concepts. In its haste to repudiate metaphysical dualism about the mind it has been tempted to assume too much similarity between psychological concepts and those of natural science. It has overlooked the centrality of the fact that other people are not just objects we may try to predict and control but fellow creatures with whom we enter into dialogue and with whom we make joint decisions. Important ramifications of these facts, for example what they show about how we arrive at our views about others' thoughts, about the logical shape of psychological concepts and about the nature of persons, have thus gone missing in much recent philosophy of mind. These, in brief, are the themes of this collection of essays. The book is aimed primarily at philosophers, but I hope that philosophically minded colleagues in psychology and other human sciences may find something of interest here too.

We have thoughts about others' thoughts. We have views about what others perceive, think, feel, care about or intend. And where we are ignorant about such things we often try to find out more, since knowing these kinds of things about each other is important to us for many reasons. These facts suggest many questions, among them these three:

(1) How do we arrive at such psychological judgements about others?
(2) How should we explain psychological concepts and what it is to possess them?
(3) What is the nature of the beings, persons, to whom the concepts apply and who are the subjects of the judgements?

1

The first question is about the process, the heuristic route, by which we arrive at our views about what is going on in others' minds. The second question is about what it is to think of a being as a thinker. The third question is ontological, and it asks what is the real nature of the beings thus thought about. The papers in this collection start from the first question and move from there to consider ideas relevant to the second and third.

The reflections initiated by our three questions form part of a long-running debate. When we think about other people do we call on the same intellectual tools and strategies as when we think about the non-human world? If we do not, why is this so and what significance does the fact have? These issues have been the focus of explicit philosophical thought since the eighteenth century at least, when the growing elaboration of the human intellectual world led to more self-conscious differentiation among branches of enquiry and to consideration of the relations between them.

These essays, however, are not directly concerned with the history of ideas. The views advocated here are broadly in sympathy with the *Verstehen* approach of those who think that human and non-human aspects of the world do merit different approaches. But there is here no discussion of Vico, Kant, Dilthey, Weber or Collingwood, nor of others working in the *Verstehen* tradition who have developed and built on their thought. The risk of not exploring the historical dimension of the debate is that we shall reinvent the wheel. Insofar as there is an excuse for running this risk it is that there is always the need to make old and valuable ideas live again by rediscovering them and re-expressing them in an idiom which makes apparent their implications for current problems. And the direction of approach in these essays is not from philosophy of history or of the social sciences, where discussion of these themes has previously tended to be located, but rather from the interests and concerns of recent philosophy of mind, philosophy of psychology and philosophy of language.

In the rest of this introduction I shall outline the shape of the collection in a little more detail, indicating which topics are treated and where. The papers are divided into four groups. The first considers the heuristic question of how we arrive at judgements about others' thoughts.

One attractive answer to question (1) above is that we are able to arrive at views about others' thoughts in virtue of possessing a body of information about thoughts. We have a theory (innate or learnt, tacit or explicit, well articulated or perhaps more jumbled) about the circumstances in which various states of mind might occur and about what upshots they might have. We call on this to work out what a person is likely to be thinking and what, as a result, he or she might do. This is often called 'the theory theory' and analytic functionalism is one familiar version of it.

But is it plausible that we possess a body of knowledge such as is postulated by the theory theory? To underpin our actual ability to think about others, this body of knowledge would have to be orders of magnitude more complicated than any other, tacit or explicit, which we take ourselves to possess (see Essay 4). Perhaps we ought to bite on this bullet and credit ourselves with this immense achievement? But if we can find a workable alternative account of how we arrive at judgements about others, then there will be no need to do so. And there is such an alternative. Moreover, it turns out to have other advantages as well, such as illuminating the attraction for us of various metaphors (see Essay 3) and helping to explain the logical form of our ascriptions of thoughts (see Essays 10 and 11).

This alternative proposal gives a central role in thinking about other minds to use of our imaginative capacity. It starts from the fact that we not only make judgements about what is actual and infer other judgements from them, but also wonder what would happen if so and so were the case and explore the consequences and ramifications of situations taken to be merely possible. This suggests a possible strategy for arriving at judgements about others' thoughts. When I want to know what you might think or decide I try to imagine the world as it appears to you and explore some of the further states of affairs and requirements for action implicit in that world. If I am successful in this, I shall (in part) re-create your point of view, your trains of thought and likely decisions. I may thus come to some views on what you are likely to think or do, and I shall do so without calling on any detailed theory about how thoughts interact or what they give rise to. Where such use of the imagination gives me insight into what another is likely to believe or intend, it does so in virtue of the fact that I and that other share the capacity to think about the world in first-order ways rather than in virtue of my possession of a theoretical, second-order, representation of that capacity.

Of the papers in Part 1, Essay 2 was the first written and supplied the starting point for some of the recent revival of interest in *Verstehen*-style themes. Essay 3, which was written somewhat later than the others and for a non-specialist audience, gives an introduction to the contrast between the theory view and the alternative, and also a sketch of one central concern of Part 2, namely the view that we, rightly, take for granted that we are rational, in one sense of that slippery word. It also links these to an outline of some themes about the nature of human interaction which reappear in more detail in Essay 12. It may thus serve as a preliminary sketch for the view which the collection as a whole seeks to recommend. Essay 4 offers the most detailed account of how 'theory' may be understood and why the theory view is implausible. It seeks to spell out what 'theory' might mean and what a detailed 'theory of thought' would have to be like. It suggests links between the complexities such a supposed theory would need to cope with and the difficulties posed by the notorious Frame Problem of Artificial Intelligence. Essay 5 considers some of the counterattacks by defenders of the theory theory, in particular the claim that attempts to judge others' thoughts are 'cognitively penetrable' and therefore must be derived from theory, and argues that they lack force.

Any reader having a passing familiarity with these debates will be aware that the approach which rejects theory theory has been given a name in recent discussion – namely 'simulation theory'. And the word 'simulation' does occur in the title of two of the essays in this collection. So why have I avoided it in the account given above, speaking instead of 'the alternative'? And why have I not boldly introduced the word 'simulation' into the title of this book? The answer to these questions is to be found in the essays in Part 2 of the collection, in particular in Essay 6. To see what is at issue here it may be helpful to step back and consider the wider context of philosophical reflection on mind and on how persons fit into the natural world.

We observe and interact with material items round us, such as sticks, stones, rivers, plants, volcanoes and clouds. We form views about the nature of the stuffs they are made of and about their structure and behaviour. We do this in part because of the intrinsic interest of the questions. But we do it also because understanding these things will enable us to predict what will happen and will sometimes also enable us to control and manipulate our environment to our advantage, forging tools, growing crops, weaving fabrics, building houses and so forth.

The information we have on these matters is organised in the various natural sciences. Each has its own distinctive subject matter and range of concepts and theories. But despite their contrasts, there is no mystery about how they fit together. Each has, so to speak, places where the findings of the others dovetail in. The special science of geology tells us about the Earth and the various stuffs and structures in its crust including, among other things, volcanoes with their magma chambers and craters. If we then want to pursue in more detail why and how magma is formed and at what point the pressures in the interior of a volcano will result in eruption, then we can call on the insights provided by the more general sciences of physics and chemistry. Similarly, genetics tells us about the heritability of characteristics. But if we want to know about the processes in more detail, then other biological sciences unravel that for us in terms of DNA and amino acids. And the behaviour of the complex molecules studied by those sciences is, in turn, illuminated by yet other disciplines. Common to all these interlocking sciences, the framework in which they fit together, is a vision of the universe as an immensely complex material assemblage developing through time in a law-governed way, under the impetus of the forces inherent in its fundamental constituents. These constituents and forces (space, time and the various forms of matter and energy which occupy them) can be described without any mention of values or of thought. They are norm-free and mindless.

We also observe and interact with people. They too are material items in our environment, the behaviour of which may impinge on us. How do they, and the ways we talk and think about them, fit into the world-view sketched above? One view congenial to analytically and scientifically minded philosophers combines two thoughts: that human beings are a kind of natural item and that psychological thinking is a kind of natural scientific thinking. It tells us that talk of perception, thought, feeling or decision is talk of items or processes in human beings which have distinctive causes and which in turn lead their possessors to behave in distinctive ways. The view anticipates that ordinary thinking about people and their thoughts will dovetail into scientific psychology and that this in turn will interlock illuminatingly with the brain sciences.

Various ideas come together to recommend this outlook and to make it seem an attractive option for a scientifically literate philosopher. One is that it secures our right to be realists about the psychological and does so in a way which is obviously compatible with the natural sciences. Another merit of this approach is that the conception of psychological notions as one sort of natural scientific notion has considerable plausibility. It is plain that what other people do is important to us and that we are often interested in predicting and controlling it. People's thoughts, feelings and deliberations are what lead to them doing what they do. Psychological states and happenings are the factors in the light of which we predict and explain others' behaviour. These commonplace remarks seem to support exactly that account of the meaning of psychological claims which sees them as claims of one particular special science.

Suppose now a philosopher who is sympathetic to the view of the psychological sketched above, and the motivations for it, but who comes to be suspicious of one central element in it, viz. the claim that we actually possess that knowledge of the workings of the mind with which it credits us. How might such a philosopher explain our ability to arrive at views about others' thoughts? What is wanted is a position which reconciles our lack of theory with our ability to make judgements about other minds, while changing the rest of the picture as little as possible.

Such a position is provided by one articulation of the imagination-invoking approach. On this articulation our use of imagination is presented as merely a heuristic device. It is something we find useful because we have not yet worked out the full theory of mind. But (on this view) there is no difficulty in supposing that such a full theory could exist and that we might come to know it. The question of whether we use theory or imagination is thus taken to be an empirical one. And, this articulation adds, what goes on when I use imagination heuristically is that I conduct an experiment on myself. I find out what happens in myself when I 'take my inference mechanisms off-line' and feed them with certain 'pretend beliefs and desires'. It is this complex of views which now goes under the name 'simulation theory'.

There is, however, another way of spelling out the non-theory view. This questions much more of the suggested naturalistic account of the psychological, starting with its assumption about the role and importance to us of psychological judgements. It is true (says this second proposal) that other people are material objects in our environment, that our inter-actions with them are of great importance to us and that sometimes we predict, control and use them as we do sticks and stones. But it is not true that this mode of interaction with them is our sole or most central one. I may do something with a stone, for example place it to wedge the door open. I might 'do something with you' in that same sense, viz. place your comatose body to wedge the door open. But the more usual sense in which I 'do something with you' is the sense in which I discuss with you whether it would be a good idea to use the stone to wedge our door open, and in which we might then co-operate to push the stone into place. When I conduct my own deliberations with a view to improving my own grasp on the world and taking sensible decisions, I cannot but take myself to be rational. So in order to see others as joint deliberators I need to credit them with the same capacity. And if other people are for us centrally beings with whom we may converse and co-operate, then what we need to know about them, and they about us, are facts which help us to locate each other as possible partners in dialogue and action. If we take psychological thoughts and remarks to occur in this context, then we shall be led to a very different articulation of the anti-theory theory view from the 'simulation' idea sketched earlier. This second articulation will see it as an a priori matter that we use the method of imagination, and it will stress also the way in which the method turns out to embody a presupposition of shared rationality.

The difference between these two articulations of the non-theory approach was not at all clear to me at the time of writing Essays 2, 4 and 5. In those papers the ways of setting out the anti-theory view, and the examples given, tend to suggest sometimes one articulation and sometimes the other. Essay 6 represents a mea culpa on this front and aims to set the record straight. Essay 7 starts from the notion of semantic holism and seeks to clarify and defend it. It does so, in part, by exploring the idea that each of us has no option but to take it that he or she is rational. It thus serves to bring out the centrality of this presupposition in our self-conception. Essay 8 pursues a contrast between the uses of imagination postulated in the two articulations and makes a case for thinking that the second is one we can and do call on.

The group of papers in Part 3 starts by turning from philosophy of mind to philosophy of language. A central theme here is that by extending ideas in philosophical logic, in particular our understanding of indexicality, we can forge some useful new conceptual tools. It is at this point that there is, perhaps, the clearest example of something mentioned earlier, namely the value of re-examining older ideas in a new context. Earlier thinkers sympathetic to the *Verstehen* approach did not have accounts of indexicality to hand. But when available they supply a tool for articulating insights which we otherwise struggle to express in more obscure fashion.

Indexical predication is, I suggest, such a tool, and it is the theme of Essay 9. We are used to the idea that the referential element of a sentence may be supplied indexically. What is suggested here is that the describing or characterising element of a sentence can also be supplied indexically. An example would be my saying "She gestured thus" and then myself gesturing in a certain manner. By this complex performance I am able to convey how she gestured. The paper argues that indexical predication is a significant linguistic tool, and one we need to recognise and account for, whatever metaphysical or semantic framework we favour in our philosophy of language.

Essays 10 and 11 seek to exploit the idea of indexical predication to throw light on the logical form of reports of speech and thought and on the nature of psychological concepts. Indexical predication is a particularly useful linguistic resource in situations where we are concerned to report the occurrence of some intricate and skilful human performance. We may find it difficult to specify in words the nature of the performance, including all the details which might interest us, while finding it easy to produce a reproduction of the performance. The reproduction may then serve as a vehicle by which the nature of the performance may be made manifest to the person with whom we communicate. Pursuing this idea leads to an account of the semantics of indirect discourse which has all the advantages of Davidson's account without the disadvantages.

Extending indexical predication from language to thought yields the idea that a person might represent another's thought in a judgement of this shape "She thinks thus: . . . ." where in the gap occurs a thought having the character which that judger aims to attribute to the other's thought. Essay 11 explores this proposal and asks whether it can throw light on question (2) of what it is to possess psychological concepts.

Part 4 returns to philosophy of mind. Rationality has played a central part in the arguments of Part 2, but it is a notoriously difficult and contested notion. Essay 12 offers a more detailed account of it than was attempted earlier. The two final papers centre round first-person authority, outlining a 'constitutive' solution to the problem of how it is possible. It is in these three papers that the themes mentioned in the first paragraph of this introduction, namely our misconstrual of our relations with each other and the distortions this produces in our philosophical accounts of mind, come most explicitly to the fore. An answer to question (3) (What is the nature of the beings, persons, to whom psychological concepts apply?) has been hinted at by the discussion of Parts 2 and 3. It is that persons are (more or less) rational agents, each having his or her own (more or less) unified point of view on the world. These final three papers offer some further sketches of how this idea might be elaborated. Essay 12 argues that adopting it provides a different way of dovetailing psychological talk with the discoveries of natural science from that favoured in the naturalistic 'theory theory' outlook sketched earlier. Essays 13 and 14 suggest also that looking at things from this perspective might help to dissolve some familiar problems in philosophy of mind.

Part One

Mind, Theory and Imagination

2

Replication and Functionalism

In this essay I want to examine two contrasted models of what we do when we try to get insight into other people's thoughts and behaviour by citing their beliefs, desires, fears, hopes, and so forth. On one model we are using what I shall call the functional strategy, and on the other what I label the replicative strategy. I shall argue that the view that we use the replicative strategy is much more plausible than the view that we use the functionalist strategy. But the two strategies issue in different styles of explanation and call upon different ranges of concepts. So at the end of the essay I shall make some brief remarks about these contrasts.

The core of the functionalist strategy is the assumption that explanation of action or mental state through mention of beliefs, desires, emotions, and so on is causal. The approach is resolutely third-personal. The Cartesian introspectionist error − the idea that from some direct confrontation with psychological items in our own case we learn their nature − is repudiated. We are said to view other people as we view stars, clouds or geological formations. People are just complex objects in our environment whose behaviour we wish to anticipate but whose causal innards we cannot perceive. We therefore proceed by observing the intricacies of their external behaviour and formulating some hypotheses about how the insides are structured. The hypotheses are typically of this form: 'The innards are like this. There is some thing or state which is usually caused by so and so in the environment (let us call this state X) and another caused by such and such else (let us call this Y). Together these cause another, Z, which, if so and so is present, probably leads on to. . . .' And so on. It is in some such way as this that terms like 'belief' and 'desire' are introduced. Our views about the causes, interactions and outcomes of inner states are sometimes said to be summed up in 'folk psychology' (Stich 1982a: 153ff.). Scientific psychology is in the business of pursuing the same sort of programme as folk psychology but in more detail and with more statistical accuracy. On this view a psychological statement is an existential claim – that something with so-and-so causes and effects is occurring in a person (Lewis 1972). The philosophical advantages, in contrast with dualism and earlier materialisms such as behaviourism and type-type identity theory, are familiar. It is via these contrasts and in virtue of these merits that the theory emerged. See Putnam (1967) for a classic statement.

This is a broad outline. But how is psychological explanation supposed to work in particular instances? What actual concepts are employed and how, in particular, are we to accommodate our pre-theoretical idea that people have immense numbers of different beliefs and desires, whose contents interrelate?

Functionalists would generally agree that there is no hope of defining the idea of a particular psychological state, like believing that it is raining, in isolation from other psychological notions. Such notions come as a package, full understanding of any member of which requires a grip on its role in the system as a whole (Harman 1973). This is true of any interesting functional concepts, even, for example, in explaining functionally something as comparatively simple as a car. If we try to build up some picture of the insides of a car, knowing nothing of mechanics and observing only the effects of pushing various pedals and levers and inserting various liquids, we might well come up with ideas like 'engine', 'fuel store', 'transmission', and so on. But explanation of any one of these would clearly require mention of the others. Similarly, we cannot say what a desire is except by mentioning that it is the sort of thing which conjoins with beliefs (and other states) to lead to behaviour.

But something more important than this is that the number of different psychological states (and hence their possibilities of interaction) are vastly greater than for the car. There is no clear upper limit on the number of different beliefs or desires that a person may have. And, worse, we cannot lay down in advance that for a given state these, and only these, others could be relevant to what its originating conditions or outcomes are. This 'holism of the mental' (Quine 1960; Davidson 1970), which is here only roughly sketched, will turn out to be of crucial significance and we shall return to it. But for the moment let us ask how the functionalist can accommodate the fact that, finite creatures as we are, we have this immensely flexible and seemingly open-ended competence

12

with psychological understanding and explanation. A model lies to hand here in the notions of axioms and theorems. We have understanding of hitherto unencountered situations because we (in some sense) know some basic principles concerning the ingredients and modes of interaction of the elements from which the new situations are composed.

What can the elements be? Not individual beliefs and desires because, as we have seen, there are too many of them; hence the view that having an individual belief or desire must be, functionally conceived, a composite state. This is one powerful reason why the idea of the possession of beliefs and desires as relations to inner sentences seems attractive (Field 1978: 24–36). The functional psychologist hopes that, with a limited number of elements (inner words), together with principles of construction and principles of interaction (modelled on the syntactic transformations of formalised logic), the complexity of intra-personal psychological interactions can be encapsulated in a theory of manageable proportions.

But, however elegantly the theory is axiomatised, the fact remains that it is going to be enormously complex. Moreover we certainly cannot now formulate it explicitly. There should therefore be some reluctance to credit ourselves with knowing it (even if only implicitly) unless there is no alternative account of how psychological explanation could work. But there is an alternative. It is the replicating strategy to which I now turn.

On the replicating view, psychological understanding works like this. I can think about the world. I do so in the interests of taking my own decisions and forming my own opinions. The future is complex and unclear. In order to deal with it I need to and can envisage possible but perhaps non-actual states of affairs. I can imagine how my tastes, aims and opinions might change and work out what would be sensible to do or believe in the circumstances. My ability to do these things makes possible a certain sort of understanding of other people. I can harness all my complex theoretical knowledge about the world and my ability to imagine in order to yield an insight into other people without any further elaborate theorising about them. Only one simple assumption is needed: that they are like me in being thinkers, that they possess the same fundamental cognitive capacities and propensities that I do.

The method works like this. Suppose I am interested in predicting someone's action. (I take this case only as an example, not intending thereby to endorse any close link between understanding and prediction in the psychological case. Similar methods would apply with other aspects of understanding, for example, working out what someone was thinking, feeling or intending in the past.) What I endeavour to do is to replicate or re-create his thinking. I place myself in what I take to be his initial state by imagining the world as it would appear from his point of view and I then deliberate, reason and reflect to see what decision emerges.

Psychological states are not alone in being amenable to this approach. I might try to find out how someone else is reacting or will react to a certain drug by taking a dose of it myself. There is thus a quite general method of finding out what will or did happen to things similar to myself in given circumstances, namely ensuring that I myself am in those circumstances and waiting to see what occurs. To get good results from the method I require only that I have the ability to get myself into the same state as the person I wish to know about and that he and I are in fact relevantly similar.

As so far described the method yields us 'understanding' of another person in the sense of particular judgements about what he or she feels, thinks or does, which may facilitate interaction on particular occasions. We may also get from this method 'understanding' in the sense of some sort of answer to a why-question. If I am capable of describing the initial conditions which I replicated then I can cite them. But the method does not yet yield any hint of theoretical apparatus. No answer is forthcoming to the question 'Certain states are experimentally found to be thus linked but why? What principles operate here?' We shall return in Sections 3 and 4 to consider what concepts and principles of connection the replication method turns out to presuppose. Could they, for example, be identical with those the functional strategy calls upon?

But I would first like to discuss in Section 2 three direct lines of attack upon my claim that replication is, at least in its method of delivering particular judgements, a real and conceptually economical alternative to the functional approach, that is, an alternative which avoids the need to credit ourselves with knowledge of complex theories about each other.

2. SOME OBJECTIONS TO THE REPLICATION HYPOTHESIS

The first line of attack concentrates on how I am supposed to get myself into the correct replicating state. One might argue as follows. The replication method demands that I be able, on the basis of looking at someone else, to know what psychological state he or she is in, so that I can put myself in the same state. To do this I must, perhaps at some inexplicit level, be in possession of a theory about the interrelations of psychological states and behaviour. But this will just be the functionalist theory all over again.

Two lines of defence against this attack are available. First, we may object that the attack presupposes that knowledge of another's psychological state must always be inferentially based and rest upon observation of behaviour, conceived of as something neutrally describable. But we need not buy this premise and may propose instead some more direct model of how we come to knowledge of others' feelings and so forth (McDowell 1982).

Second (and this is the more important line of defence), the attack misdescribes the direction of gaze of the replicator. He is not looking at the subject to be understood but at the world around that subject. It is what the world makes the replicator think which is the basis for the beliefs he attributes to the subject. The process, of course, does not work with complete simplicity and directness. The replicator does not attribute to someone else belief in every state of affairs which he can see to obtain in the other's vicinity. A process of recentring the world in imagination is required. And this must involve the operation of some principles about what it is possible to perceive. Visual occlusion is the obvious example. But a theory about what one can know about the world from what viewpoint is not the same thing as a theory about how psychological states interact with each other or about what behaviour they produce.

It is worth remarking here that we need not saddle the replication theory with a commitment to the absurd idea that we are all quite indistinguishable in our psychological reactions – that any two persons with the same history are bound to respond to a given situation in the same way. Replication theory must allow somewhere for the idea of different personalities, for different styles of thinking and for non-rational influences on thinking. It is not clear what shape such additions to the core replication process would take. But there is no reason to suppose that they would take the form of the reimportation of the proposed functionalist-style theory.

Someone might try to press or to reformulate the objection by conceding that looking at the world rather than the subject might be a good heuristic device for suggesting hypotheses about his or her beliefs, but insisting that, nevertheless, we must employ (implicitly or explicitly) some criteria for the correctness of these hypotheses. What shows me that I am thinking of the world in the same way as the person I seek to understand? I must have some theory about what constitutes sameness of psychological state, and this theory, it will be suggested, could well, or indeed must, take a functionalist form.

But why should we accept the foundationalist epistemological presuppositions of this argument? Is it not enough for us to credit ourselves with the concept of 'same psychological state' that we should, first, be able to make generally agreed judgements using the notion and, second, that when our expectations are falsified we are usually able to detect some source of error when we cast around for further features of the situation, and hence to restore coherence among our own views and between our views and those of others?

We touch here on large issues in epistemology. But at the weakest we could say this: that there is not in this area any quick knock-down argument in favour of functionalism as against a claimed economical replication view.

Let us turn to a second reason for supposing that replication cannot be more economical than functionalism. Dennett (commenting on something similar to the replication view which he finds hinted at by Stich [1982b]) writes:

> How can it (the idea of using myself as an analogue computer) work without being a kind of theorising in the end? For the state I put myself in is not belief but make believe belief. If I make believe I am a suspension bridge and wonder what I will do when the wind blows, what 'comes to me' in my make believe state depends on how sophisticated my knowledge is of the physics and engineering of suspension bridges. Why should my making believe I have your beliefs be any different? In both cases knowledge of the imitated object is needed to drive the make believe 'simulation' and the knowledge must be organised in something rather like a theory. (Dennett 1982: 79)

Of course Dennett is quite right that the psychological case as I have sketched it is not one of strict replication, unlike the drug case. It would clearly be absurd to suppose that in order to anticipate what someone else will do I have actually to believe what he or she believes. But Dennett is wrong in thinking that what he calls 'make believe belief' is as alien a state – and hence as demanding of theoretical underpinning – as making believe to be a suspension bridge. Make-believe belief is imagining. And we do this already on our own behalf. The sequence of thought connections from imagined state of affairs to imagined decision parallels that from real belief to real decision. If it did not, we could not use the technique of contemplating possibilities and seeing what it would be sensible to do if such and such as part of our own decision making. So to make the replication method work I do not require the theory which Dennett mentions. I require only the ability to distinguish real belief from entertaining a possibility, and the ability to attribute to another person as belief what I have actualised in myself as imagining.

16

The third attempt to show that replication and functionalism coincide takes a bolder line. The replicator supposes that some working out is to be done in order to find out what it would be sensible to do in the situation the other person envisages. Similarly the functionalist also supposes that working out is to be done. It is from a knowledge of particular states together with general principles or laws that a judgement on this case is to be reached. Why should we not suppose that the working out involved in the two cases is, contrary to superficial appearances, the same? The description of the replication method given so far suggests that sequences of thought states occur in me without mediation of any further thought, just as the sequences of reactions to drugs do. But perhaps this is a misleading picture, perhaps transitions from one thought to another occur in virtue of my awareness of some principle or law requiring the occurrence of the one after the other. Doing the actual thinking, which the replicator represents as something entirely different from functionalist-style thinking about thinking, is not in fact fundamentally different. Making up my own mind is just the first-person version of what, in third-person cases, is functionalist-style causal prediction.

But this will not do at all. For a start an infinite regress threatens. If any transition from thought to thought is to be underpinned by some further thought about links, how are we to explain the occurrence of the relevant thought about links without invoking some third level and so on? But let us waive this objection. More substantial difficulties await.

It is indeed tempting to suppose that whenever I draw a conclusion, that is, base one judgement on another, I must implicitly know or have in mind some general principle which links the two. But whether or not we think it right to yield to this temptation, the only sense in which the claim is plausible is one in which the principle in question is a normative one ('one ought to believe so-and-so if one believes such-and-such') or relatedly a semantic one ('the belief that so-and-so would be true if the belief that such-and-such were true'). In neither case is the principle in question a causal law, such as the supposed axioms of the functionalist theory are to be. The terminology I used above in arguing my opponents' case (a 'principle' or 'law' by which the occurrence of one belief 'requires' the occurrence of another) is designed to obscure this vital difference. If we try to restate the proposal being quite explicit that the connections in question are causal we arrive at the most bizarre results. It amounts to supposing that it makes no difference whether a thinker asks himself or herself the question 'What ought I to think next?' or the question 'What will I, as a matter of fact, think next?' On the proposed view, these are just different wordings of the same question.

Suppose, then, that I do infer that q on the basis that p, and that my knowledge that belief that p causes belief that q is integral to the process. We seem to have the following choice. Either we could say that the inference that q is based not just on the premise that p (as prima facie but misleading appearance has it) but also on the (implicit) premise that belief that p causes belief that q. This amounts to endorsing the principle of inference 'I will be caused to believe that p, therefore p'. Alternatively we could suppose that drawing the inference just is making the prediction. And this amounts to identifying belief that p with belief that one is being made to think that p.

Clearly none of this will do. It makes judgements about the world collapse into or rest upon judgements about me; and moreover they are judgements about me which have quite disparate truth conditions and roles in thought from the judgements about the world they are required to stand in for.

There are certain conditions under which the assimilation would appear less ludicrous. These are that I could isolate causal factors constitutive of my rational thinking from interfering ones; that I am a perfect thinker (that is, I rely on no confused concepts or plausible but unreliable rules of inference) and know that I am a perfect thinker. In other words, if I knew that physiologically I embodied a logical system and I knew the meta-theory for my own system, then causal-syntactic knowledge about myself would have semantic equivalents. The discussion of fallibility below will indicate some of the reasons why this is unacceptable.

So far I have been examining attempts to show that the replication strategy cannot be a real alternative to the functionalist one. And I maintain that none of them has undermined the plausibility of the original claim that the two approaches are different and that the former is more economical than the latter.

3. PROSPECTS FOR A RECONCILIATION

I turn now to a different line of thought, one which concedes the above claim but argues that nevertheless a replicative style of psychological understanding is compatible with a functionalist style. The use of the one does not preclude the other. A functionalist theory could develop out of and dovetail smoothly with use of the replicating strategy. Perhaps it is already doing so; or perhaps it will, when cognitive science is more advanced.

In the case of reaction to drugs something like this is clearly possible. At one stage of the development of knowledge I may be unable to anticipate others' reactions except via the replication method and be unable to conceptualise them except through ideas appropriate to that method. For example, I ask of another person, 'Why was she sick?' An initial answer might muster all the relevant information I have like this: 'I was sick; she took the same drug as I did and she is like me.' Or we might express it more naturally: 'She is like me and she took the drug which made me sick.' But this is not a stopping point. When I become reflective I shall ask, 'In what respects is she relevantly similar to me?' and 'What feature of the drug connects with this feature of us to make us sick?' There is no reason in this case why the answers should not be ones the finding of which precisely does amount to my finding a causal theory which will emancipate me, wholly or partially, from the need to replicate. The key feature here is that the relevant similarity will probably turn out to be something about body chemistry. When I have these physiological concepts to hand I can specify directly what sort of creatures will be affected by some drug without mention of myself as a standard of similarity. And I can describe directly what the drug does to them instead of pointing to myself and saying, 'It makes you like this.' Now why should this not also be the case with psychological replication?

Perhaps replication is a method by which primates unreflectively facilitate their social interactions. But we, it might be said, are in the process of emancipating ourselves from this primitive approach. (This is a view suggested to me by some remarks of Andrew Woodfield [1982: 281–282].) So when one unreflectively attributes a thought to another creature one may replicate that thought, and at the first attempts one may be unable to characterise the state in question in any other way than by pointing to oneself and saying, 'Well, it is like what I am doing now.' And one will be unable to anticipate others except by re-creating and attempting to rethink their thoughts, because one has no access to the nature of the thought as it is in itself or the respects in which the other subject and oneself are relevantly similar. Nevertheless, reflection shows us that there is such a thing as the nature of the thought in itself, some intrinsic character that it has, and some non-demonstrative specification of relevant similarity. So when we use psychological terminology reflectively it is to these things that we intend to refer. And cognitive science is about to fill in the actual detail of what they are.

But I want now to argue that this will not do. When we reflect on the notion of 'relevant similarity', as it needs to be used in psychological explanation, we discover an insuperable bar to imagining it being superseded by the sort of physiological or structural description which functionalism requires. And, relatedly, we find that we cannot get at the nature of the thought as it is in itself but continue to have access to it only in an indirect and demonstrative fashion.

The difference between psychological explanation and explanation in the natural sciences is that in giving a psychological explanation we render the thought or behaviour of the other intelligible; we exhibit the thought or behaviour as having some point, some reasons to be cited in their defence. Another way of putting this truism is to say that we see them as exercises of cognitive competence or rationality. (I intend these terms to be interchangeable and to be understood very broadly to mean what is exercised in the formation of intention and desire as well as belief.)

It is this feature of psychological explanation which the replication method puts at the centre of the stage. When I start reflecting upon the replication method and trying to put the particular judgements and connections it indicates in a theoretical context, it is the notion of cognitive competence, of the subject struggling to get things right, which must present itself as the respect in which I and the other are relevantly similar.

But what further account can we give of rationality? Could it be discovered to be identical with and replaceable by something which would suit the functionalist programme? Initial thoughts about rationality or cognitive competence suggest that it surely has something to do with the ability to achieve success in judgement (that is, truth for belief and whatever the analogous property or properties are for desires, intentions, etc.). But the nature of the link is difficult to capture. Is rationality something which guarantees the actual success of judgement in particular cases? Arguably not, since the question 'But have I got this right?' can always be raised. We must recognise ourselves to be thoroughly fallible. This is one important implication of the extreme complexity of interaction of psychological states which our earlier discussion did not bring out. In our earlier remarks about functionalism the complexity served merely as a spur to thinking of psychological states as molecular rather than atomic. That move was needed because we could not specify in advance what beliefs might be relevant to any other – as premises or conclusions. Thus, given enough background of the right sort, any belief could bear upon the truth of any other. It is this which prevents the individuation of beliefs as atomic units by their placement in some specifiable pattern of a limited number of other psychological states. But a further implication of this (as Quine constantly stresses) is that we cannot pick upon any belief or beliefs as immune to any possible influence from future information.

So cognitive competence is not the claim that for at least some sorts of judgement success is guaranteed. Could it be defined, then, in terms of inference rules relied on or judgement-forming procedures – for example, by mention of specific rules like *modus tollens* or inductive generalisation or, more non-committally, via the idea of inference rules which are generally reliable? This again will not do, and its failure is crucial to the incompatibility between replication and functionalism. I can fail to follow simple and reliable inference rules and can adopt some most unreliable ones, and recognise later that this was what I was doing, quite compatibly with continued trust in my then and present cognitive competence. The only constraint is that I should be able to make intelligible to myself why I failed to notice so-and-so or seemed to assume such-and-such. And, as with the case of individual judgements, enough scene setting can do the trick. This is not to say that I can make sense of my past self – or of someone else – even where I can find no overlap at all between my present judgements and inference procedures and those of the other. Rather my claim is that we cannot arrange inference procedures (or judgements) in some clear hierarchy and identify some as basic or constitutive of rationality.

We may have models or partial views of what constitutes rationality (in logic, decision theory, etc.) but thinking in accordance with the rules or standards there specified cannot be definitive of or exhaust the notion of rationality. This is not only because our current views on these matters may be wrong, but for another reason also. If rationality were thus definable, then the claim that I myself am rational would acquire some specific empirical content, would become just one proposition among all the others which form my view of the world. It would thus be potentially up for grabs as something falsifiable by enough evidence of the right character. But, notoriously, any attempted demonstration to me by myself that I am a non-thinker must be absurd because self-undermining. Hence any account of what it is to be a thinker which seems to make such a demonstration possible must be at fault.

How does all this bear upon the idea that as we gain more knowledge and conceptual sophistication some primitive replication method could gracefully give way to a more scientific functional understanding? It is relevant because this idea does require exactly the assumption that rationality can be given a complete formal definition in terms of syntactically specifiable inference rules. It is only if this is the case that the replicating

21

assumption of relevant similarity – 'they are like me in being cognitively competent' – can be replaced by the functional assumption 'they are like me in being systems with inner states structured and interacting according to so-and-so principles'.

I have used as a premise a strong version of fallibilism which some may find implausible. Surely, one might protest, some propositions (that I exist, that this is a desk, that here is a hand) are in some sense unassailable, as are also some rules of inference. Am I seriously suggesting that the law of non-contradiction or universal instantiation might be overthrown?

Suppose we concede the force of these remarks; does it then become defensible again to maintain that functionalism will turn out to be compatible with the replication approach and will ultimately replace it? It does not. As long as we admit that there are any parts of our implicit inferential practices which may be muddled – that is, as long as we admit (as we surely must) that the world has some funny surprises in store for us as a result of which we shall recognise our earlier thinking patterns as muddled and inadequate, then we must also admit that our formal grip on rationality is not complete.

It is the position within the network, defined by the supposed formal account of rationality, which provides the functionalist account of what a thought is in itself. Thoughts are, for functionalists, identified and individuated by causal-explanatory role. So a corollary of the non-existence of a formal account of rationality is the non-availability of that mode of characterising thoughts which functionalism counts on – a mode imagined to be independent of our entertaining or rethinking those thoughts.

4. COROLLARIES OF THE REPLICATION STRATEGY

I turn finally to some sketchy and programmatic remarks about the concepts and modes of explanation which will be called on under the two strategies, replicating and functionalist. Recent writings in the functionalist school have produced powerful arguments to show that upon their approach the semantic properties of psychological states, that is, their referential relations to particular objects or sorts of stuff in the world, are not directly relevant to their explanatory roles. We think of psychological states (they say) both as things which are true or false in virtue of semantic connections with the world and also as things which are explanatory of behaviour. But these two ways of thinking about them are in some sense independent. So that-clauses are systematically ambiguous;

sometimes we use them to ascribe truth conditions and sometimes to ascribe causal-explanatory roles (Fodor 1980; McGinn 1982; Field 1978).

I shall not fully rehearse the arguments for this view here. The nub of the matter is just this, that admission of the referential as explanatory in the functionalists' causal framework would amount to admitting a very mysterious action at a distance which goes against all our causal assumptions. Distant objects exert their causal influence over us via chains of intermediate events, where these events could occur from other causes even if the distant object did not exist. The functionalist views as explanatory a state which could exist even if the supposed referent did not. Thus he claims to unite economically, in one form of account, actions guided by true beliefs (i.e., ones which are referentially well grounded) and also actions which are based on illusion. The functionalist claims that we have a concept of what is common to referentially well-based cognition and illusory cognition, a concept which is specifiable without mention of referential success; and that referential success is thus a conjunctive notion (cf. McDowell 1982).

But what is this something else, this non-referential content which we sometimes use that-clauses to ascribe? One thing which is clear is that in attributing non-referential content to someone's thought I do not commit myself to the existence of any particular thing (or natural kind) outside him. I merely characterise him as he is intrinsically.

But obscurities remain. One of these has been noted (Bach 1982). Non-referential content could be something thought of merely syntactically – that is, to be labelled 'content' only in an exceedingly stretched sense. On the other hand, the notion of non-referential content could be recognisably a notion of meaning in some sense. In reporting it we report the subject's 'mode of representing the world', but without commitment to the existence of anything outside him.

But within the latter option there is also an important further obscurity. Is non-referential content strongly conceptually independent of reference and truth, in that someone could have the former idea without the others so much as having crossed his mind? Or are they only weakly conceptually independent, in that ascription of non-referential content does not commit one to an actual referent or truth conditions but does commit one to some disposition concerning reference and truth? On the second view, in thinking of something as having non-referential content we are thinking of it precisely as something which in a certain context or under certain other conditions would have such-and-such referent and truth conditions.

There are thus three options. Non-referential content is:

(*a*) a merely syntactic notion;
(*b*) a notion of meaning strongly independent of truth and reference;
(*c*) a notion of meaning only weakly independent of truth and reference.

Which of these do the functionalists propose? It is claimed that classification of beliefs as explanatory and classification of them as truth bearers are 'independent' because such classifications can crosscut, as in the case of indexicals or Twin Earth situations. And in the discussion of why we are interested in reference at all, it sometimes seems to be assumed that this 'crosscutting classification' argument has established (*a*) or (*b*), that is, has established 'independence' in a strong sense of complete conceptual detachment. These discussions proceed on the assumption that grip on the non-referential notion of content has provided no foothold at all for truth and our interest in it has to be motivated totally ab initio. But in fact the crosscutting classification point does not establish this. Consider 'fragile' and 'broken': these classifications crosscut. But this would hardly show that we could understand 'fragile' without understanding 'breaks' or that our interest in breakage needed to be motivated independently of our interest in fragility. On the other hand, the notion of non-referential content is sometimes elucidated in terms of notions like subjective probability, inference, Fregean sense, or Kaplanesque 'character'. And these notions are ones which prima facie have conceptual links with reference and truth. Thus Kaplan's notion of the character of an indexical utterance or belief is precisely the notion of something which, placed in a certain context, determines a referent and hence a truth value (Field 1978: 44–49; Fodor 1980: 66–68; McGinn 1982: 208–228).

Whichever of these options the functionalist takes there will be difficulties. On (*a*) and (*b*) it turns out that a view which I earlier offered as a truism, namely that in psychological explanation we exhibit the explanandum having a point or being at least in part justified, is false. The explanatory notions postulated in (*a*) and (*b*) are ones which provide no foothold for talk of justification or point. So, if presented as a view about everyday psychological talk and explanation, this philosophical theory has the problem of explaining where the semantic and related justificatory aspects of the practices fit in and why they seem to loom so large for us. I do not say that this cannot be done, only that attempts so far have not been convincing.

Field suggests that we attribute reference and truth conditions to the inner states of others because we find it useful to 'calibrate' them; we can then use facts about their inner states, in conjunction with some reliability theory, to gain information about the world for ourselves (1978: 44–49). McGinn objects to this that it makes assignment of reference to others' beliefs and utterances too contingent. On Field's account, McGinn notes, we would not bother to do it if we thought that the other person, through limitations of his knowledge or his unreliability, had nothing to teach us. Yet surely we might assign reference even in these circumstances. So McGinn proposes that we need the notion of reference in characterising the practice of communication. 'A hearer understands a speech act as an assertion just if he interprets it as performed with a certain point or intention – viz., to convey information about the world' (1982: 225–228).

But this, by McGinn's own lights, will hardly do. The phrase 'about the world' would itself be subject to the bifurcation of role which McGinn claims to find in all that-clauses or content ascribers. So when I ascribe to another an intention to "convey information about the world", on McGinn's account I may understand this attribution of content to his or her intention in either of two ways. I may take it, first, as ascribing an inner explanatory state, grasp of the nature of which requires no semantic concepts, or second, as ascribing an inner state with semantic relations. But only the former is needed for psychological explanation and hence for understanding of communicative behaviour. So, failing some further account of 'characterising the activity of communication' (an account which shows it to be other than psychological explanation of it), we are no further forward.

What is odd about both these accounts, Field's in particular, is that they take for granted that we want true beliefs for ourselves. But once this is acknowledged the attempt to anchor the notion of truth and our interest in it by pointing to some complex of causal facts and correlations observable in third-person cases seems strange. The interest in truth is already anchored as soon as a person comes to express reflectively his or her own beliefs and to ask, 'But is that right?'

So the idea that we take a theory endorsing (a) or (b) as an elucidation of our everyday notion of content runs into serious problems. Our everyday notion of content seems to unite explanatory and semantic in a way such a theory does not allow. On the other hand, if the theory is presented not as an account of the notion we now employ but as a blueprint for a future, highly abstract version of neurophysiology, then it is not faced with those difficulties. Its relevance, however, for philosophical accounts of current practice is non-existent.

If the functionalist adopts (*c*) as his account of non-referential content, then his problems are different. This content notion is one in which two elements are linked – namely the idea of a 'a mode of representing the world' and the idea of a 'causal-explanatory role'; moreover, they are linked in such a way that the one 'is constitutive of' the other (McGinn 1982: 210). The 'mode of representing' notion now invoked has enough link with truth for notions like justification and seeing the point to get a grip. So it would not be absurd to offer this as an account of part of what we are ordinarily doing with psychological statements. But, if the arguments centring on fallibilism in the earlier part of the essay were persuasive, the difficulty will be to show convincingly how there can be a notion which dovetails this 'mode of representing' idea with the 'causal-explanatory role' idea. Grip on a causal-explanatory role is grip on some pattern, thought of as fixed and where the relata are known. But grip on justificatory content is confidence in my power to see the point, to understand arguments and justifications involving this notion when I am called upon to do so, without supposing that I now know what those other related thoughts are. That such a functionalist notion – that is, one in which the two elements are dovetailed – is called for by a plausible version of functionalism is not an argument for its coherence, unless functionalism itself is unassailable.

In summary, then, in this section I have been arguing that much work needs to be done to clarify the notion of non-referential content which functionalists ought to espouse and to demonstrate that such a notion is coherent.

What will be the theoretical apparatus and modes of explanation which the replication account calls for? In stressing that a person is only in a position to understand another psychologically by rethinking his or her thoughts, I am putting the idea of 'doing the same thing oneself' in a prominent place. And it may thus seem that Cartesian introspectionism is reappearing on the scene. But this is not so. And the crucial difference is that, on the view I maintain, one has no more access to the intrinsic nature of one's own thoughts than one does to the intrinsic nature of those of others. Thinking about my own thoughts is not, on my model, direct and intimate confrontation with something about whose nature I cannot be deceived. It is, in my own case as for others, replicating – that is, putting on a certain sort of performance, rather than being in possession of a certain kind of quasi-perceptual knowledge. Psychological ascriptions – the use of that-clauses – might better be called re-expression than description. I do not by saying this mean to outlaw the phrases 'psychological knowledge' or 'psychological description', but rather to put us on our guard against a certain way of conceiving of such knowledge or descriptions. We may agree that a person knows of himself or herself what he or she is thinking more easily than he or she knows this of others. In one's own case one does not have the complexities of recentring to deal with, so replication comes very easily. But the technique for doing it, namely looking at the world, and the outcome, namely placing oneself in a position to put on a certain sort of performance, are just the same whether one thinks of oneself or another. And the emphasis on fallibilism shows that my easy replication of my own thought gives me no privileged position in connection with claims to understand it, see what follows from it or the like.

I have argued that the notion of rationality or cognitive competence is central to the replication account. But equally I have argued that no substantive definition of it can be given. It is not that rationality has no conceptual connections with other notions. The idea of cognitive competence must have something to do with the idea of attaining success in cognition, that is, truth for beliefs and whatever the analogous properties are for other intentional states. Hence the idea that semantic notions such as truth have no importance in psychological explanation will clearly be mistaken on the replication view. Rationality cannot be understood without a grip on the semantic notions which define success or failure in cognition.

But one might still wonder about the point or usefulness of deploying the notion of rationality. If I affirm of myself that I am rational, what point can my action have if I am not offering something with a testable content, a description of the world? I conjecture that we have here one of those items at the limits of our conceptual scheme which present themselves sometimes as statements but at other times rather as programmes of action or announcements of a stance. One thing that I might be doing in affirming myself to be rational is acknowledging the necessity of taking success as the norm in my cognitive enterprises, that is, taking success as what is to be expected unless evidence of mistake appears. I suspect that pursuit of this clue might lead to a more illuminating picture of what psychological explanation is than attempts to elaborate a functionalist account.

3

Understanding Other Minds from the Inside

Can we understand other minds 'from the inside'? What would this mean? Many have felt an attraction to the idea that creatures with minds, people (and perhaps animals), invite a kind of understanding which inanimate objects such as rocks, plants and machines do not invite, and that it is appropriate to seek to understand such animate creatures 'from the inside'. What I hope to do in this essay is to introduce and defend one version of the so-called simulation approach to our grasp and use of psychological concepts, a version which gives central importance to the idea of shared rationality, and in so doing to tease out and defend one strand in the complex of ideas which finds expression in this mysterious phrase. Talk of persons 'having a point of view', and of there being such a thing as 'what it is like' to be that person, are also part of the same set of ideas. (But I would like to stress that the whole issue of the existence of 'qualia' is not touched on at all in what follows.)

I would like here to introduce the salient ideas of the simulation approach. Simulationism is best understood by contrast with another approach in philosophy of mind which has, at least among Anglo-American analytic philosophers, been the dominant one of the last decades and which has also been an important influence on psychologists and cognitive scientists. We may call this familiar alternative the 'theory theory'. The version best known to philosophers is functionalism in philosophy of mind. This says that to grasp psychological notions is to grasp that there are certain inner states of persons, which are typically caused by such and such external events, which interact among themselves to cause further inner states and events, and which finally combine to cause behaviour. To possess the concept of some particular mental state is to grasp the particular causal-explanatory role associated with that state. When we use our

28

understanding of psychological notions, for example in predicting what another will think or do, we deploy this theoretical knowledge. Block has usefully collected some of the classic readings which present these ideas (1980).

There are many ways of elaborating this general approach, depending on what view we take of how we acquire and represent this supposed theoretical knowledge – whether it is innate or learnt, whether explicitly or tacitly known, and so on. But let us leave all these issues on one side, just noting, however, that the theory theory does not seem at all hospitable to the 'from the inside' idea. Indeed, part of its motivation is to find an account of the psychological which is naturalistic, that is, which does away with certain deeply suspect forms of dualism and sees human beings as part of the natural order. Theory theory does this precisely by claiming the similarity of psychological concepts to non-psychological concepts such as those of natural science, presenting the former merely as particular complex and interesting cases of the general style of thought invoked in the latter.

So much for theory theory. Now for a thumbnail sketch of its rival, the simulation approach. This is by no means an entirely new idea. A version of it goes back to Vico in the early eighteenth century; it gets a passing mention in Kant; it is associated with Dilthey and is force-fully defended by Collingwood (Berlin 1976; Kant 1953: 336; Dilthey 1976; Collingwood 1946: esp. 282–302). And under the name *Verstehen* one broadly simulation-style approach is familiar, and has been exten-sively debated, in the philosophy of history and social science. But in the last ten years the idea has been revived in the context of psychology and philosophy of mind. And here it provides a new perspective on a great number of familiar topics – for example, the nature of imagination, the differences between practical and theoretical reasoning, the nature of emotion – as well as initiating an interesting body of empirical work in psychology and suggesting new models in cognitive science. I shall touch on only a very small part of this.

A way of putting the central idea of the simulation approach is this. When we think about another's thoughts or actions we somehow ingeniously exploit the fact that we ourselves are or have minds. What we do is to make our own mind in some way like the mind of the one we seek to predict or understand. We simulate his or her thoughts, we re-create in ourselves some parallel to his or her thought processes. Many simulationists further articulate this by talking of my having 'pretend be-liefs' and of my 'inference mechanisms' being run 'off-line'. But others

29

(and here I include myself) would prefer to use more everyday vocabulary and to talk of my using my imagination and thereby entertaining the same thoughts and making the same inferences as the others. We shall come to the significant differences here in due course.

I shall not here consider in detail the reasons for preferring a simulation approach to a theory theory one. Let me just indicate one central and immediately apparent advantage of simulationism. It is this. Others' thoughts are very varied and numerous, and interact with each other in countless different ways. The remarkable thing is how successfully we deal with this, correctly adjusting our expectations of others' thoughts, feelings and actions in an immense variety of circumstances. Clearly any theory adequate to systematise our competence here would itself be immensely complex. But simulation can explain our competence without crediting us with knowledge of any such vast, and very probably unwieldy, body of information. Rather, in thinking about another's thoughts, in order, for example, to predict his or her intentions, we harness our own cognitive apparatus and make it work in parallel with that of the other and then use the result we arrive at to ground our prediction. And for this to occur all that is required is, first, that we have cognitive apparatus which is sufficiently similar to that of the other to produce usefully similar results and, second, that we can make it work in a parallel way. It is *not* required that we have some representation of the apparatus itself or its workings. We do not need to possess a 'know that' about the processes of thinking, what thoughts lead to what others and so forth, provided that we can harness relevantly our own 'know-how' of doing the thinking itself and can thus follow through in ourselves the same train of thought as the other has pursued. The economy of the proposal is striking.

The phrase 'thinking about others' thoughts' covers several different kinds of reflection which we now need to distinguish. There is something importantly right in functionalism, namely its stress on the facts that psychological states may be caused by events in the world, that such states interact with each other to give rise to further states and that they may give rise to bodily behaviour. This gives us a useful framework for considering the different sorts of issue which may arise for me concerning another's thoughts.

First I may wonder what effect the circumstances around her will have on the psychological states of another. (E.g., She is being whirled round on a fairground ride; will she feel sick? There is a disturbance in the corner; will she notice it?) Let us call these connections 'world-mind links'.

Second, I may wonder what further thoughts she will have, given some thoughts about which I already know. (E.g., She believes thus and such about the cash flow of our firm; will that lead her to think that we are about to go bankrupt? She endorses these and those principles; what decision will she reach in this particular case?) Let us call these 'mind-mind' or 'intrapsychic' links.

Third, I may wonder what behaviour, that is, what actual bodily movements, she will exhibit, given her thoughts. (E.g., She hears a balloon popped behind her; will she jump? She intends to smash her opponent's ball away to the sideline; will she succeed in springing high enough to get the needed angle?) Let us call these 'mind-world' links.

But let us note also that there is a fourth thing I may be doing under the general heading 'thinking about another's thoughts'. I may try to work back from the behaviour she has produced to a view about the psychological states from which the behaviour arose. (E.g., She pulled a funny face; was she really amused? She said that such and such; was she annoyed?)

These are four extremely different contexts in which psychological concepts are used; and competence at each of them may well call upon different aspects of the skill which is a grasp of those concepts. We should beware of lumping them all together and supposing that a philosophical account of our competence with such concepts, whether simulationist or theory theory, should say the same about each. And the claim I want to make about simulationism is that it is particularly at home, its strengths and plausibility particularly apparent, in the second of the listed circumstances, namely in an account of our grip of mind-mind or intrapsychic links. And this will be mainly what I shall discuss below. I do not think that simulationism has anything distinctive to say about our ability to answer the third sort of question. It probably has distinctive ideas to contribute on the first and fourth, but I shall not discuss them in detail here. However, a few remarks about the fourth may help to ward off some misunderstandings.

It is important to note how, on any view, the fourth context − that of interpreting and explaining behaviour − will plausibly be a very different matter from the others. All philosophers, whatever their theory of mind, acknowledge that many alternative explanations of the same behaviour are possible. For example, even if we can identify something with fair confidence as an intentional raising of the arm, when we seek to identify the purposes behind the raising, and penetrate to the feelings, goals, beliefs which in turn lie behind that purpose, it is clear that many accounts could be given.

31

Even on a functionalist or theory theory view there is no such thing as just 'applying the theory' in some fixed and algorithmic way to derive an interpretation. In the other cases (with the first, second and third sort of question noted above) as conceived by functionalism, there is such a fixed and algorithmic procedure. If one has suffficient information about the prior conditions, then one just has to identify the parts of the theory which deal with those conditions and apply them. One's prediction may be hedged because one knows that further information may reveal the case as more complex than it at first appeared or as requiring adjustments in the light of subsidiary theoretical principles. But (these kinds of complications aside) forward-moving theory-invoking prediction is quite a different matter from backward-looking theory-invoking explanation. An account of how we do the latter cannot just call on 'our knowledge of the theory', but must also tell some story about how we generate a range of possible explanations compatible with the theory and how we assess them.

The same general kind of point needs to be made in connection with simulationism. Even if we accept a simulationist account of how prediction about others' thoughts or behaviour are arrived at (e.g., in cases of type 2 above), this does not of itself tell us how backward-looking interpretations and explanations are arrived at. So we should beware of taking simulationism to be the idea that mere awareness of another person – of his or her circumstances and behaviour – automatically produces in the observer, via some natural sensitivity, a simulation of the other's mental state. Simulationism is not the claim that we have some kind of quick route to knowledge of other minds, or that we can empathetically 'tune in' to others, or anything of this kind. Perhaps such an empathetic 'tuning in' occurs in a few basic cases. For example, in normal infants we find very early a disposition to attend to what others attend to, to be frightened if adults in their company are frightened and the like. It is plausible that such basic patterns of response are central to our ability to understand other minds. But this does not take us very far. Patently other people are often difficult to understand. Often we know that we are ignorant of their thoughts and feelings, or we have little confidence in our conjectures about what they may be. Simulationism is not the promise of some easy answer to these difficulties.

Let us now turn to consideration of the distinctively simulationist story about mind–mind links, that is, about how I might come to some prediction or further belief about another's thoughts on the basis of knowledge of some subset of her thoughts. To take a very schematic case, suppose that the other believes that p_1–p_n and is interested in whether or not q. How might I work out her likely opinion on whether or not q? Theory theory of course says that I, so to speak, look up what the theory tells me about what is the likely upshot of the combination of believing p_1–p_n with an interest in whether q. I invoke the relevant axioms about beliefs and interests of that kind and apply them to this particular case. So it is by using my knowledge about thoughts and their effects that I work out what to expect.

Simulationism will say something different. But there are two contrasted ways in which the simulationist story can be told. One story starts with a picture of the mind which is very congenial to the theory theorist and is derived to a considerable extent from cognitive science. The mind, on this picture, consists of a number of sub-systems which perform various functions. For example, there are two stores in which beliefs and desires are kept. There are various processors which produce beliefs and put them in the belief store. These include a sensory analysing system, which takes sensory inputs and transforms them into beliefs. They include also some inference mechanisms, which take beliefs and derive other beliefs from them. There is also a practical reasoning system, which takes beliefs and desires as input and produces intentions as output. And so forth. Each processing system is designed to accept certain kinds of input. Receiving input of the appropriate kind causes it to go through its distinctive evolutions and to produce output of distinctive kinds. These inputs and outputs – sensory states, beliefs, desires, intentions, and so forth – are realised or coded in vehicles which are, in fact, brain states, for example neuronal patterns described at some suitable level of abstraction. And on this picture what really drives the evolution of the inference mechanisms, practical reasoning system and the like are the intrinsic properties of the vehicles, the brain states or neuronal patterns, which are the beliefs, desires and so forth.

Given this view of what goes on in the mind, simulationism is now spelt out in the following way. Suppose, as in the schematic example above, that I wish to work out what the other is likely to think about whether or not q, given that she believes that p_1–p_n, when I myself do not share her beliefs. What I do is first construct some 'pretend' beliefs that p_1–p_n. These are items which do not, in my mental architecture, play the role of beliefs; they do not come from my belief store. Nevertheless they are like beliefs, at least as far as concerns the nature of the vehicle in which they are coded. I now take my inference mechanisms 'off-line' – that is, I detach them from their usual links with my belief store. I feed in the pretend beliefs I have constructed, at the same time making some adjustment to the mechanisms to make them search for q-relevant consequences. I then wait to see what the mechanisms produce as output. If they output a pretend belief that q, then I attribute to the other the belief that q. Of course I do not do all this consciously. Nevertheless, this is what is going on at the level of the operations of my sub-personal cognitive machinery.

Simulation theory presented in these terms is conceived of as an empirical hypothesis. Those who articulate it like this suppose that it has empirical consequences different from those of the theory theory, that we can already see what those consequences are and that we can set about testing them.

But I would like to suggest that there are considerable problems with this conceptualisation of the issue. Consider first the fact that we do not have any well-backed-up and detailed view about what kind of functional 'systems' are to be found in the brain or how the various kinds of mental state and process recognised in common sense are in fact implemented at the sort of level envisaged. Many kinds of architecture are imaginable other than the one sketched above. For example, is it necessary to distinguish between theoretical and practical reasoning in the way proposed? To insist that we should is to make substantive and controversial philosophical assumptions about the relation of belief, desire and value. Another, and for our purposes more important, question is whether we have to take it that 'inference mechanisms' operate on beliefs, that is, the whole complex state including both content and the attitude to it. A different articulation would take it that 'inference mechanisms' operate on mental representations minus their attitude determiners – on, so to speak, 'thought radicals'. There is surely some case for thinking that we can reason with representations which we do not believe. How do we explain what we are doing in arguing by reductio ad absurdum or reasoning hypothetically if every piece of reasoning needs a belief as a starting point? But if we thus reconceptualise the 'inference mechanisms' as operating on thought radicals, then simulationism, formulated in terms which presuppose the existence of inference mechanisms operating on beliefs, turns out to involve a false picture of the mind and so to be worthless.

Consider also the fact that (even supposing that the original sketch of the architecture of our cognitive machinery is the right one) we have very little idea of what would be involved, neurophysiologically or functionally, in taking a system 'off-line'. We do not know what features of operation would remain the same and what would be different. It may be that we are seduced by the image of a machine made of cogs, levers and pistons, where we can make sense of things like disengaging the gears, detaching the drive belt and so forth. But is the brain like that in any sense? Who knows?

I am not here seeking to make difficulties for the whole project of trying to understand the mind by breaking up its overall operation into various different functions and looking for the biological structures and processes which subserve those functions. Good luck to the cognitive scientists, psychologists, neuroanatomists and so forth who grapple with these fascinating and difficult tasks. The point I am urging is rather that we do not yet have enough grip on how that project might actually work out in detail to have any confidence that we are working in terms of the right architecture when we talk of 'pretend beliefs' and 'off-line running'. Nor do we have enough understanding of how that proposal could be implemented to see what the talk of 'off-line' running would actually amount to. The latter point means that we do not really know how to test simulationism, regarded as this empirical hypothesis. The former means that simulationism, when articulated in terms of this particular architecture, is made hostage to future discoveries in brain science and might, given unfavourable developments there, turn out to be a total mistake. (This issue, and its significance for ways of conceiving the theory/simulation debate, is discussed elsewhere [Heal 1994]. The problems there raised are also considered further by Martin Davies [1994] and by Davies and Stone [2002].)

But it seems that the simulation hypothesis has considerable plausibility quite independent of any empirical developments in brain science, a plausibility noted by Kant, Dilthey, Collingwood and others who were not at all in the business of speculative cognitive science or high-level neuroanatomy. This suggests that there ought to be a reading of the simulation proposal in which it is articulated in quite different terms, terms which place it nearer the a priori end of the spectrum and on which it is effectively insulated from how things turn out in neuroanatomy and the like.

Let us also note that the idea of 'off-line' use of inference mechanisms and the like does not offer any particularly congenial setting for the idea of 'understanding from the inside'. The attraction of the idiom is not at all illuminated by the simulationist story as spelled out above. If I wish to predict how another person will react to some new supposed cholesterol-lowering medication, I may try to find out its effects on her by taking a dose myself and observing the results. Or (indulging in some science fiction) I might be able to unhook a part of my circulatory system and run an experiment on that. In either case I could 'simulate' in myself the operation of the drug on her. But the fact that it is a bit of my own bodily apparatus which is being run in experimental fashion gives no special insight 'from the inside' into the workings of the drug. And we have been told nothing which entitles us to think the case of the mind – that is, the brain – to be any different. But the idea of simulation did seem to have some resonance with the idea of 'understanding from the inside'. So again we are led to the thought that there may be an alternative way of conceptualising the idea.

So now let me sketch such an alternative. Consider a normal person who is capable of having beliefs about a certain subject matter, that is, of forming them appropriately and reasoning from them appropriately, among other things. Let us take Charles as an example. He is an investment expert and can form the belief that the base rate will rise on seeing evidence that it will and can make sensible inferences from this, for example to a fall in the value of shares. Now we take it entirely for granted that if Charles is capable of doing these things then he is also capable of reasoning hypothetically about what would happen if base rate were to rise. It is difficult to make any sense of the opposite supposition. Remember that Charles is a normal human being, so that in dealing with most subject matters, cups of tea, rain, buying a house and so forth, Charles can cope with both actual and hypothetical. Suppose that we now try to graft on the supposition that, for example, when faced with sentences beginning 'Suppose that base rate were to rise . . .' Charles goes deaf, or berserk or in some other way just fails to cope, although he does respond normally to the straight assertion 'Base rate has risen'. Or suppose we try to add on the idea Charles can appreciate the need for contingency planning in connection with most kinds of events but never seems to indulge in any kind of contingency planning about base rate rises, although, remember, he copes with great competence when they actually occur.

Can we really fill in the details of such a story in a coherent way? I do not say that it is provably impossible that we should do so. We are familiar with the extremely bizarre and disconcerting way in which what are normally treated as unitary abilities can unravel in the case of brain damage and disease (agnosias, aphasias and the like). But the interesting point is that such cases are extremely rare and that our ordinary psychological concepts do not allow for them. Our ordinary concepts are, quite properly I suggest, tailored to the outward, behavioural contours of the normal case, to the kinds of successful performances and achievements one can regularly expect of persons. They are not tailored to respect or record the structure of the machinery which realises those abilities.

In our thinking about other people one fundamental question we can and often do ask is what subject matters they are familiar with, that is, roughly what concepts they possess and in what kind of detail. Do they understand about tables and chairs? About royalty? About snow? About car engines? About income tax? And how well do they understand about each? If a person is familiar with a subject matter and understands it to some roughly indicated level, then we take it for granted that this ability to think about the subject matter will manifest itself just as much in coming to counterfactual beliefs, in considering possibilities and their upshots, as it does in forming and reasoning from categorical beliefs. The ability will show itself also in desires, intentions, emotions, dreams and fantasies. Competence in thinking about a subject matter is a multifaceted ability. It is an error, a distortion of our central psychological notions, to think of concept possession as something which shows up only or centrally in the formation of categorical beliefs. Rather, belief formation is just one facet of an ability which naturally manifests itself also in other kinds of thinking.

Note here a further important point, implicit in what has been said already but needing emphasis. A parallelism between certain psychological processes is already presupposed in the everyday conception we have been spelling out, namely a parallelism between, on the one hand, the inferences a person makes with categorical beliefs in virtue of his or her grasp of a subject matter and, on the other, the counterfactual conditional beliefs he or she would form as a result of making suppositions and the like. So Charles infers from 'Base rate will rise' to 'Share prices will fall'. But it is also the case that when he wonders 'What if base rate were to rise?' he will come to the conditional belief 'If base rate were to rise then share prices will fall'. This parallelism must stay more or less in place on pain of our losing our right to describe the content of Charles' wondering as 'What if base rate were to rise?' It cannot be base rate and its possible rise that he is wondering about if he does not at this point come up with the same idea, to figure in the consequent of his conditional belief, as he would come up with in a straight belief-to-belief inference. The fact that this parallelism exists is what makes viable the whole conceptual structure we use in talking of others' thoughts, plans, desires, reasonings and so on. What we assume is the existence of multifaceted abilities or, in other words, that the same content can occur embedded in various contents and as the object of different attitudes.

Someone might here offer a hypothesis about how it is that we have such a multifaceted ability, that is, about the nature of the systems or devices in which the ability is realised. Perhaps what goes on when I wonder 'What if p?' is that I take some inference mechanisms 'off-line' and feel in a pretend belief that p (Nichols et al. 1996). But to pursue the line of thought I am proposing we do not need to get embroiled in issues like this at all. The parallelism between thinking about what is taken to be actual (having a belief) and thinking about what is taken to be merely possible (wondering, hypothesising, imagining and the like) exists, whatever its underpinnings turn out to be. And we are entitled to invoke it in our account of thought about other minds.

So back again to simulation and other minds. We can now present the simulation hypothesis like this. Ability to think about another's thoughts, for example, to reason from the existence of those thoughts to conclusions about the existence of further thoughts, is an extension or redeployment of the ability to think about the subject matter of the other's thoughts.

How does this work? Let us take the following way of spelling things out. Let us revert to our schematic example in which the other believes that p_1-p_n and is interested in whether or not q. I know this and I am interested in whether or not she comes to believe that q. What she will do is wonder 'In the light of p_1-p_n is it the case that q?' that is, she will direct her thought to answering the question whether q, having in mind the evidence that p_1-p_n. If the propositions that p_1-p_n imply that q, and she comes to be aware of them as so doing, then she will come to believe that q, taking this to be a belief to which she is entitled, in the light of the facts (as she sees them) that p_1-p_n. What will I do? If I share her beliefs I may, in effect, pose myself just the same question, viz., 'In the light of the facts that p_1-p_n is it the case that q?' But if I do not share her beliefs, then the question I should address is, rather, 'If it were that p_1-p_n would it be that q?' But in either case the other person and I share a central aim, namely trying to get a sense of the relations of implication or otherwise between p_1-p_n and q. We carry out this aim by exercising our ability to think about the subject matters of p_1-p_n and q. And it comes to seem to me that if it were that p_1-p_n then it would be that q, then I attribute to the other the belief that q.

Let us now reflect on the concepts implicit in the story I have just sketched. I have spoken of us as having 'a sense of' some thoughts as implying or being implied by others. Much recent philosophy, influenced perhaps by cognitive science models, tacitly operates with a picture of the progress of thought through time, when a person is reasoning and reflecting, as a matter of there being one thought (perhaps quite a complex one) occupying the conscious mind at one instant and of its being entirely replaced by another thought at the succeeding moment. So, for a schematic example, at first I think 'p and if p then q; but is it the case that q?' and then this complex thought is swept away and replaced by 'q'. But this is surely a distortion of our experience as thinkers. A slightly more accurate narrative is one in which I first think 'p and if p then q; but is it the case that q?' and then next think 'Well, clearly q, since p and if p then q'. That is, I judge that q in a light of a sense of it as following from p and if p then q. And I take my new belief that q to be justified by my beliefs that p and that if p then q.

So far only beliefs have been considered. But the above is a structure which we find in numerous intrapsychic connections, for example between desires, intentions and emotions (or at least some important aspects of them) and other contentful states. So my fear of something consists, at least in part and in central cases, of my taking it to be dangerous and threatening. But when I so take it, it is in the light of my belief that it may explode or may bite. So my fear, insofar as it is to be identified with taking the feared thing to be dangerous, is experienced by me as justified or appropriate in the light of other thoughts. Similarly, I make take a resolution to perform an action in the light of that action seeming to me to be advantageous and to have no drawbacks. Again, it is not just that first I think about the advantages and lack of drawbacks and then the next instant these considerations are entirely swept away from my conscious mind and replaced by the thought 'I'll do it!' Rather, the ensuing thought is more like 'I'll do it (since it is advantageous and has no drawbacks)'.

And what goes for me goes for others, on the account of the use of psychological concepts which I am sketching. We do not think of others primarily or solely as extremely complex biological machines containing many physical structures interacting in elegant ways. In thinking of a person as a person, these aspects of human existence are not to the fore. Of course there is complexity in others' psychological states, and this complexity is implicated in temporal development which it is quite proper to think of as causal, in some sense of 'causal'. This is what makes the 'biological machine with complex innards' story, and the related functionalist view in philosophy of mind, seem plausible at all. But when we think of persons the complexity we are aware of is, I suggest, unified in a particular way. It is not unified just as 'the states of the bits of stuff inside that skull' but rather as 'the elements of the coherent worldview constructed by the person whose body that is'. And the person is unified inasmuch as her mind is unified, that is, inasmuch as the elements of it are seen as cohering and are brought to bear on one another to suggest new conjectures, to correct misconceptions, to provide mutual support through their rational connection and so forth.

A person becomes aware of her world and builds up a picture of it, through perception, memory and reasoning. And that view must be unified in the way sketched. But let us note also that her view will necessarily include, woven in among the rest, many indexical thoughts, defining her beliefs about herself, her placement, role, capacities and so forth. For example, they will include beliefs of the form 'I am in such and such a location', 'I am capable of these or those actions', 'I occupy such and such a role', 'These and those achievements, dangers, disappointments or pleasures are possible for me' and so forth. These elements may be said to define 'a point of view' on the world, in both a literal and a metaphorical sense. So when I attempt in simulationist style to re-create another's thoughts, insofar as such indexical thoughts are included, then I have, to some greater or lesser extent, attempted to re-create her point of view.

The suggestion I would like to pursue now is that it is this complex of ideas which makes the adoption of the idiom of 'understanding from the inside' so natural and attractive. There are a variety of strands in this metaphor. The mind of other is 'inside' in the sense that (sometimes at least) it is not immediately apparent in behaviour what a person thinks, and hence it takes reflection to see what her thoughts are. A mind is also 'inside' in the sense that mental events and states are capable of moving the body to spontaneous (i.e., not immediately externally caused) movement. In these senses the mechanism of the alarm clock is inside it. We come to something more distinctive of mind in the fact that, on the view sketched, when I consider the nature of what is 'inside' another person, in the senses suggested by these two earlier points, what I find myself postulating is a set of thoughts which represent the world from a point of view. So the 'inside' which I find is not mere mechanical or biological complexity. If the inside were of that kind, there would not be any question of anything being 'from' it. But things can be 'from the inside' with a person because what is 'inside' is itself outwardly directed. It is an interlocking complex of items with indexical representational content concerning the world around that person. The existence of this kind of outward-directed content is bound up with the person's ability to respond to changing perceptions and reasoning by modifying and enlarging the worldview in rationally intelligible ways. We think of the content as having been built up by the exercise of the person's cognitive capacities, her perceptual awareness and her abilities to remember and reason. The idea of reason then provides a further strand which enriches the 'from the inside' metaphor, inasmuch as in deploying it I represent other people as beings capable of recognising and responding to norms. Their thoughts and behaviour therefore have sense and can be justified in ways which have no analogue in the explanations provided for the behaviour of inanimate items.

What is the status of all this, you might ask. I have just outlined very roughly a picture we have of ourselves and others – each of us a rational subject with a point of view, having multifaceted abilities to think effectively about many subject matters and so forth. And this picture is, I have suggested, the one presupposed by the form of simulationism which I have tried to outline and defend. I would also like to suggest the converse, namely that this kind of simulationism is the natural theory of the understanding of other minds for someone who conceives of persons as unified rational subjects. It is clear, then, that a presupposition of rationality, that is, the ability to appreciate what follows from what, to respond to reasons by grasping their force, is central to this whole complex of views. But could it be that this presupposition might turn out to be recognisably false? If so, then either we must say that, contrary to what I have urged, there is no conceptual link between the mental and rationality, or we shall have to reconfigure our idea of the mental so as to extrude the rationality assumption. Might it be that it transpires that mental notions are so inextricably bound up with the illusory idea of rationality that this separation cannot be made? If so, the upshot of the empirical discovery of our non-rationality would be the need to eliminate the mental altogether. This form of scepticism about the mental is too big a topic to address here. But I would like to conclude by offering a few reflections.

The idea that we are rational has received some excellent probing and clarification from philosophers. Psychologists have also undertaken fascinating empirical investigations bearing on the actual workings of our inferential processes. The joint upshot of this philosophical and empirical work is that it is quite clear that there are a number of grand and demanding senses of 'rational' in which we cannot properly claim to be rational. Such ability as we have is imperfect, limited by the finitude of our memories and by the amount of complexity we can take in. We do not have the time, energy or attention even to do all of the comparatively simple thinking and inferring which would be useful to us, let alone many elaborate reasonings, and even further the grandiose projects of achieving total consistency or coming to recognise all the logical consequences of what we accept. And, worse, we seem to be prone to systematic errors in elementary reasoning; there seem to be inferential versions of perceptual illusions such as the Mueller-Lyer case, where we are gripped by the conviction that something follows from something else when it does not (Cherniak 1986; Stein 1996).

So our rationality, if it exists, does not amount to anything very grand. But then, we do not need anything very grand to defend the picture sketched above, any more than we need to credit ourselves with illusion-resistant eyesight of eagle-like acuity in order to defend the claim that in vision we have a sense which enables us to become aware of the placement and properties of things about us. Sight is reliable enough for us to be able to become aware, when we reflect, of when it is prone to illusion. So we can use it in increasingly subtle and well-focused ways (involving cross-checking, self-critical awareness of possible sources of error, help-fully devised instruments and the like) to progressively improve our grasp on the layout and properties of objects. The central claim we need about rationality is closely analogous. We need to be entitled to the assumption that thinking about a question, deploying all that we know which bears on it, will generally tend to improve our grasp on that issue rather than the contrary. And, as in the case of vision, what makes this central idea defensible is that we are capable of such things as reflecting on our reason-ing practices, recognising mistakes through cross-checking and turning, where need be, to various aids. And thus we are capable of progressively improving our sense of what follows from what. No empirical evidence currently to hand shows that we are not entitled to the assumption that our basic thinking capacity is not fundamentally pointed in the right di-rection, namely, in the direction of leading us, when we employ it, to a better grip on things. Indeed, the empirical studies which identify our inferential shortcomings are precisely evidence to support the assumption. And how would anyone who did not make it proceed with his or her thinking? What is the practical alternative to making it? There is none.

Consider finally something about our relations with other people. It is often taken for granted in the discussions of philosophers and psychologists that the central role of psychological concepts is to enable us to predict inner states in others so that we can, in turn, predict and sometimes influence the behaviour those states bring about. But this is a serious distortion. Our relations with other people do not have the same structure as our relations with inanimate objects, plants or machines. We do not deal with our family members, friends, colleagues or fellow citizens as we do with volcanoes, fields of wheat or kitchen mixers, namely, by trying to figure out the nature and layout of their innards so that we can predict and perhaps control them.

Prediction and control may (sometimes rightly and sometimes wrongly) be the name of the game for psychiatrists, prison governors or dictators, in some of their dealings with some people. But it is not the name of the game for most distinctively human interactions. A much more central pattern occurs where one person offers to another some articulation of how things strike him or her – a remark, gesture, action or expression – in the course of pursuing some more or less well-defined joint project. Certainly this will be offered in the expectation (or at least the hope) that it will be identified for what it is. Thus far a prediction will probably be made. And also a prediction will be made that a response of a certain very broad class will be forthcoming. So in a philosophical debate one will expect to get back a philosophical question or observation; in a chess game one will get a chess move; in a game of mud pies one will get an elaboration of the mud-pie world; in a courtship one will get a move to deepen the intimacy; and so forth. But the specific nature of the response is not predicted. Social life would be utterly boring, completely different from the communicative reality we experience, if it were. What we hope of another with whom we interact is not that he or she will go through some gyrations which we have already planned in detail, but that he or she will make some contributions to moving forward the joint and co-operative enterprise in which we are both, more or less explicitly, engaged.

There will be, in any particular case, many moves which would fit the general bill; which move an individual makes depends upon his or her individual appreciation of the situation, to which he or she brings not only differences in temperament, inventiveness and the like but, nearly always, differences in awareness both of empirical facts and of what follows from what. In a philosophical discussion the parties will probably share a good deal of common ground; but they will not be, psychologically speaking, identical twins. That is why there is a point in discussion; we engage in it so that we can pool our knowledge, insights, inventiveness and so forth. This is one way of combating our finitude, namely, by having different of us pursue different lines of thought, since there is typically more labour in discovery than in appreciation of the discovery once made. Division of intellectual labour is not something which comes on the scene merely with large accumulations of knowledge and specialisation in the sciences. It is built right in to the idea of conversation and co-operation in the most everyday activities and plans.

The way in which we carry on such activities shows that we presuppose the rationality of others, presuppose that we share standards of what follows from what and what is relevant to what. Our first move, on finding another's response not immediately intelligible and helpful, is to search round for an interpretation which makes it so. And if others disagree with us about what constitutes good reasoning, making moves which show that at some level they do not share standards about what follows from what, we seek to put them right in the expectation that they will acknowledge the mistake (or perhaps they will show that it is we who have made the mistake). Let us further note that when a mistake is agreed to have been made, we will often look for, and find, a reason why it was made, not just in the sense of a cause or regularity in its making, but in the sense of some excuse which reconciles the making of the mistake with the idea that, even in making it, the perpetrator was exercising his or her rationality. This may be done by pointing to the false presuppositions which were accepted, the misleading analogy which was unduly prominent or some similar factor. Few mistakes, whether factual errors or mistakes in reasoning, are just opaquely and blankly completely unintelligible when reflected on. Some shred of justification can nearly always be found.

And how well this general orientation to others serves us, how well things work out, on the whole. And how completely lacking we are in any conception of how things could be differently conducted. Empirical studies of our limitations and proneness to error (together with such factors as awareness of the differences of our own outlook from those of other cultures and times, or Freudian insights into the deeper workings of our motivations and self-conceptions) may all enrich the mixture and make us aware that the intelligibility we seek is not always to be found easily or on the surface. But such facts do not prevent us looking for reason and intelligibility or stand in the way of our thinking, in most cases, that we have found it. The conclusion is that rationality, in the schematic but still powerful sense outlined, is a very deeply entrenched assumption in our picture of ourselves and others, and hence that the understanding of other minds which calls upon the simulationist framework is not to be easily dislodged or replaced.

4

Simulation, Theory and Content

1. INTRODUCTION

Some, the theory theorists, say that when we make judgements about the psychological states of others and use such judgements to predict or explain, we employ some theory about the psychological. But others, the simulationists, say that we possess no such theory, or at least none complete enough to underpin all our competence with psychological notions. Rather, they say, what we do in such situations is 'simulate' others' mental states and processes in ourselves and thus gain insight into what others are likely to do.

My aim in this essay is first to offer an argument in favour of simulationism and second to suggest possible limits to the simulationist strategy. I shall suggest that simulation must be central as far as dealing with the contents of others' mental states is concerned, but is much less clearly of relevance in dealing with non-content. Thus, philosophers and psychologists should not oppose simulation to theory, but rather should ask what is the appropriate realm of each and how they interact.

The topic throughout is the nature of the fully developed adult competence with psychological notions, in the context of predicting others' future psychological states and actions on the basis of knowledge about their current psychological states. I shall not discuss the (it seems to me) importantly different question of how we arrive at judgements about others' thoughts, feelings and so on from knowledge of their placement in the environment or bodily behaviour. Also, I am not concerned here with the issue of what psychological concepts are and what it is to have possession of them. And I shall not touch at all on developmental issues or questions of how children's competence with psychological language grows and changes. I believe that there are implications for many of these questions in the considerations which follow, but I shall not pursue them here. (For more on the second question, on what it is to have psychological concepts, see Essay 11.)

In more detail the structure of what follows is this. Section 2 offers some further clarification of the three central notions 'simulation', 'theory' and 'content', and some remarks on why simulation is at least an option. Section 3 reminds us of some important facts about thought. Section 4 builds on these to offer the main argument against theory theory. Section 5 returns to the contrast between content and non-content, suggesting that even if the earlier argument persuades us as to the importance of simulation, we should not overextend our claims on its behalf.

2. THE CENTRAL NOTIONS

By a simulation of X we shall understand something, Y, which is similar enough to X in its intrinsic nature for tendencies to diachronic development which are inherent in X to have parallels in Y. Hence, given suitably analogous stimuli or circumstances, their histories unfold in parallel, and properties of the one can be read off from properties of the other according to some simple correlation scheme. The classic example is the model aircraft in the fanned draught of the wind tunnel, which is a simulation of the real aircraft in the real wind. (Thus 'simulation' as I intend it here is equivalent to 'process-driven simulation' as introduced by Goldman [1995a: 85].)

Given this notion, the central simulationist claim is that the thinking which occurs when one person reasons, in all seriousness, to some theoretical or practical conclusion, can be simulated in a second person, who need not however be in the same way committed to the thoughts entertained. Simulationists have also claimed that this similarity can be accessed or employed so as to enable the second person to arrive at judgements about what the first will think or do.

By 'theory' we shall understand an articulated structure made up of elements, each of which either makes a claim of a kind expressible in a public language (perhaps with some extended vocabulary or notational system) or expresses a rule of inference. We are, of course, allowing that theories may be tacitly as well as explicitly known. But the kind of thing theories are is shown by the explicit specimens, for example in physics or linguistics. The use of 'theory' advocated here thus differs from the very generous construal offered by Stich and Nichols (1995a: 133) on which any process subserving our capacity to predict others which is not simulation counts as a theory, even if it contains no sentence- or rule-like items. For Stich and Nichols' polemical purposes at that point, their wide definition is entirely appropriate. But intuitively it is a considerably stretched usage to call something a 'theory' when it lacks articulated contentful structure.

One thing which possession of a psychological theory would explain is our ability to make predictions about people from knowledge of their psychological states. But a theory is not a mere conjunction of such individual judgements. It must embody the information not as a mere list but in some more compendious way. So the theory will contain generalisations which can be applied to individual cases.

But what form will they take and how will they be organised? Let us make a contrast here which will later be important. Consider two possible bodies of medical knowledge about diseases, their symptoms and likely developments. The aim here is to clarify how bodies of knowledge may be contrasted in their completeness and organisation. We shall concentrate on knowledge which is explicitly available to the knower. First we can imagine a wise woman who is able to offer some general remarks about symptoms and their seriousness. ('High fever is often dangerous', 'Laboured breathing is generally a bad sign', 'Many skin rashes are trivial') and can also, surveying a patient, select from among the visible symptoms the ones which are in fact important in the particular case. So she can say, correctly, 'This patient will recover, because the fever has broken in a sweat' or, in another case, 'This patient will not recover, because the breathing is now very laboured'. But it may well be the case that the patient who will recover is also exhibiting very laboured breathing. Our imagined wise woman, however, is unable to say explicitly why the breathing is not so sinister in that case. She knows that she is entitled to ignore it in arriving at a prognosis. But she does not know why, at least not explicitly. And it is only the content of explicit claims which we are considering here.

Second, we can imagine another practitioner, say a doctor with modern training, who possesses as part of her explicit knowledge what the wise woman lacks, namely a framework within which the various symptoms are listed and systematically related to each other. This practitioner can talk of the interrelation of symptoms and of the contexts in which each is important. She can not only predict what will happen in a particular case, but locate that case among other possible ones, by saying what would have happened in other circumstances and why.

Considering these two bodies of explicit knowledge, I suggest that there is at least one use of the word 'theory' where it is only fully at home in describing something with the structure and power of the second example. The wise woman has some explicit knowledge which we might well call 'theoretical', knowledge of the kind that could figure in a theory. But the totality of what she can deploy explicitly does not amount to a full-fledged theory of symptoms and disease. Now, of course, it may be that when we add in what she knows tacitly then she can be credited with knowledge of a fully fledged theory. But as far as explicit knowledge is concerned, the modern practitioner knows a theory, whereas the wise woman possesses only a scrappy collection of bits of theoretical knowledge.

In what follows I shall take it that when the theory theorist claims that we possess a theoretically based ability to predict psychological states, he means 'theory' in this sense of 'fully fledged theory'. So his claim is that we possess, but probably only tacitly, some body of knowledge with the kind of organisation and richness which is exhibited in the explicit knowledge of the modern practitioner. So he acknowledges that, as with the wise woman and medical knowledge, our explicit psychological knowledge is scrappy; but he maintains that, tacitly, we deploy something much richer. (You may object that this is to lumber the theory theorist with commitment to tacit knowledge of theory in an overly demanding sense of 'theory'. We shall return at the end of Section 4 to consider how the debate goes if we agree with this objection.)

By 'content' we shall understand the representational aspect of a mental state, that in virtue of which it carries some specification of how the world is (or might be) and in virtue of which it can be assessed for fit with the world. We shall return in Section 5 to the distinction between content and non-content. For the moment it is enough to note two things. The first is that it is extremely implausible to suppose that full specification of content exhausts what can be said of a mental state. To say it did would be to take it that there is only one mode of occurrence of content and that every psychological state, whether a propositional attitude or a perceptual state, can be seen on investigation to consist of some content (perhaps immensely complex) entertained in this one mode. I do not say that I have an immediate knock-down argument against this view. (It may be that some have held it. Spinoza is a plausible candidate.) But it has an overintellectual flavour, and it seems extremely likely that we shall need to recognise non-content to account both for the differences between propositional attitudes and also for the nature of perception and sensation. The second point to note about content is that examples of it are specified by that-clauses when we attribute beliefs, intentions, desires and emotions to people. And it is this kind of content with which we are primarily concerned in what follows.

Are we in possession of some theoretical knowledge, whether tacit or explicit, about persons and their states? And does this provide the whole of what we call on when we predict others? The answer to the first question must surely be 'yes'. We are capable of stating a fair amount about the sort of beings we take people to be, the factors which influence them and how those factors interrelate. For example, people acquire beliefs in various ways, perception and inference among them, and retain through memory many of the beliefs they acquire. They have desires and, under the guidance of their beliefs, form projects on how to fulfil them. They feel emotions which are liable to influence their patterns of reasoning. And so on. (Wellman provides a fairly full and plausible sketch of our folk psychological framework [1990: chap. 4].) Being a normal adult human being with competence in using psychological notions requires grasp on this kind of thing. Some of it we clearly know explicitly, and perhaps there is more of the same sort which we grasp only tacitly.

But it does not follow from this that the answer to our second question is also 'yes', namely that we possess a theory, tacit or otherwise, in terms of which the whole of our ability to make predictions about individuals can be explained. What we set out above were only generalities about beliefs, perceptions, emotions, projects and so on as broad classes. Such generalities say nothing directly on beliefs or projects about particular subject matters, for instance, under what circumstances a doctor will believe that a patient has measles or a restaurant customer will order soup rather than salad. If the theory we possess, when spelled out, is to be one which underpins such particular predictions, it must grapple with content. And the claim I wish to defend is that we cannot be taken to know a theory (in the sense outlined above) which deals fully with content. Of course we know bits of theory about some contents and their relations. But my suggestion will be that our primary competence with content is of the 'know how' variety and that only a small part of this can be reflected in any theoretical 'know that' about how contents relate.

The nature and possibility of simulation have been explored in the existing literature, so I shall not rehearse the issues here. The key point is that we think and reason about situations using the same capacities, whether we take those situations to be actual or merely possible. So if I take on merely as a hypothesis what someone else actually believes, then what I do in further thought simulates what he or she does, inasmuch as we both exercise the same intellectual and conceptual capacities on the same subject matter and so may move through the same sequence of related contents to the same conclusion. The ability to think about the non-actual is very remarkable. But the point worth stressing is that once it has been conceded we need very little more (merely a grip on the general picture of the person sketched above, says the simulationist) to enable us to use our ability to think about the non-actual for the very different task of predicting others' thoughts.

3. FOUR IMPORTANT FACTS ABOUT THINKING

I turn now from elucidating the idea of psychological simulation and defending its possibility to putting in place some of the ideas which will enable us to argue its attraction, namely by undermining its rival, the theory theory. It will help us to get clear first what a theory adequate to deal with content would have to cope with. So I shall introduce four important facts about thinking: (1) the amount of information we possess; (2) epistemic holism; (3) our actual rationality; and (4) our actual success in predicting others.

Let us take information first. Each normal adult human being knows (or believes) an enormous number of things. He or she has a worldview (history, physics, politics . . .) together with information about personal history (family, friends, career . . .) and perceptually given information about current physical surroundings (the location and properties of objects, people . . .). A psychological account of a person at an instant would specify all this and would say whether the information was merely dispositionally possessed or occupying conscious attention. In addition, such an account would spell out the person's tastes, values, ambitions, emotions and so on. To write all this out in a natural language would take volumes and volumes. I shall ignore here questions about whether indeed there could be such a thing as a complete articulation of a person's thoughts, or whether, at the end of the day, we have to fall back on pointing to our lives and everyday surroundings and saying that our thought is what enables us to cope with all this. (On this, see Dreyfus and Dreyfus 1986.) Clearly there is such a thing as trying to make a start on the project of articulation, and that is enough for our current argument.

A person's psychological state evolves diachronically, partly under the impetus of external stimuli and partly as driven by internal factors, for example, what problems she is thinking about. So a person frequently acquires new propositional attitudes, which are derived from ones already possessed. And this brings us to our second important fact about thinking, namely that justification or epistemic status is a holistic notion.

This is particularly important for what follows, so we should consider it further. The central claim is that the status of a thought as justified or not is determined by features of the whole set of thoughts from which it arises. An answer to a question may seem to have good support from some subset of thoughts. But if we look wider we may find further thoughts in the light of which the prima facie force of the subset is modified. Hence it is something about the nature of the whole set of thoughts, viz., the presence or absence of such disruptive modifiers, which determines the status of the new thought as justified or not.

One familiar observation which gives some limited support to this claim concerns the extreme causal complexity of the world. If I am seeking to tell what some object has done or will do, I need to look not just at it and its close surroundings but also more widely to see if the circumstances are normal, or if there are further factors which will disrupt normal developments or correlations. For example, if I have the information that you are about to release the spoon you hold, then I may sensibly judge that the spoon will fall. But if I also know that the spoon is suspended by a thread from the ceiling, then I should not form that belief – not, that is, unless in addition I know that the thread is just about to be cut. And so on.

But it would be consistent to acknowledge this and also to think that for some particular phenomenon we do have a complete story and so can offer generalisations and make claims with no 'ceteris paribus' cautions. At this point we need to note a different and more radical reason for acknowledging holism. This is the possibility of contradiction or tension in a worldview. Drawing out an implication of a subset of thoughts may serve to make such a tension or contradiction manifest; and then the right response could well be to abandon some or all of the subset rather than to adopt the implication. What this shows is that a view about whether something is or will be the case should be sensitive, not only to obviously relevant considerations (e.g., about the causes of or evidence for the thing in question), but also to information relevant to whether one's views about the causes and evidence are themselves correct.

This more radical point can be deployed in tandem with the earlier one to suggest that no thought, whatever its subject matter, can be ruled out a priori as certainly irrelevant to any given question. For any given question, any pieces of information might bear on it, if there were any one of an indefinite number of suitable patterns of other thoughts to link them.

For example, suppose I am a doctor investigating whether a patient has measles. I have a great deal of information about symptoms and the results of physiological tests in this particular case, and also some general beliefs about the signs of measles. These pieces of information are obviously relevant to my question. Let us suppose further that when put together they entail that the patient does not have measles. For example, one of my pieces of information is that a standard and supposedly entirely reliable diagnostic test has produced a negative result. It may seem obvious that the question is now settled. I do not need to offer the verdict with any 'ceteris paribus' rider, and further information I possess that Henry VII of England was a Tudor could not possibly be relevant to the issue. However, we need to insert only a few further ideas (not outrageously bizarre) into my belief set to put in place a connection and to make the information about Henry bear on the medical question.

Here is one way of making the link. I may already be aware of a few odd cases (hitherto ignored or shrugged off as failures of apparatus) which suggest that we are perhaps wrong in thinking the standard diagnostic test conclusive. But when we focus on these cases they hint at the idea that in people of a certain genetic constitution the disease runs a non-standard course in which the test is unreliable. This genetic constitution is common in Wales, and in particular in the Tudor family. And perhaps my patient has boasted of his royal ancestor, Henry VII. Given all this, the information that Henry VII was a Tudor is the crucial fact which links the odd case of my current patient to the other odd cases. The discovery of that link might be the final piece of the jigsaw which stimulates me to reassess the previously accepted view of the reliability of the test. And having done so, I then judge that the patient does indeed have the disease, despite the negative result. This is a possible scenario. And it is only the absence of any linking pattern of this kind which would entitle me to pay no attention to the history of England when trying to diagnose my patient's condition.

Similar arguments show the need for practical decisions also to be sensitive to the possible bearing of considerations beyond those which are obviously relevant. For example, my judgement that I am now seated in a restaurant, that I am hungry and that I have been given a menu provides good support for my decision to read the menu with a view to choosing a dish. But if I also recognise the waiter as a wanted criminal, from a distinctive scar on his hand, then I have reason to telephone the police rather than read the menu. But, again, if I also have further information that my movements are being watched by the criminals who suspect that

I am a police agent, then perhaps I have reason to sit tight and (at least pretend to) read the menu. And so on. Or again, working out the means needed to secure a goal might show me that pursuit of it conflicts with other objectives and so lead me to abandon the goal rather than to resolve on those means.

Let us summarise the central thoughts here. Given a question in which I am interested and a body of information which bears on it and strongly suggests an answer, it does not follow that I ought to accept that answer. There may be, elsewhere in what I accept, considerations which supplement or undermine those already in hand and which, when taken into account, will suggest a different answer. Moreover, we cannot lay down in advance restrictions on the subject matter or logical shape of such thoughts, since (for all we have seen) anything could bear on anything, given suitable links. So coming up with the justified answer to a question requires a certain kind of sensitivity to the shape of one's whole body of thought, viz., the ability to detect in it the presence or absence of other relevant considerations.

This epistemological and justificatory holism is a quite different matter from semantic holism and ought to be accepted even by semantic atomists or molecularists. It does not arise from some essential interconnectedness which thoughts of their nature have with other thoughts. Rather, what underlies it is the potential complex interconnectedness of things, both causally and evidentially, together with the fact of our fallibility and liability to harbour tensions in our views.

Often, of course, circumstances are normal, other things are equal, latent contradictions are not lurking. Then we shall arrive at a correct judgement or decision, even if only paying attention to only some limited part of what we know. But how do we cope when things are not so straightforward and when factors prima facie very distant (the scar on a man's hand, Henry VII being a Tudor) are relevant to a question (whether to study a menu, whether this patient has measles) because of the existence of one of those patterns of linkage mentioned earlier? Are we then stymied? This brings us to the third important fact about thinking which we need to recognise.

Sometimes, of course, we are caught out by the unusual. Much recent literature about cognitive functioning emphasises how limited, fallible, habit-bound and irrational we are. We overlook matters, fail to follow up clues, get confused and so forth. But not always. A striking fact about us is that when we seek answers to questions, all the information in the volumes and volumes of our worldview is, to remarkable degree, appropriately available to us. It is available not just in the sense that each of us knows what he or she thinks about the matters on which we have information. It is available, rather, in the more important sense that, if there are configurations in the total view which make proper something other than a stereotypical answer to some question in hand, then that information may well become prominent to us and influence our judgement appropriately. So we do arrive at opinions and decisions which are justified in the light of our total worldview, in cases where this has required us to range widely and to see the relevance of new kinds of factors which we have not taken into account before.

Fourth and finally, we must note that, in predicting the thoughts of others, we take account of the fact that they have this ability to cope in these kinds of situations. In other words, we expect of them that, sometimes at least, they will make the judgements which are justified in the holistic fashion sketched. Consider again the cases of the doctor or restaurant customer, from the point of view of someone attempting to predict what they would do. In setting up these cases I earlier relied upon the fact that you would have no difficulty in seeing that a person with the thoughts sketched could well respond in the way I outlined.

4. SIMULATION, RELEVANCE AND THE FRAME PROBLEM

Having set in place accounts of our key terms and drawn attention to some important facts, we are now in a position to consider why the theory theory, when it embodies a claim to be able to deal with content, is unattractive and simulationism is correspondingly strengthened. We may put the issue this way. The theory theorist is committed to the claim that we have – tacitly at least – solved an extremely important precursor problem to the famous Frame Problem in Artificial Intelligence, namely the problem of providing a general theory of relevance. And this claim is highly implausible.

The Frame Problem (or at least one of the problems which goes under this name) is, roughly, as follows. Artificial Intelligence (AI) aims to outline how we might build machines which can perform similarly to human beings with respect to such things as sustaining a conversation or coming up with some plan of action. The object is to show how to endow a machine with knowledge and the ability to process that knowledge in such a way as to enable it to derive appropriate answers to questions it is set. But any assemblage of information has many implications, the bigger the assemblage the greater the number; and only a few of them will bear on a given question. The difficulty AI researchers have run into is that of finding a format for coding knowledge and questions, and a way in which a machine can process its knowledge in the light of its question, so as to enable it to come up reasonably quickly with the required answer rather than with some one of the vast number of other true but irrelevant conclusions which its knowledge base and inference rules license. Possibilities for deriving these other conclusions have to be allowed for, because they might be needed in other cases, if other questions were posed. But how do we get the device to ignore them in this case? (See Dennett [1984] for a good account. Other papers collected by Boden [1990] also provide an introduction to the extensive literature.)

The Frame Problem in some version arises even if we do not believe in epistemological holism of the kind already described. Someone who thinks both that we can ignore the possibility of our being inconsistent and also that knowledge is organised in deductive systems is still faced with the problem of finding a way through the multiply branching set of consequences to the needed conclusion. But the sort of holistic justification structure sketched earlier threatens a much tougher version of the problem than a deductively based system. When deduction (from a set of premises guaranteed consistent) is central, we might hope to use some combination of vocabulary and formal features in the shape of the question to narrow down the range of axioms and inference rules to be considered; and thus we might find some strategy for homing in speedily on the needed route through from information to answer. But if holism is the order of the day then relevance becomes context relative. We need not only to locate the obviously important materials but also to survey systematically the whole of the rest of the assemblage to see whether or not it contains any of the indefinitely large number of configurations of information that might also be important.

My claim is not that the theory theorist must suppose that the theory he postulates itself provides a solution to the Frame Problem. That problem is about how to represent and process knowledge in an artificially created system, and it largely concerns the implementation level. Those studying the Frame Problem have to deal extensively with non-intentional subject matter, such as the virtues of different computer languages, the attempted syntactic specifications of various inference procedures and the like. By contrast, the imagined psychological theory need deal only with items, viz. thoughts, specified intentionally.

But theory theory and the Frame Problem are nevertheless closely connected. One thing which makes the Frame Problem so difficult is our inability to say much of a structured or systematic kind about the central notion of relevance. We want to mimic human intelligence. We can say at a high level of generality that it is characteristic of that intelligence that, given a question and a worldview, a person will respond to what in that view is relevant to the question. We can also give detailed examples of relevance, and so of how people actually should and do respond to this or that question. But an intermediate-level competence – on which we could group the cases in a revealing way or classify kinds of relevance or point to some finite number of structural possibilities for relating information or the like – is strikingly lacking. If we had it we might at least see how to think about implementing a similarly structured ability on a machine. But this intermediate-level grip, a systematic way of treating relevance, is what the theory theorist supposes we do actually, even if only tacitly, have.

To see this recall the claim of Section 2 that a theory is something which enables us to locate a given case among the range of possible cases. It specifies the possible factors bearing on outcomes, how they interrelate, and why some and not others are actually influential in a given case. Such a theory need not, of course, itself tell us what happens in unusual circumstances; to handle these we need to integrate the information provided by the theory into a wider picture. But a theory of a phenomenon ought to give us systematically based insight into the behaviour of the items theorised in normal circumstances.

When a question on a particular subject matter (medicine, restaurant behaviour) presents itself to us, our remarkable cognitive system serves up to us information obviously relevant to the question. Supposing that the subject matter is theorised, then it will serve up the theory (or the required section of it). If there are no unusual circumstances, then we apply the theory and come up with an appropriate answer. But if circumstances are not usual, the system may well serve up that information also. It will tell us that perhaps we need to look beyond the normal theory, or to modify it.

Matters will be just the same with the supposed psychological theory. We need to have it, rather than some other irrelevant theory, come to mind when required. And its predictions are as liable as those of any other body of information to be in need of correction or supplementation in the light of extra information. Suppose, for example, I am applying the theory to predict whether or not someone will raise his arm by thinking about what the theory tells me is relevant, say his beliefs and desires. If I also know that the subject has a brain tumour which makes him liable to seizures, or that someone has attached his arm to a pulley, then in making my prediction I must operate flexibly and holistically, modifying the expectation suggested by the psychological theory in the light of these further considerations. So in operating the psychological theory, as with any other, we shall need to rely upon the amazing powers which consideration of the Frame Problem has made us aware we have.

There is nothing so far to worry the theory theorist. Simply by acknowledging that we are entitled to rely on those powers, he is not committed to supposing that he has solved any part of the Frame Problem – any more than a doctor or theorist of restaurant behaviour is so committed. But there are two factors which make the psychological case crucially different and which mean that a claim to have a psychological theory of content does involve further commitments.

The first is that the subject matter of psychological theory is precisely thoughts themselves and their upshots. The second, and crucial, consideration is that dealing with the unexpected or unusual is an expected and usual part of human thought. As we stressed at the end of the previous section, we can cope when circumstances are not entirely straightforward and we understand very well that others can do so too. So if our imagined psychological theory is to account for our competence in these cases, it must give systematically organised insight into the difference between our responses in usual and unusual cases – that is, insight into a whole range of worldview/question pairs and their possible upshots. It must specify the range of psychological factors which influence what answer is returned to a given question. It must lay out how those factors interact. It must say why some are important to outcomes in some settings and not in others. It must be able to tell us how and why things would have been different, given this or that variation in the starting conditions. But, given epistemological holism and our actual rationality, what all this amounts to is precisely a general and systematic theory of relevance.

I do not say that it is impossible that we do possess tacitly a theory of this character. But I suggest we should be very unwilling to postulate it. One difficulty is the oddness of supposing that we possess it tacitly while at the same time having no inkling of how to set it out explicitly. But another, and much more important, consideration is the quite mind-boggling richness and complexity of the theory postulated. It needs to be able to handle worldview/question pairs and come up with a systematically supported prediction about what answer will be given, in every case where, in practice, we can predict what another, who had that view and was faced with that question, would conclude. Let us remember that the worldviews are volumes and volumes long. We may, if we like, summarise much of the information very briefly with phrases like 'what most people know' or some such. But even when disguised in this way and made to look less threatening, the volumes and volumes must still be handled by the theory. So it must have ways of separately registering every difference in content between two worldviews, which we can see could result in their possessors giving different answers to the same question. It must also have ways of appropriately classifying these differences and systematically setting out how they contribute to the outcomes they influence. As an information storage and processing task, and given the range of our possible worldviews and actual psychological competence, dealing with this imagined theory is orders of magnitude more formidable than dealing with any other tacit theory that has been proposed – for instance, for grammar or folk physics.

The theory theorist may try to avoid this unpleasant outcome by denying that we have this systematic theoretical grip on relevance. (Here we revert to the thought that the sense of 'theory' with which we have saddled the theory theorist is unfairly demanding.) Instead, he says, there is a non-theoretical background machinery – our remarkable cognitive system – which delivers to us the factors relevant to any given problem. It thus enables us to pick out from another's worldview the particular thoughts important to determining his or her behaviour in a specified case. For example, taking the customer in the restaurant who recognises the criminal, it says that the other is thinking: 'Here is a menu. I am in a restaurant and want food. Therefore it is sensible to read the menu. That man is a criminal. Criminals ought to be reported to the police. Catching criminals is more important than studying menus'. The background machinery also serves up a relevant general principle, namely, 'People faced with reasons for two actions tend to do the one they judge more important'. And, applying the principle to the presented data, we arrive at the prediction that the customer will call the police.

There are, however, two problems with this picture of what is going on. The first is merely verbal. It is just that the tacit theory now postulated falls considerably short of what the use of the word 'theory' suggests. The content of the supposed theory has dropped back to what was explicit in the wise woman's medical knowledge. Much work which we would expect to be done by a theory (e.g., keeping a systematic count of all potentially relevant features, specifying which are important in which circumstances and why) has been shuffled off onto the background ability. The second problem is more substantial, given the dialectical position. It is that, in presenting this picture of matters, the theory theorist has conceded the primary point that the simulationist is urging with respect to content. To apply the remarkable machinery to someone else's worldview so as to extract from it the thoughts relevant to answering a particular question is precisely to simulate his or her thought. His or her remarkable machinery is doing exactly the same, namely sieving through varied contents to find and use the relevant ones. Each of us is relying on his or her understanding of the question and of the content of the worldview to drive forward the thought process which delivers the answer.

5. CONTENT AND NON-CONTENT

Let us now turn to the distinction between content and non-content, and consider the question of whether use of simulation could explain our competence in handling the non-content-based aspects of psychological predictions of others.

By definition non-content is an aspect of a mental state in which it differs from another mental state, but where the difference does not consist in either state representing something different from the other. We should, I suggest, look for non-content in two places; first, in whatever makes the difference between different propositional attitudes, and, second, in the nature of sensation and perception. These are prima facie very different. The former has to do with the intuition that content plays different explanatory roles in different kinds of state, and that grasping the role is different from grasping the content. The latter has to do with the plausibility of the idea that there are aspects of mental states possessing a felt 'qualitative' character, where that cannot be cashed out in terms of representational content.

Although the distinction between content and non-content is (more or less) clear in principle, it is not entirely easy to draw in practice. The difficulty is to decide when a state has representational content, that is, when it is liable for assessment for fit with the world. With attitudes this takes us into issues about realism (e.g., on values, necessity, etc.). With felt character it takes us to the issue of qualia and of distinguishing between sensational and representational elements in perception. Since these are controversial, there is a difficulty in finding unproblematic examples to illustrate the argument. But I hope that we can get at least some grip on the issues.

It seems clear that (if the idea of non-content is well grounded at all) each distinctive kind of non-content has a set of properties which are linked in a recurrent and stable cluster. For example, craving as a distinctive sub-variety of motivational state is, typically, marked by the following features. It arises from such conditions as illness or repeated ingestion of certain substances, rather than from detailed rational appraisal of the value of the craved item. It is not extinguished by knowledge of the lack of value of what is craved. It is manifested in episodes which are urgent and unpleasant. It tends to lead to actions to secure what is craved. And, to take a case of the other type, visual non-content is caused by light falling on the eyes, can be associated with spatial representational contents and has a distinctive quality space, in which it differs from those associated with hearing, taste, touch and so on.

An important assumption I shall make is that this clustering is a posteriori, both in the sense that possession of one feature in a cluster does not entail possession of the others and (more important for the argument) in the sense that it is not an a priori matter that a state with a particular cluster of properties exists in any creature which is a proper subject of psychological attributes. The claims that I am in effect making here are, first, that there are real psychological kinds and, second, that what these kinds are in any actual type of creature is a matter of the contingent facts of the physiology and of the cultural formation of that type of creature. The very general conception of mind, of an active subject of experience, may fix that certain broad categories (information processing, motivation, perception . . .) must find application. But how this works out in detail, what kinds of perception, motivation and so on a given creature has, is not given a priori in the very notion of a psychology.

If non-content is to be simulated, then we must allow that people can put on a kind of reproduction of non-content which will enable new information about that particular sort of non-content to be derived. The idea is that we can, for example, thus 'simulate' craving or visual perception and, by noting the nature of what then goes on in us, we can learn, for example, new things about what craving or visual perception can lead to.

The obvious candidate for such a reproduction is imagining, where we mean by this not 'falsely believing' nor yet 'merely supposing' but rather 'vividly imagining'. This is the kind of imagining which in the case of visual experience takes the form of having visual images, and in the case of such things as craving takes the form of what we are inclined to describe as 'really thinking what it would be like'. The idea that this sort of imagining is the occurrence of a (faint) copy of what is imagined is familiar and attractive. It is also notoriously controversial. But I shall suggest that simulationist claims are not significantly advanced, whichever side we take in that controversy.

Suppose first that we deny the 'faint copy' view of imagining. We think it is a naive muddle to suppose that, say, having a visual image of a rose is anything like actually seeing a rose. Rather, having such a visual image is a matter of a certain sort of conceiving of the seeing a rose. What makes the difference between mere conceptual supposing and what we call 'having a visual image' is that in the latter case a great amount of further detailed content (about colours, angles, etc.) is specified. Application of this view to 'imagining craving' is that what is described by this phrase is not a faint copy of craving but a matter of exercising the concept of craving in some particularly richly contentful supposition.

It is no surprise that this view is inhospitable to the simulationist idea, since no one takes it that what occurs in supposition, namely mere representation, has a significant degree of intrinsic causal resemblance to what it represents. Indeed, in general, we do not want our representations (whether these are sentences on a page or structures in the mind) to be too causally lively under their own steam; otherwise they might start dictating our empirical theories and our thoughts to us. We want them to help in calling up further representations only when (a) we have, through our own empirical investigations, put in place linkages, for example in the form of laws, between the original and the subsequent phenomena represented, and (b) we ourselves direct our thoughts in such a way as to allow some of their implications to emerge. So representations of particular phenomena are, in general, causally neutral with respect to calling into existence other representations.

But what if the 'faint copy' view is, after all, defensible? I want to suggest that, contrary to what one may initially think, this does not make matters substantially better for the simulationist. Let us allow that having a visual image is not just having a representation with the content 'such and such is seen' but also involves the occurrence of further non–content events, significantly resembling those of actual vision. More generally, let us allow that when someone vividly imagines X, and X is a mental state, then something which is like X with respect to the phenomenal qualities of immediate experience occurs in the mind of the imaginer. The crucial point, however, is that in allowing this we have not allowed that the item need belong to the same real psychological type as X, in the sense of having the nature from which the cluster of X-distinctive causal properties flow. From the point of view of further properties, it may be mere delusory fool's X which occurs.

61

And when we consider actual cases they strongly suggest that this is so. For example, visual experience has the further property, which we did not mention earlier, of giving rise to afterimages. But I do not believe that someone who was unfamiliar with the phenomenon of afterimages could be got to be aware of it by imagining closing her eyes after seeing a bright patch. A physiological account of this is easily forthcoming. Real seeing involves processes in the retina which give rise both to events deeper in the brain, events associated with the characteristic experiences of sight, and also to liability to afterimages. Having visual images may resemble seeing in that it involves visual experience-type events deep in the brain without resembling it in involving occurrences in the retina. Similar remarks can be made about craving. A further and hitherto unmentioned feature of it is that it sets up sensitivity to the most tenuous thought associations. One who craves X (in the dispositional sense) is liable to be reminded of X and have the active craving re-awoken by all sorts of flimsily associated items, even when the mind is focused elsewhere. But, again, it seems to me highly implausible that someone who was unaware of this could have it brought to his or her attention by vivid imaginings of craving.

Do the above arguments throw any doubt on the idea that simulation is possible, and indeed required, for the handling of content? They do not. Defence of simulation with respect to content starts from an undoubted fact, namely our ability to think – with awareness of logical implication, relevance and so on – about the non-actual. To simulate another's belief that p by engaging one's own mind on the hypothesised content that p is not to have some faint experiential copy of a belief that p occurs in one. Neither the belief nor the content are reproduced in this way. This is because, to put it briefly, belief is not there in that way at all, and content is wholly there. To spell this out just a little further, what we call 'simulating belief' is something we label 'imagining'. But it is not vividly imagining believing (i.e., something which might be thought to be a faint phenomenal copy of believing) which is required, but imagining or supposing that p. And in such imagining the content that p is fully, and not merely faintly or apparently, present. Any simulationist story must of course postulate resemblance between what is done by the subject who believes that p and what is done by the simulator who imagines that p. And there is resemblance between my hypothesising that p and your really believing that p, namely the identity of content. But this is quite different from the 'faint copy' kind of resemblance postulated between seeing and having an image.

5

Simulation and Cognitive Penetrability

1. INTRODUCTION

'We would maintain that, for any cognitive capacity, demonstrating that that capacity is cognitively penetrable indicates that the capacity derives from an information base rather than from an off-line simulation'. So write Nichols, Stich, Leslie and Klein (1996), echoing some earlier claims of Stich and Nichols (1995a, 1995b). But are they right? I shall argue first that they are not, and that a simulationist may admit the possibility of cognitive penetration. This discussion will comprise the next three sections of the essay, Section 2 setting the scene and Sections 3 and 4 presenting the main considerations against the quoted claim.

But following that I shall ask whether cognitive penetration of the kind outlined is, in fact, likely to be the source of error in the cases cited by opponents of simulation, and I shall suggest that it is not. In understanding the causes of these errors it is probably more important to grasp what simulation can and cannot plausibly claim to deal with and certain potential complexities of its operation. The domain of simulation is considered in Section 5, where I urge that rational connection of content is the matter that simulation should centrally be expected to cope with. Section 6 summarises possible sources of error that a simulationist can acknowledge without embarrassment and offers some comments on the errors discussed in the literature.

The general moral I would like to urge is that there will be no quick empirical knockdown for simulationism of the kind that its detractors might have hoped. Empirical findings will doubtless be stimulating and useful. But the debate also needs more conceptual sophistication in clarifying the possible differing understandings of 'simulation' and their ramifications.

63

'Theory theory' and 'simulation theory' are rival accounts of what is involved in possession of psychological concepts, in the ability to apply them to ourselves and others, and the ability to use judgements invoking these concepts in arriving at predictions of the thoughts and actions of others. Both theory theory and simulation theory have a considerable number of different variants which are presented in the literature (Davies and Stone 1995a, 1995b; Stone and Davies 1996).

The core ideas of theory theory are that mastery of psychological concepts is grasp of a theory, and that when I predict the thoughts and actions of another person using my competence with psychological concepts I do so by calling upon this theory, that is, a body of information about the nature, causes and effects of psychological states. This theory may be explicitly known or (much more probably) in large part only tacitly known. It may consist of some structured set of nomological generalisations or just be a melange of low-level rules of thumb. It may be internally represented in sentences or, alternatively, in pictures or rules. But whichever of these variants we go for, individual predictions, for example of the decision of another person, are arrived at by taking information about that person, integrating it with the information of the theory and deriving the prediction (Stich and Nichols 1995b).

The simulation theory is not quite so easy to summarise, since the differences between its versions range more widely. But as we need to deal here only with what simulation theory has to say about the basis of our ability to predict others we can ignore differences between simulationists over other matters. We shall also leave aside much variation on how exactly simulationist prediction proceeds. What follows is intended to be neutral between the views on that favoured by the various proponents (Goldman 1995a; Gordon 1995a, 1995c; Heal, this volume, Essay 2; Harris 1995a). I shall come later to one difference between simulationist views which is of importance for the debate; but for the moment I aim to extract an agreed core, at least as far as prediction is concerned.

We can get at the key idea by considering the familiar example of the model aircraft in the wind tunnel. (The case has some misleading features, which we shall need to remark later, but it will serve to get us started.) Suppose that we know, in general terms, that aerofoils provide lift, that aircraft are liable to become unstable in some circumstances and the like, but lack any detailed quantitative theory of aerodynamics. We do not have a set of usable equations relating all the significant variables, such as body shape or wind speed, to the upshots, such as lift and stability, in which we are interested. How can it be that we may nevertheless arrive at detailed quantitative predictions on these matters? Here is a possible method. If we are convinced (for example, by inductive generalisation, or as a consequence of theoretical assumptions) that a model aircraft will behave similarly to a real aircraft of the same shape, at least in a usefully wide range of circumstances, then we may test models with varying shape in varying wind speeds and so on, measuring the quantitative outcome in various respects and using those figures as a basis for the needed detailed predictions of actual aircraft. We use the model aircraft to simulate the real aircraft.

The simulationist hypothesis is that something analogous to this takes place in many cases when we arrive at predictions about the thoughts and actions of other people. We call upon our similarity to other people, in particular the similar functioning of our minds. So we play that role vis à vis another whom we predict which the model aircraft plays vis à vis the real aircraft. In more detail the idea is that we possess certain capacities to develop new thoughts (beliefs, feelings, intentions, etc.) from given thoughts, by reasoning and becoming aware of connections. These capacities we can exercise both on straightforward beliefs and desires, and also (very importantly) on thoughts that are mere suppositions or imaginings. So, for example, I can infer an actual belief that p from existing beliefs that q and r, or I can hypothesise q and r and then see that p would follow.

We can harness these capacities to work through the implications of thoughts, not only on our own behalf but also to enable us to predict others. To do so we take the contents of the beliefs and desires of the other as material for our own reasoning and reflective capacities. When this occurs, the mind of the would-be predictor and the mind of the person to be predicted (if all goes well) proceed through parallel evolutions and arrive at similar end states. Each of these persons develops thoughts from thoughts, using his or her capacities. Of course, in the simulated person the upshot will be a real belief, feeling or decision, whereas in the simulator the upshot will be something of a merely imagined or hypothetical character. But the content will be the same and the simulator can thus use the upshot, as it occurs in him or her, as a basis for prediction of the other. The prediction is derived by a simulation process, not by calling on some theory about how minds work.

There is possible muddle that needs warding off at this point. On the simulationist view, a judgement about what someone else will think is, of course, 'derived from an information base', namely information about the subject matter with which the other's thoughts are engaged. For example, my prediction of your answer to the question of whether p, given that I know you believe q and r, is based on my knowledge about what is involved in the states of affairs that p, q and r. So 'being derived from an information base' and 'being derived from an off-line simulation' are not exclusive rivals, as the quotation at the start of the essay may suggest. But of course the important dispute is whether the judgements about others' thoughts are derived from an information base *about thoughts*.

As I have presented it here, simulationism has a story to tell about how we arrive at a wide range of predictions about others, concerning their beliefs and feelings as well as their intentions. The opponents of simulation whose arguments I shall be discussing talk for the most part as if they regarded simulationism as a view concerned only with how predictions about intentions (and so actions) are derived. But it seems unnecessary in our discussion to observe this restriction. These opponents of simulation theory recognise that simulation can and has been proposed as relevant in other kinds of prediction, and they take it that the considerations about the importance of cognitive penetrability would have full weight in these cases as well (Stich and Nichols 1995a; 1995b: 96). And I agree with them that if cognitive penetrability refutes simulationism about intention prediction then it would also refute it as an account of these other kinds of prediction. Moreover, I believe that the arguments to be advanced against their contention apply across the whole range of cases. So what follows should be taken as bearing upon the viability of simulationism as an account of psychological prediction taken with a wide brief.

Another point worth setting out explicitly at this stage is who wins, the theory theorist or the simulation theory, under various envisageable outcomes. This is a terminological rather than a substantive issue, but it is one where we need to know what we mean. Consider again the aircraft case and imagine that we get the figures in our quantitative predictions by using a model, because we lack knowledge of or cannot use any relevant detailed equations of aerodynamical theory. Suppose someone now says: 'We are using theoretical assumptions here. For example, we know that an aerofoil shape in a wind stream generates lift and other generalities of this kind. Moreover, our knowledge that the model and the real aircraft behave similarly is derived from our aerodynamic theory. These bits of knowledge are important in guiding our use of the model and in underpinning our confidence in the predictions we arrive at. Therefore these detailed quantitative predictions we arrive at are derived from a theory. So theory theory wins in this case'.

I think our reaction ought to be that this is an odd move. After all, we set up the aircraft case as a paradigm of simulation-derived prediction. But now the fact that we call also on propositions of the kind which figure in theories is being used to relocate the case in the theory camp. What has gone wrong is that the sense in which the predictions are now said to be 'derived from' a theory is different from that which was originally invoked. The theory theory, as implicitly understood on its original appearance, was the claim that predictions, in all their detailed contents, are derived from theory. So if theory theory is to win, then the supposed theory must contain enough in its axioms, generalizations, rules, or whatever, to explain every feature of the content of the prediction, for example the actual quantities it mentions. If there is no such fully competent theory, and some important features of the content of the prediction are derived instead from a simulation, then simulation theory wins.

This, at least, is how I shall use the terms in what follows. Thus, in this context of discussion, theory theory is imperialistic. It says, 'Everything comes from theory'. Simulation theory is the contradictory of this; so it says only the more modest 'At least some important things do not come from theory but come from simulation'. Simulation theory is thus compatible with the view that what we might call an outline or sketchy proto-theory has an essential role in our conception of ourselves and others, and in our ability to use simulation effectively. I am fairly confident that Stich and Nichols understand the distinction in the way set out here. For example, they too use the aircraft analogy to illustrate the simulation approach (1995a: 125–126). But I labour the point, because it is not so clear that other authors of the paper cited in my opening quotation have the same usage. Thus Leslie, in another paper, seems to suggest that what he understands by 'theory theory' wins if what generates predictions is a theory plus simulation mixture (Leslie and German 1995: 124).

The position with the psychological that I believe to hold has roughly the shape of the above-sketched position with aircraft. We do possess a proto-theory about the kinds of psychological states we can be in (beliefs, desires, feelings, etc.), how they typically arise and what they give rise to; and we know such important general things as that beliefs can be true or false, desires fulfilled or unfulfilled, and so forth. But what we do not have is theoretical knowledge about the contents of psychological states and how they interact to give rise to states with further contents. Our ability with contents is of the 'know how' kind and not of the 'know that' kind. We know how to think about states of affairs, how to work out the implications of our beliefs and desires, how to detect relevant connections, and so on. But we do not possess any full and detailed theory of how this or that actual content or set of contents is potentially related to these or those other contents. It is instead our capacity to think things through, to detect relevance, that we must rely on in moving from our grip on what the other person believes or wants to our prediction about what further thoughts he or she will have.

So what is 'cognitive penetrability' and why might its occurrence or non-occurrence be relevant to the dispute between theory theory and simulation theory?

3. COGNITIVE PENETRABILITY

The central ideas are put very clearly by Stich and Nichols:

According to the theory theory, predictions about people's behaviour are guided by a rich body of mentally represented information (or misinformation) about the ways in which psychological states are related to environmental stimuli, other psychological states and behavioural events. If that information is wrong or in-complete in various areas, then we should expect the accuracy of predictions in those areas to decline. According to the off-line simulation theory, we generate predictions of people's behaviour by running our own decision-making system off-line. If we are ignorant about how people's minds work, or if we have mis-taken views, this should not affect the accuracy of our predictions about how people will behave, since our views about how the mind works are not involved in generating the predictions. So if the off-line simulation theory is right, what we don't know won't hurt us – predictions about people's behaviour are 'cognitively impenetrable'. (1995b: 99–100)

So to say that a process of deriving a judgement is 'cognitively impen-etrable' is to claim that neither the absence nor the presence of further opinions about the subject matter of the judgement (thoughts in the case of the psychological, aircraft lift in the aerodynamic case) can affect what is predicted by that process. And the claim is that the process of deriving predictions of thoughts and so on by simulation must be so impenetrable. (The notion of cognitive penetration called on here is based on that in-troduced by Pylyshyn [1980]. There are differences between the idea he defines and the one invoked here. But we need not enter into these complexities.) The argument against simulation theory then proceeds by pointing to cases where we make false predictions about what others will believe or decide. It is urged that if simulation were the method of generating these predictions then they ought to be correct, since appropriate inputs to a simulation are available and the simulation process needs nothing else to run properly. What, then, could be the source of the error? The most plausible hypothesis is that it is some (perhaps tacitly held) false opinion about what is to be expected in these cases. But that would show that whatever is generating the prediction is penetrable by these false opinions; and since simulation is cognitively impenetrable, the predictions must have been generated not by simulation but by theory.

But should we accept this argument?

Let us start by making one very obvious point using the aircraft parallel. Even if I derive, and must derive, most of my detailed predictions about the aircraft from simulation using the model, this is no bar to my occasionally using some (perhaps false) generalization as the basis for some specific prediction. This prediction could then be regarded as generated by a kind of mini-theory, which I think to be applicable to the kind of case in hand. Here my faith in the mini-theory leads me to take a shortcut and neglect simulation. One might say that because people can (sometimes rightly and sometimes wrongly) adopt such shortcuts the simulation process as a general method has been 'cognitively penetrated'. But to admit this would not in any way tend to support the idea that all aircraft predictions do or could come from theory. Analogously, the falsity of some psychological predictions might be explicable by the predictor's reliance in those cases upon a psychological mini-theory, derived from overhasty generalization, folk prejudice or what not. But to allow this would not at all discredit the idea that simulation is a useful, indeed necessary, method in many other cases. The Principle of Charity directs us to suppose that Stich and Nichols are not recommending that we make this fallacious move.

So let us consider the more interesting question (which I take it is their prime concern), namely whether individual episodes of simulationist prediction could be cognitively penetrated. Note that two distinct and independent claims are in effect made in the crucial initial premise concerning cognitive impenetrability. We shall call them 'Absence' and 'Presence'.

Absence: If a prediction is derived by simulation then ignorance (e.g., of a theory about the workings of what is simulated, of what to expect in this case, etc.) will not prevent arrival at a prediction and arrival at a correct one, if the simulation is correctly set up and the particular process goes smoothly.

This must surely be accepted by a simulationist. The central claim of the simulation theory is precisely that we are indeed ignorant of a (detailed) theory of interrelations between mental states, but that this is no bar to our ability to predict correctly in many cases.

But what about the second claim?

Presence: Belief in positive misinformation about what will happen in a case could not affect a prediction arrived at by using simulation in that case.

We have not been given any reason to accept this claim. Stich and Nichols just assert it, as though it were obviously true, but on reflection it is far from so. Certainly the striking thing about the cases for which Pylyshyn's coinage 'cognitively penetrable' proved so useful is the truth there of a principle analogous to 'Presence'. A familiar example is the Mueller-Lyer illusion. The visual system serves up to the perceiver the impression that the lines are unequal, and this illusion persists in the face of knowledge that they are equal. But for simulation-based prediction 'Presence' would be true only if both the operation of the simulation process and also the delivery of its outcome to the simulator were necessarily impervious to any influence from other beliefs. And what shows that these things are so? Nothing we have been told so far. Indeed, we can see that the second of them is not so by constructing an example.

Consider again the model aircraft. Suppose I am running a simulation to measure some quantity generated by a particular novel combination of shape and wind speed. I am already convinced (perhaps by overhasty inductive generalization) of the falsehood that the outcome must be of a certain order of magnitude. I do not have a belief about what particular figure to expect, but I am convinced that it will be below 100. I run the simulation and take a glance at the instrument giving the final reading. It says 222. But my pre-conception leads me to read this as 22.2. I thus arrive at a false prediction about some feature of the real aircraft – that the quantity there will be 22.2. I arrive at it by running a simulation and the outcome of that simulation has contributed importantly. But the actual judgement I end up with has been distorted, cognitively penetrated, by my false belief.

For all we have seen, the upshot of a simulationist psychological prediction might similarly be shaped, as it appears in the mind of the simulator, by a false preconception. And although in the aircraft case we shall not find that belief about the outcome can affect how the simulation itself runs, and so influence the final reading of the instruments, let me repeat that we have not been shown why cognitive penetration of this further and even more radical kind could not occur in the psychological case.

The aircraft case alone is enough to show the invalidity of the inference on which Nichols et al. seem to rely, namely, 'This prediction is arrived at by simulation. Therefore it is cognitively impenetrable'. But is it actually the case that psychological predictions generated by simulation can be cognitively penetrated? To see that this may well be so, it will be helpful first to consider why and how the aircraft analogy, although useful for many purposes, must not be pressed too far.

4. SIMULATION AND THE EXERCISE OF SKILL

At least two things are, I suggest, misleading in the aircraft analogy. The first is that it encourages the idea that the running of a psychological simulation is a passive process: I just feed inputs into some system, sit back and wait. But in the psychological case this is not how it goes. When I set up the simulation, by engaging my mind with the contents of the other's thoughts, I am then required to think about the subject matter of those thoughts. This is an active matter. It involves, minimally, the appropriate direction of attention and the exercise of sensitivity to the relevance or otherwise of further thoughts which arise in me. In more intricate cases it involves such things as working out connections, keeping track of alternatives, checking for accuracy and completeness, and so on. (Consider, for example, the case where I try to predict someone else's belief about the total of some numbers by doing the sum myself, or the case where I try to anticipate an opponent's chess move by considering the position from her point of view.) So psychological simulation involves the active exercise of skills in thinking about some subject matter.

If we take this point on board it makes the second potentially misleading feature of the aircraft analogy easier to identify, namely the idea that a psychological simulation can 'run' on some isolated subsystem in the mind, the functioning of which is unaffected by the cognitive and emotional setting provided by the rest of the person's mental states. This idea is reinforced by the 'boxological' representation of the mind favoured by Stich and Nichols and used extensively in their articles. They present the differences between theory theory and simulation theory by a diagram in which various parts of the mind – 'inference mechanisms', 'beliefs', 'decision making system' and so on – appear as labelled boxes which are connected by (rather few) arrows standing for causal influences. For example, an arrow goes from the belief box to the inference mechanisms box, and another goes in the reverse direction, and these are the only arrows entering or leaving the 'inference mechanisms' box; similarly, the only inputs recorded to the 'decision-making system' come from boxes labelled 'beliefs' and 'desires'.

But, as their own account makes clear, what is represented by the separate boxes are (mainly) capacities or abilities we have, viz., to make inferences, to remember things, to make decisions and the like (1995a: 123). There may well be some mental subsystems which function in an isolated modular way (e.g., bits of the visual system). But such elements as our capacities to reason or remember do not seem plausible candidates. Quite the contrary in fact, since common sense and psychological experiment both show the openness of our reasonings and memories to influences from an immense variety of sources such as emotion, mood, subliminal suggestion, and so forth. So the skills and capacities represented by the boxes are ones the exercise of which can frequently be variously influenced, and where exercises of one and the same capacity can result in interestingly different performances on different occasions. Another way of putting this point is to say that if you like the boxological notation, to avoid risk of being misled you must be sure to put in a realistically large number of boxes and a realistically large number of arrows connecting them. Do not be seduced into the idea that the output of a box is determined by one sort of input only – for example, the output of the 'inference mechanisms' box only by the premises one has fed in. Let us consider this theme further.

It is a familiar fact that tiredness and emotional disturbance can affect the success with which a skill is exercised. For example, if I am tired, angry, depressed or overexcited I may make a mistake in elementary arithmetic which normally I would avoid. But given that this is so, then a simula-tionist will expect simulation-based prediction of another's arithmetical calculations to come out incorrectly sometimes, even when I start with the right inputs, because my simulation of the other's (correct) addition goes wrong through my tiredness or emotional upset. The example can clearly be generalized to apply to all types of reasoning, both theoretical and practical. To allow this is not to allow that what is going on is not simulation or that simulation is not central in delivering many successful predictions. (If 'simulation' is, for you, a success word and 'inaccurate sim-ulation' a contradiction in terms, then speak here instead of 'attempted simulation'. But I shall continue to use 'simulation' more liberally.)

Consider another kind of influence of setting on the exercise of a skill, starting with a non-cognitive example. The ability to play tennis is something that can be exercised either in an actual game or in such activities as practising one's shots. But the exercise of the skill may issue slightly differently in the two cases. Perhaps the intensity of the real occasion brings out effort, and so success, which are absent in the routine of practice. Alternatively, the knowledge that it is an actual game may make the player nervous, so she misses shots that she could easily hit in practice. We can find analogues to this in more intellectual skills. Take meditating on what it would be like to have a certain job. It may be that merely hypothetically one is inclined to think that it would be rather fun, but that as soon as the reality looms it becomes apparent that it would be a most unpleasant responsibility. How can this be? Although in both circumstances one understands quite well what the job entails and thus is in a position to think about what it would be like, perhaps one does not exercise that skill in an urgent or serious enough way unless in the service of forming real beliefs; one is lazy and inattentive in one's merely hypothetical thinking. Or, in a reverse kind of case, perhaps one could see, in cool hypothesis, that a certain action would be base and shameful but is hindered from grasping this fully when actually believing the action to be open to one by the feelings and temptations that come along with the belief.

It cannot be that the abilities to discern connections diverge substantially between imaginative thought and actual belief-based thought. If they did we would lose our justification for saying that it was the same content that was at one time hypothesized and at another believed. This general point is something it is important for simulationists to defend. But acknowledging it is consistent with the kinds of contrast noted above between the upshots of deployment of concepts in imagination and in actual belief. And because these contrasts exist, there is again room for error to creep into simulationist prediction of others, inasmuch as the others entertain real beliefs and desires and the simulator mere suppositions.

These cases illustrate the general fact of the influence of setting on the success with which a cognitive skill may be exercised, and they have thus enabled us to identify various ways in which simulation-based predictions of others might go wrong. But we have not yet shed light on the crucial question of whether the exercise of the intellectual skill of thinking about a subject matter, in the interest of simulationist prediction, could be influenced in its outcome by an independently motivated false belief about the expected outcome. The aircraft example suggests one direction to look, namely for last-minute contamination of the output of the simulation. But although I do not rule this out in the psychological case it is not a line I will pursue here. To go down this path is to be embroiled rapidly in contentious matters about exactly what the output of a simulation is and how it gets to be employed in the judgement of the simulator. We cannot give the matter proper treatment here. So I will offer instead some considerations pointing in another direction, namely to the possibility of the actual working of a simulation process being affected by the presence of a separately based belief about the subject matter it deals with.

Let us start obliquely. Suppose I am debating some course of action for myself, for example whether to accept a job offer. The situation is slightly non-standard in that I have already, in a roundabout way, acquired a belief that I shall accept. I have overheard a friend, whose opinion I respect, saying to someone else that she thinks I will accept. But this current deliberation of mine is supposed to be quite independent of that. I intend to be entirely open-minded. I would repudiate the idea that 'My friend thinks I will take the job' is functioning for me as any kind of premise in my thinking. My aim is to see, just on the basis of the pros and cons of the job itself, whether I should take it.

This is not an absurd plan. Compare the situation where I am checking arithmetic. I believe that some previously reached answer is correct and that I shall reach that answer. But the check is designed to deliver its result quite independently of that belief. It is perfectly feasible to embark on such checks, whether of one's own or others' workings. And this is how I expect it to be with me and the job offer.

Unfortunately, however, my intention is not fulfilled. The belief does (in ways of which I am unaware) affect how I consider and evaluate the pros and cons of the job. At the simplest level we might say that what has gone on is that I did my thinking lazily and inattentively because I thought I already knew the answer to which the deliberation was tending. This links this case back with a possibility already mentioned. But subtler versions of the situation are at least imaginable. Perhaps the extra belief induces a kind of mind-set in which I fail to register the full force of the disadvantages of the job and am overimpressed by the advantages. This might occur even when my checking is genuinely conscientious and laborious. But, however the extra belief operates, the upshot is that I reach the decision to accept, whereas in its absence I would have decided to refuse.

Now only a little transposition is needed to get a simulationist case where a belief leads me astray. Change the position so that I am now trying to anticipate the decision of another. As before, I already have a belief about what she will decide; as before, this belief is independently derived from mere hearsay; but also as before, I am trying to do an open-minded check on it. My method is the simulationist route of thinking through the advantages and disadvantages as they will present themselves to the person making the decision. Unfortunately the belief acts, as in the previously imagined case, to influence the way I proceed in my simulation. So I end up predicting that she will take the job, whereas she, more clear-eyed and unencumbered by knowledge of the prediction, has weighed the factors differently and decided to decline.

Are these stories, or ones of similar shape, actually true? This is difficult to ascertain without empirical investigation. But it would not be surprising if instances were found. And the more important point is that the stories clearly do represent what is at least an empirical possibility. Hence cognitive penetration of simulation-based prediction cannot be ruled out.

Does this conclusion matter? Doubtless it is better to have a true opinion rather than a false one on whether or not simulation necessarily excludes cognitive penetration. And it is important also to inject a little more sophistication into the overly simple picture of simulation (as the 'off-line' running of isolated 'mental systems'), which made the 'no cognitive penetrability' claim seem so plausible. But, to be frank, it seems to me unlikely that the kind of cognitive penetration outlined here is the explanation of the wrong predictions about others which have been discussed in the literature so far. To shed light on them I suggest that we need to look elsewhere. So I turn next to consider the domain over which simulation may be expected to work.

5. THE DOMAIN OF SIMULATION

No simulationist should claim that every prediction about another's psychological states, even every prediction about someone else's practical decisions, is or could be arrived at by simulation. To see that this is so consider the following question: 'This person has just drunk a pint of whisky. How will he feel in five minutes' time?' We should not expect simulation to be able to deal with this question. The idea that I could get a good answer by, for example, imagining drinking a pint of whisky, then waiting five minutes and seeing what I feel like, is absurd. An answer to the question needs rather to be got from physiology or from experience.

Why is this so? If simulation-based prediction of some outcome is to be possible, there must be some other existing item which is similar to the item to be predicted and in which processes are going forward closely analogous to those in the target item, at least in the respects relevant to determining that outcome. With the aircraft, both the system to be predicted and the model are rigid structures, with a certain sort of shape; so both are capable of being acted on by currents of air and thereupon developing lift, instability and so forth. In the psychological case, both the person to be predicted and the simulator are entertaining thoughts with content, and both states are capable of being developed through the exercise of reflective capacities and thereupon of giving rise to other thoughts. But in the whisky case, what occurs in the non-drinker is not relevantly like what occurs in the drinker with respect to production of bodily feelings. Alcohol circulates in the blood of the one who has actually drunk the whisky, alterations in brain chemistry are thereby caused, which in turn give rise to feelings, abnormal behaviour and so forth. What we can offer in attempted simulation is merely vivid imaginings of the taste and other sensations of drinking the whisky. However vivid this is, it does not correlate with any alcohol analogue circulating in any blood analogue, in a way capable of causing any drunkenness analogue. So imagining drinking whisky is not a simulation of it for the purposes of predicting giddiness or aggression, let alone torpor or cirrhosis of the liver. It may be a simulation of it for purposes of predicting other outcomes, for instance, whether it would be an acceptable accompaniment to haggis. But, if so, this will be because in the respects relevant to that outcome the real and the imagined drinking are appropriately similar (Heal 1995b: 48–49; Stone and Davies 1996: 19–20; Harris 1995: 218-219).

So simulation should not claim to be able to deal with all predictions of psychological states. But should it claim to cope at least with all predictions of practical decisions? No, because these predictions can depend upon prior answers to questions that simulation cannot handle. Consider: 'This person is drinking a pint of whisky. If he is asked in five minutes' time whether he would like to lie down, what will he say?' The answer here depends upon the answer to the question of how the person will then feel. Hence we should not expect simulation to help us.

So then what kinds of psychological states should the simulationist say can be simulated, and with respect to the production of what kinds of outcomes? The kind of simulationism I would like to defend says that the only cases that a simulationist should confidently claim are those where

(*a*) the starting point is an item or collections of items with content;
(*b*) the outcome is a further item with content, and;
(*c*) the latter content is rationally or intelligibly linked to that of the earlier item(s).

It is at this point that the proposals of this essay differ from those of some other proponents of simulationism, who either explicitly see simulation theory as a rival to rational interpretation theory (Goldman 1995a), or proceed in a way which, by omitting any emphasis on rationality, strongly suggest that the scope of simulation is not to be so limited. On the other hand, the view defended here is in line with the earlier writings of the *Verstehen* tradition, which are the forerunners of simulationism (Collingwood 1946).

I do not say that it is impossible that there should be psychological simulation involving non-content or non-intelligible linkages. The claim is only that there can be no a priori assumption in favour of the existence of such cases. When starting point and/or outcome are without content, and/or the connection is not intelligible, there is no general reason to suppose that the process linking the two can be simulated, that is to say, there is no general reason to think that there exists any state simulating the starting point with respect to the property that leads to the outcome. Let us consider this further, as it is important.

If I imagine that an X exists we may say that, in virtue of this imagination, a 'pretend X' is brought into being, viz., the intentional object of my imagining. But it would be a horrible muddle to assume that this guarantees the existence of a 'pretend X' in another sense, viz., that in which 'pretend X' just means 'item fit to serve as a simulation of X with respect to most important outcomes'. It is obvious that this would be a muddle in the case of non-psychological (or partly non-psychological items) like tigers, waterfalls and whisky drinkings. But it is equally true for psychological items. So the question of whether a kind of psychological state can be simulated, and if so how fully and with respect to what kind of property, must be looked at separately for each kind of state. We must also beware of supposing that we can just help ourselves to the idea that there are 'mental systems' subserving each kind of psychological state and there is such a thing as running these systems 'off-line'. To suppose that we make clear to ourselves what we mean by simulating some kind of psychological state by using this kind of talk is to be taken in by language. If we favour the 'off-line running' idiom, the right to use it must be established separately for each sort of state by establishing that what is to be simulated involves the running of a system and making clear what its 'off-line' running would amount to. And simulationists should be particularly wary of compounding these two mistakes by making the simplistic equation of 'imagining that psychological state S occurs' with 'having S occur off-line'. This equation is wrong even in the central cases where simulation seems least contentious, namely belief. If you simulate my belief that p by imagining something, it is not by imagining a belief that p but by imagining that p.

When we consider content, however, we see that these kinds of challenges to demonstrate the defensibility of the simulationist picture can be met. Content is exactly the sort of thing that can be present in both actual states such as belief and in other psychological states such as imagining. Moreover, it is fully and effectively present in both states with respect to its ability to enable the thinker to become aware of links of intelligibility and relevance. Our whole conception of ourselves as creatures with limited but improvable epistemic grasp and with choice between possible future actions is inextricably bound up with commitment to this idea. Hence there is little doubt of the feasibility of harnessing this ability – namely to deal with content in imagination as well as belief – to enable us to derive simulation-based psychological predictions of others. Even Stich, Nichols et al. admit that this is an intelligible and defensible proposal (Stich and Nichols 1995b: 93–97; Nichols et al. 1996: 53–55). Moreover, arguments can be given, rooted in deep-seated and general features of our outlook, that our competence with detailed content-related psychological prediction must be simulation-based.

In summary then, the idea of simulation centred round intelligible links in content can be articulated and defended in a way that makes clear its possibility (indeed perhaps even its necessity). But the idea of any other kind of simulation is far more problematic.

What, however, makes a link rational or intelligible? What is content? And what psychological states have it? I would like to offer just a few observations and tentative speculations on these substantial questions, by way of indicating the demarcation lines this approach might draw and the kinds of issues that will need to be tackled if it is to be spelt out more fully.

First 'rational' should not be interpreted in a narrow and demanding sense, where some linkage counts as rational only if it withstands leisurely scrutiny by logically acute and formally aware minds and thus conforms to, or even improves on, the practice sanctioned by current best accounts of deductive logic, statistics and probability theory, decision theory, and so on. One reason this notion is inappropriate for the simulation approach is that the approach recognises that people do their reasoning, form their stances and take their decisions in real time, often under pressure and facing the need to handle a great amount of complex material. We, quite properly, rely on shortcuts, on the analogies and saliences that strike us, on the intellectual habits encouraged by our communities and so forth. Hence not everything 'irrational' in the strict sense falls outside the domain of simulation. For example, being taken in by fallacious reasoning is something we can often sympathise with, find intelligible and predict by simulationist methods. The important issue for the applicability of simulation is whether we can see what went on as the upshot of the exercise of cognitive skills, not whether it was a flawless exercise of those skills. It is a corollary of this that intelligibility is not an all-or-nothing matter. One may see some sense in another's response and yet be puzzled by certain aspects of it. One may have some sympathy with it without fully endorsing it and so forth. As far as prediction is concerned, the clearer-cut the rationality the more likely is simulation to be able to handle matters on its own. Where we have partial intelligibility, then, perhaps, simulation will need to be supplemented with non-simulation-derived information about the subject's situation or individual style of thought.

Another reason that the narrow sense of 'rational' is not the one we need is that it seems to get no grip over a great swathe of very important behaviour, namely that which it is natural to call 'expressive'. Thus there is an intelligible link between the content of belief and the intentional actions of utterance to which it may give rise. And similarly for emotion and the many expressive actions to which it gives rise, for example, hugging someone in affection or shaking the fist in anger. But the link between state and behaviour in these cases is (often) not one of instrumental rationality. These actions may well not serve any purposes other than the extremely general ones of helping us to articulate to ourselves and others what our states of mind are and giving some outlet to feelings (Hursthouse 1991). Nevertheless, we can sometimes see, 'from the inside' so to speak, why such actions are done. Hence at least some aspects of some such expressive behaviour falls within the remit of simulationism. So here again the simple word 'rational', narrowly understood, may not serve our purpose very well. Phrases like 'such that some intelligible sense or point can be seen in it' or 'such that some justificatory account of it can be given' might serve better to summarize the simulationist's notion.

And finally, let us remember that the rationality or otherwise of some contentful states or actions may not be easily discoverable. There are sometimes beliefs or attitudes (such as those lying deep and unarticulated in an unfamiliar culture, or even unconscious ones discoverable by psychoanalytically oriented consideration) which will serve to reveal as intelligible another's prima facie bizarre thoughts or actions. But such beliefs or attitudes may make themselves apparent only when we have made ourselves sensitive to them by relevant investigations and reflections.

The kinds of states that have content include at least perceptions, images, beliefs, desires, fantasies and imaginings, emotions and intentions.

What sort of content they have and the many ways in which states of all these kinds and their content can link is too big a topic for here. But let us note that there are at least two areas of controversy which the simulationist will need to consider.

One is the content of perception and how to draw the line (if there is one) between content and non-content properties of perceptions. Clearly the simulationist may allow that there could be simulation of perception – in the sense of a state (having images?) which shares (some of) the content of a perception – and that this may form the basis for predicting what another will do. So, for example, if you can see the layout of a maze and so how to escape from it, I, knowing this, may predict your choice of route if I can form an image of the maze as you see it. But if there are links between perceptual contents that are entirely non-rational, or links involving at one end non-contentful states, then simulationism would not claim to cope with them. (The causing of afterimages of contrasted colours might be an example of the first sort and the causing of headaches by long exposure to bright light an example of the second.)

The second very large problem to which simulationism needs to address itself is the connection between desires, emotions and intentions on the one hand and value judgements on the other. Recent thought in moral psychology, and philosophy of action more generally, has emphasised the links between the whole affective and motivational side of our nature and the concept of the valuable. So it will not do to conceive of the desire that p merely as a state that tends to cause actions bringing it about that p. This conception is incapable of explaining how desire rationalises action or what the difference could be between mere compulsions (such as kleptomaniacs or obsessives, at least on the popular conception of them, are supposed to experience) and more normal motivational states. The better picture is of a close link between desiring that p and conceiving that it would be valuable in some way, for example enjoyable, amusing, health-promoting, just and so on, if p (Anscombe 1997; Smith 1994). One does not have to be a believer in objective value to acknowledge this link. One may be an error theorist or a quasi-realist about value and still recognise it. Differences between these positions will come out in the more general metaphysical positions within which the link is located and what kinds of explanations for it are offered.

The general realisation has ramifications in the treatment of emotion and intention. Roughly, emotion connects closely with the recognition that something conceived as valuable exists, or has been destroyed, or is threatened, or is to be hoped for (Kenny 1963; de Sousa 1987). Intention connects with the judgement that the intended action is a way of promoting or defending some value and, perhaps, with judgement that the action itself has some value character – for example, being prudent or permissible, or obligatory or best all things considered (Davidson 1980: essays 1–5).

The importance of this for simulation theory is its possible implications for how we should conceive of simulating desires, emotions and intentions. It would certainly be wrong to make a simple identification of these states with the judgements about value with which they are linked. Phenomena like depression, akrasia, overreaction and the like show that strength of motivation or feeling can get out of line with what is rationally licensed by the associated judgements, in being either too weak or too strong. Hence there is more to desire, emotion and intention than such judgements – there are the characteristic causal links with purposive action and with disposition to expressive behaviour. But it does not follow from this that there is more to simulating a desire, emotion or intention than entertaining the content of the associated value judgements. As far as rationalising and making intelligible are concerned, it is the value judgements that do the work.

A good deal of the simulation debate hitherto has ignored these issues. It has proceeded rather as though it were obvious what was involved in simulating a desire, emotion or intention. One picture is that such simulation involves a kind of faint version of what is simulated, conjured up by imagination. Another (and not incompatible) picture, which is explicit in some presentations (e.g., those of Stich, Nichols et al.), is that the simulation is just the thing itself, but occurring in the relevant 'mental system' while it is being run 'off-line'. These ways of looking at things may encourage the idea that all kinds of upshots of these mental states, whether rational or not, can be expected to be predictable by simulation. They encourage it because they lead us to imagine that the whole of the state, and not merely its content, is present in the simulation.

But the earlier strictures (about the lack of close connection between imagining X and simulating X and about unsupported use of the 'off-line' idiom) should make us wary of these pictures. Moreover, the above reflections about the centrality of value judgements encourage a different conceptualisation. On it we say that the crucial element in simulating a desire or emotion or intention is the ability to exercise one's cognitive powers on the content of the other's value judgements. Conceiving things in this way makes it clearer how we can maintain the demarcation that puts rational connections within the remit of simulation and excludes other kinds of connection. This view says that simulation will be applicable and will cope when the links of value judgement to the other elements of the situation (e.g., strength of motivation and feeling) are all intelligibly in order, but will fail when there is akrasia or other non-intelligible or non-content-involving factors affecting the outcome.

6. SOME WRONG PREDICTIONS AND WHY WE MAKE THEM

In the light of the discussion so far, together with common sense and suggestions from the previous literature, let us now assemble a list of possible sources of error in a simulation-based prediction of another person.

(1) The input to the simulation may be inappropriate or incomplete. Perhaps the simulator has not got access to some relevant information about the subject. Or perhaps theoretical preconceptions affect the input.
(2) A simulator can fail to exercise his or her thinking skills in a way that matches that of the person to be predicted because of his or her own tiredness or emotional disturbance.
(3) The simulator may fail through lack of taking the imagined situation seriously enough.
(4) The simulator may fail through not allowing for disturbing influences on the other, for example, tiredness, emotional disturbance.
(5) The simulator may fail through distorting influences of other beliefs on the actual simulation process, that is, cognitive penetration of the simulation process.

Let us also note two further possibilities:

(6) Simulation may be supplanted in a case, or class of cases, where it could operate by the tempting shortcut of an incorrect mini-theory.
(7) A prediction may be wrong because it comes from a false theory, dealing with a situation in which simulation cannot be employed.

Cases (l)–(6) show how error may occur in predictions suitable to be arrived at by simulation. And three of these cases – (1), (5) and (6) – involve, in different ways, errors in some theory, which interacts with the simulation process to distort or inhibit it. Thus a simulationist has plenty of options in accounting for error, as well as that of claiming that the case in question falls under (7), and so is not in the remit of simulation at all.

It is worth noting also other possible sources of error, for example, inability to handle the intricacies of entering and exiting the simulation process (perhaps because of immaturity or insufficiency of thinking capacity) or inability to set up a simulation correctly because of lack of a correct or complete proto-theoretical framework in which to do it. These seem profitable areas for simulationists to explore in attempting to explain young children's errors in predicting others, for example in the famous false-belief tasks. I am doubtful that the factors listed in (1)–(6) are significant in these cases. There is another whole large and important set of questions here.

So what are we to say of the cases mentioned in the literature which are supposed to make difficulties for simulation? Stich and Nichols present three cases where our predictions of others' behaviour or beliefs are wrong (1995a). Some of these are discussed again later, with further refinements and consideration of earlier objections (Stich and Nichols 1995b; Nichols et al. 1996). Another discussion adds a fourth case (Nichols, Stich and Leslie 1995). I shall discuss the first two cases only briefly since I have little to add to existing comments on them.

The Case of the Shopping Mall Questionnaire: When presented with an array of products, e.g., nightdresses, which are in fact qualitatively identical, and asked to rank them, people show a marked rightward bias, i.e., they tend to rank more highly those items which are towards the righthand end of the array. But when subjects are asked to predict what other people will do in this situation (i.e., when asked, 'What will people do when presented with an array of products which are in fact qualitatively identical and asked to rank them'), they entirely fail to anticipate this rightward bias, predicting instead that people's high-ranking choices will come randomly in the array.

The obvious move, given my assumptions, is to say that the rightward bias is irrational and hence not something we need expect simulation to cope with. It is true that in the light of the conscious thoughts that the questioned people have, their choices are not irrational; they think that they detect differences between the items that justify their rankings and they repudiate the idea that they are influenced by position in the array. But it is surely plausible that these thoughts are post hoc confabulations of some kind, generated to provide a veneer of defensibility to an impulse coming from somewhere else. And why should we expect a mere simulation of the experience of the questioned persons to have similar non-rational impulse-producing power? (A similar response is urged by Harris [1995] and Gordon [1995b], although in somewhat different terminology.)

The Case of Belief Perseverance: In the course of psychological experiments, subjects have sometimes been given evidence that they were good at a task (e.g., telling real from fake suicide notes), put through some tests and then 'debriefed' by being told that the evidence was faked and their abilities in reality not outstanding. The assumption was that the debriefing would remove the induced false belief without remainder. But this turns out not to be the case: despite the debriefing the induced belief persists. This is an unexpected phenomenon which only came to light through observation. Clearly the psychologists who originally conducted the kind of experiment that involved inducing false beliefs had not anticipated it; and it comes as a surprise to the rest of us too.

One natural way of describing the phenomenon is this. In virtue of being actually believed, certain kinds of content get firmly embedded in the mind in such a way that revelation of the ungroundedness (irrationality) of the belief does not shift them. Given this kind of description, the kind of simulationism I favour clearly has an explanation of our failure to anticipate the effect. If simulation has as its central domain the area of rational linkages, then this particular result is not one it should have been expected to anticipate, since it is a striking case of irrationality. Merely contemplating a content allows one to exercise one's abilities to see what it supports and what supports it. But such contemplation has of itself no tendency to do anything analogous to the firm embedding, the setting up of habits of thought and so on, which holding an actual belief for a length of time induces.

On these cases I would like to endorse the comment of Blackburn that, in seeking to make difficulty for simulationism by pointing to our lack of success in anticipating the irrationalities revealed in the cognitive dysfunction literature, Stich and Nichols are looking in exactly the wrong place (1995: 289, n. 1). If intelligibility plays a central role in simulation, then they are looking just where simulationists will agree that we may well go wrong.

The Case of the Lottery Ticket Buy-back: People are asked to take part in an experiment on judging the grammaticality of sentences and are offered a lottery ticket as a reward. Of those who agree to take part, some are just given a ticket while others choose theirs. Neither group knows that others are getting slightly different treatment, that is, those who are given their tickets do not know that others can choose for themselves, and vice versa. At the end of judging the sentences the organiser tells the participants that it has turned out there are not quite enough tickets to go round and that he would like to buy some back. The participants themselves are asked to set a price. The price asked by those who chose their own tickets is strikingly higher than the price asked by those who were just handed their tickets, about four times as much on average. Now we shift to the subjects in the second-level or prediction experiment. Each of these is shown a videotape of the original experiment, that is, a video of a person having the grammaticality questionnaire and the lottery-ticket reward explained and of that person acquiring his or her lottery ticket, by one or other method. Again these subjects do not know that others are shown slightly different films. They are asked to predict what answers about grammaticality the other will give; they are told about the offer to buy back lottery tickets and are asked to predict what price will be demanded by the person they have seen on the film. [The description just given is of the more elaborate second version of the experiment from Nichols et al. 1996, presented by them in response to criticisms of the earlier version by Goldman 1995b, Gordon 1995b and Harris 1995.]

This experiment is carefully set up to make the likelihood of an accurate simulation as great as possible. Each predictor shadows, so to speak, the one he or she is asked to predict, and on just the same time scale. But the upshot is that, despite this great parallelism in their positions, the predictors failed to anticipate the prices their targets would ask. Those who had observed people choosing their tickets, as opposed to being given them, did not predict the high prices in fact demanded. Rather, the prices predicted for choosers and non-choosers were very similar. But, say Nichols et al., if simulation theory were right, surely we would expect the predictors to do much better. They seem to be in a remarkably good position to simulate accurately without the influence of distracting factors. Why, then, do they get the answer wrong?

One important question is clearly whether the reported first-level result is robust and under what circumstances, if any, it can be reproduced. A recent attempt to reproduce the effect, reported by Kuhberger, failed to do so on four successive trials (Kuhberger et al. 1995). He and his collaborators found no significant difference in the price asked by the choice and the no-choice subjects. If, as this suggests, the original effect was a freak phenomenon, then failure to predict it in the second-level experiment is of doubtful significance. But resolution of this issue awaits further empirical study. So let us for the sake of the argument assume that there is a genuine effect, even if it appears only in certain delicately adjusted circumstances. And let us further assume that Nichols et al. were indeed successful in setting matters up in such a way that those in the second-order experiment were in a position to simulate.

On this assumption the next important question is the extent to which the responses of the subjects in the first-level experiment are rational or intelligible. Is there a right price to ask for a ticket that one has been given and another, and different, right price to ask for a ticket one has chosen? On discussing the issue informally with a number of people, and asking them how they would go about fixing a price, a frequent response was a demand for more information. What chance of winning does each ticket have? How much money does the organiser have to buy back tickets with? How many must she get? How will she choose which to buy? Lacking this, and further relevant information, it is not clear that subjects can make any sensible choice about what price to set. They may well be reduced to plucking a figure out of the air. (One interesting feature of the results reported by Kuhberger et al. is the very wide spread of prices asked.)

But still the issue remains of why the numbers thus plucked should be higher on average for the choice than for the no-choice subjects (still taking this to be a genuine phenomenon). Are they responding intelligibly to one of the few relevant factors of which they are allowed to be aware? Or are they in a situation where, precisely because of the lack of relevant information, non-rational factors come strongly into play?

It looks at first sight as if the latter is the case. I have yet to come across any convincing articulation of why the ticket choosers felt so attached to their tickets. Perhaps the relation between choosing and attachment is like that between drinking whisky and feeling giddy. If so, the failure of simulation to predict it is entirely to be expected.

But it may be that, as we reflect more and delve deeper, a sort of intelligibility in the ticket attachment will loom into view. Perhaps we shall see how it connects with, and springs from, deep but inarticulate conceptions of the self, the nature of our control over things, the need to be committed to our enterprises or what not. If so, the simulationist can say that the simulation did not run properly because the simulator did not take on board a wide enough range of considerations, and did not make him or herself open to the possibility of these less clear-cut kinds of rationality. He or she did not activate and so make effective in the simulation those thoughts (conceptions of the self, views about control, commitment to enterprises or whatever) which are in fact doing important work. And why is this so? Perhaps because of the influence of some (tacit) theoretical assumption, for instance, that matters as deep and inarticulate as the ones mentioned could not bear importantly on such a trivial seeming decision. Here we diagnose an error of the first type distinguished at the start of this section. Either way, simulationists have resources with which to deal with the case.

The Case of the Presentation Mug: Subjects are shown a mug and asked what price they would ask for it, if they owned it and were invited to sell. They are then given the mug and asked to set a price for selling it. The interesting result is that they substantially underpredict their own future demands. There is, it seems, an 'endowment effect' according to which people set a higher value on things when they own them than the value they set when they do not own them.

Nichols et al. comment that 'it is not plausible for the simulation theorist to suppose that the Pretend Belief and Desire Generator would have a problem generating the pretend beliefs and desires that result from being told that one now actually owns the mug' (Nichols, Stich and Leslie 1995: 443). They therefore urge that the failure to predict raises a serious difficulty for simulationism. After all, in this case the psychological mechanisms of the target and the predictor could hardly differ, as they are identical.

They are certainly right that generating the relevant 'pretend belief' (i.e., the state that simulates the belief) by imagining that one owns the mug, is surely something that simulation theory must suppose to be done and done easily. This is a trivial adjustment to an obvious possibility. But are they equally right in supposing that generating the 'pretend desire' that will be present in the imagined circumstance must also be unproblematic? The question is what desires concerning the mug will arise, given the changed situation. Our approach says that intelligible desires arise out of the perceived presence of value. Now the claims 'this mug is elegant', 'this mug is useful' and the like point to valuable features of the mug which make it intelligibly an object of desire. But does 'I own this mug' report on a further value feature that ought to make the mug an object of yet stronger desire? At first sight this is not at all a plausible view (unless we add in more circumstances, e.g., that I have owned the mug for a long time and it has acquired many sentimental associations). 'Being owned by me' is not, in any clear way, a feature that makes a mug better as a mug – more beautiful, better at retaining heat, less likely to break or whatever. So the simulation theorist may say that this is a case where desire and the value judgements on which it could intelligibly be based fall out of line. Hence it is not a case which the simulation approach can predict. Alternatively, as with the lottery-ticket example, we may say that what makes the attachment to the mug (at least partly) intelligible are factors which lie deep and are not likely to be drawn on in a rapid and superficial simulation.

Either way, the case does not present the insuperable difficulties for simulationism which Nichols et al. suppose. They think that it does only because they are operating with an overly simple account of simulation theory, one that ignores the important role of intelligibility and does not delve deeply enough into what such a theory should say about value, desire and emotion.

Part Two

Thought and Reason

6

Co-Cognition and Off-Line Simulation: Two Ways of Understanding the Simulation Approach

1. INTRODUCTION

The central aim of this essay is to articulate and recommend the idea that the simulationist view about what is involved in grasp and use of psychological concepts may be understood in two different ways, namely as an a priori claim about the relations of certain personal-level cognitive abilities or as an a posteriori hypothesis about the workings of sub-personal cognitive machinery. I hope also to show that this contrast has important implications for the simulation debate in general, in that it suggests there is a potentially serious confusion lurking in the way the 'theory versus simulation' question is often posed and discussed. The stimulus for the attempt to clarify these matters has been the desire to respond to some of the points made in a recent paper by Stich and Nichols (1997), which is in turn a response to an earlier paper of mine (this volume, Essay 5). So, in the final sections of this essay, 1 shall comment briefly on some aspects of this exchange. But one major issue raised there, namely the role of (some notion of) rationality in defining the domain of simulation, is not fully considered here. I seek rather to provide the context in which a more adequate discussion of that topic might occur.

Put slightly more fully, my central suggestion is this. It is commonly taken that the inquiry into the existence and extent of simulation in psychological understanding is empirical, and that scientific investigation is the way to tell whether simulation theory or theory theory or some amalgam is correct. But this perception, I shall argue, is confused. It is an a priori truth, and not an a posteriori one, that theory theory (at least on one strong but natural understanding of 'theory theory') is unacceptable as an account of our personal-level abilities. Correlatively it is an a priori truth that simulation, in some sense, must be given a substantial role in our personal-level account of psychological understanding. Given this, what is up for scientific investigation is not whether this sort of simulation plays an important role, but rather the exact boundaries of that role and how the simulation is realised or embodied. It is as an answer to this 'how' question that simulationism, understood now in a very different way as a hypothesis about sub-personal machinery, comes on the scene. It is one hypothesis among many possible ones as to how the simulation, recognised on a priori grounds, is realised. Thus both simulationist lines of thought are intelligible and of interest; we do not have to choose between them as rival interpretations of the one true simulationism. Moreover, they may both be true. But it is important to be aware of their differences.

I have pointed to the contrast between these two construals in earlier papers and expressed my preference for concentrating on the a priori issue. But those papers did not clarify the contrast or bring out its significance. Hence the likelihood of debates at cross-purposes with other thinkers whose primary interest is in the empirical question and whose assumptions about the structure of the debate are different. This essay is aimed, in part, at remedying these potentially muddling inadequacies of the earlier discussions. The likelihood of misunderstanding is increased by the availability of only one word, 'simulation', for the expression of several different ideas. In what follows I shall try to avoid this difficulty by tightening up on terminology and introducing one new word. I shall use 'simulation' as a general term to cover both approaches, to gesture in the direction of the vague idea that grasp and use of psychological concepts is bound up with the ability to re-create (in some sense) others' thoughts and reasonings. I shall use 'off-line simulation' to talk of the idea that is the focus of the a posteriori hypothesising about what is implicated in thinking about others' thoughts; and I shall coin a new term, 'co-cognition', to talk of what the a priori claim says is central to such thinking. (My 'off-line simulation' is thus roughly equivalent to Stich and Nichols' 'pretence-driven-off-line-simulation' [Stich and Nichols 1997].)

Using this terminology we may restate the central claim of this essay as follows. There is an a priori question as to whether we should adopt a strong version of theory theory or a co-cognition view about what underpins use of psychological concepts. If we settle that question in favour of co-cognition, there is then an a posteriori question as to how our co-cognitive abilities are actually realised. Here off-line simulation may be part of the answer but is certainly not the only possibility. Hence the truth or otherwise of the off-line simulation view is an a posteriori matter. Its a posteriori rivals do not, however, include strong theory theory but are, rather, hypotheses about sub-personal machinery which could realise co-cognition. If I am right about this being the most revealing way of setting out the structure of the issues, then the general-purpose term 'simulation' is of limited usefulness. It has a role only where the a priori and a posteriori aspects of the issues have not yet been disentangled. But since that is where we now are, I shall for the moment continue to use it.

Here is an overview of the structure of the discussion. Section 2 sets out some background, formulates the co-cognition proposal and contrasts it with the off-line simulation proposal. Section 3 sketches the a priori grounds on which the co-cognition view is to be preferred to strong theory theory. Section 4 considers the case of conditional judgements, which provides an instructive parallel to the case of psychological judgements and helps to clarify and strengthen some of the earlier claims. Section 5 turns to consider explicitly the relations between the a priori and a posteriori simulationist claims. It examines the conditions under which they are compatible and under which the a priori might lend support to the a posteriori. It also considers what alternatives we can envisage to the a posteriori claim, given that theory theory, being already ruled out on a priori grounds, cannot be such an alternative. Finally, Section 6 brings out some of the implications of the foregoing for the debate between Stich and Nichols and myself.

2. SOME BACKGROUND IDEAS AND THE TWO PROPOSALS

I shall not here attempt to summarise the recent debate concerning the possible role of simulation in the grasp and use of psychological concepts, assuming familiarity with at least the outlines of that discussion. But two points do need to be brought out. First, in arguing that strong theory theory is untenable I do not mean to suggest that co-cognition can carry the whole burden of explaining what is involved in grasp and use of psychological notions. Much of what theory theorists urge has force, and consequently the truth may well invoke some combination of co-cognitive and theoretical elements. Second, I shall in the following discussion (as I have done previously) confine myself to considering only one part of the whole area, namely what is involved in our arriving at further psychological judgements about others, given information about some of their existing psychological states. For example, provided with information about some of a person's beliefs and interests ('She believes p_1-p_n and is interested in whether q'), I may well arrive at a view about some likely further belief ('She believes that q'); or given information about ambitions and beliefs, I might infer an intention; or given information about a general intention and belief, I might infer a more specific intention. So I am setting aside all the following questions: How does information about persons' circumstances support judgements about their psychological states? How does information about their behaviour support such judgements? What is distinctive of psychological explanation and how do we arrive at such explanations? What is it to possess psychological concepts? What is the course of children's development of competence with psychological concepts? It is not that I suppose that the ideas of co-cognition or off-line simulation could have nothing to contribute on these issues. Quite the contrary. But it seems to me that our best hope of real clarity and hence progress is to keep our reflections tightly focused.

Before introducing the notion of co-cognition and the a priori claim, a brief word about how 'a priori' is to be understood in what follows. To say that something is a priori, as I mean it here, is not to say that it is susceptible of proof in some formal system. The idea is rather that the a priori is that which is deeply embedded in our worldview, in the sort of way Quine points to, or Wittgenstein (Quine 1953; Wittgenstein 1969). An a priori claim is one we rely on unhesitatingly in making inferences. In cases where it seems threatened, our automatic assumption is that the threat is illusory and we seek ways of explaining it away. If challenged, we are thoroughly at a loss to describe realistically or in any detail how we would carry on intellectually if we could not rely on it. Hence the a priori is not something the testing of which could be the object of a realistic scientific project. To say that a judgement is 'a priori' in this sense is not to say that it will never be abandoned or replaced, nor is it to say that we know that the concepts invoked in it could not mutate into what are recognisably successors in terms of which the claim is false. But it is to say that at the moment we have no serious idea about how such replacement or mutation might go, and hence that little powerful argumentative work can be done by invoking such shadowy and perhaps illusory possibilities. The idea that some claims are a priori in this sense is not itself controversial in the way in which ideas about analyticity may be, nor does it commit us to other controversial positions like the existence of some sharp contrast between philosophy and science.

Let us introduce now a distinction which is important in what follows, namely the distinction between subject matters of thought which are independent of each other and those which are not independent. 'Subject matter' is (intentionally) an extremely vague and catch-all term. A subject matter of thought is any kind of thing, property, stuff, situation, event, quantity, action, and so on which we can think about. So subject matters are immensely various in their logical category and degree of specificity. Examples include stars, money, investment, emotions, flowers, numbers, machines, cars, colours, water, energy, paintings, interest rates, military coups in Africa, Queen Anne's death, detective stories, Jack the Ripper, negation, totality, the past, determinism, and so on.

Two subject matters are independent of each other when the principles of classification, knowledge and conceptual skills relevant to dealing with the one are of little help in dealing with the other and vice versa, and when, in consequence, a person may have rich and adequate grasp of one subject matter but no or very little grasp on the other and vice versa. As an example consider as subject matters vegetables on the one hand and stocks and shares on the other. A person brought up in the country might have a great deal of information about vegetables, their varieties, patterns of growth, required nutrients, soil types, climate and so on while knowing very little of stocks and shares. Conversely, a person brought up entirely in a built environment might have an excellent grasp of stocks and shares, their varieties, legal complexities, profitability and so forth, while being extremely ignorant of the vegetable world. The share dealer who wishes to go into market gardening has got it all to learn, and similarly for the market gardener who would like to go into share dealing. The only overlaps between the two bodies of knowledge and skills are provided by the very general subject matters specified by such concepts as 'object', 'cause' and 'time' and by the basic logical notions such as quantification and conditional.

To say that subject matters may be independent is not to say that the world comes in isolated packages. On the contrary, it is richly interconnected in many ways. Full grasp of any subject matter, as opposed to a grasp which is merely rich and adequate, will bring in many other subject matters, often ones which are prima facie remote. (Vegetables are grown with the help of chemicals produced by companies which are quoted on the stock exchange, etc.) So independence is a contingent matter and comes in varying degrees. But, as the world and our interests actually are, there exist important subject matters where a rich and adequate grasp on one is, in practice, independent of all but a minimal grasp on the other and vice versa.

Clearly, however, not all major subject matters are so independent. For example, while one may be competent in elementary arithmetic without any grasp of advanced number theory, the converse is not the case. Here we have an example of asymmetric dependence. Another case of asymmetric dependence, particularly interesting for our purposes, is provided by the relation between X and photographs of X. Take vegetables and photographs of vegetables as an example. A person may have an excellent understanding of vegetables without having any sort of grasp on photographs of vegetables, indeed without so much as knowing that photographs exist. A person may also have knowledge about photographs in general (their varieties, how they are taken, how printed, how used, etc.) without knowing that vegetables exist. But a person cannot be credited with rich and adequate knowledge of photographs of vegetables without knowing such things as what colour is likely to predominate in a close-up colour photograph of a well-lit pile of clean carrots, as opposed to a pile of cabbages. This knowledge cannot be supplied merely by grasp on the general notion of a photograph. To arrive at detailed and specific judgements about photographs of vegetables a person needs to call upon her grasp of the nature of vegetables as well her grasp of the nature of photographs. Knowledge of photographs in general includes a schematic element, for example such principles as 'A colour photograph (taken close up, in good light, etc.) will exhibit the same colours as what it is of'. These call out for supplementation by knowledge of the colours of what is photographed if they are to help to constitute grasp on a more specific subject matter such as that of photographs of vegetables. Hence photographs of vegetables are not a subject matter independent of that of vegetables.

We need next to introduce an important assumption about thinking. In what follows I take 'thought' and 'thinking' in a wide sense to cover all propositional attitudes and the kinds of reflective development they enter into. The assumption is this: a person's grasp on a subject matter provides her with a multifaceted ability which shows itself not only in the beliefs which she forms and her belief-to-belief inferences but also in her other propositional attitudes and the patterns of transition which they sustain. When a person thinks about a particular question, she calls on whatever knowledge she has of the subject matter, or subject matters, of that question. The more information she has and the better she is at deploying it relevantly, the better the outcome of the thinking. But all this is true not only of the thinking which is belief-to-belief inference but also of the thinking in which desires are clarified, fantasies are elaborated, plans are worked out in detail or hypotheses are developed.

We can see this easily in connection with the extremely minimal or limiting case of grasp of a subject matter, namely grasp on the logical connectives. If an intention is conjunctive – for example, is the intention that p and q – then it enters into certain relations with other intentions – for example, that of potentially sustaining an intention that p and an intention that q. Its doing so is connected with the fact that it is conjunctive, i.e., that the intender exercises the concept 'and' in having this intention. But similar points may be made in connection with more specific subject matters. Consider a person who has an intention that her cabbages should grow to be more than one foot in diameter. One central fact about this intention is that the drive to action it sustains will cease when she acquires the belief that the cabbages have so grown. This is because of the way in which intention and belief interrelate in the overall structure of the mind. (To understand 'intention' and 'belief' we need to know this kind of thing, as theory theorists so rightly emphasise.) But the intention plays other roles also. It will lead to more specific intentions in a way which is guided by the person's grasp on the causal aspects of growing vegetables and growing large cabbages in particular. Also it will lead to precautionary measures to forestall possible but undesirable side effects of its fulfilment. The kind of mental activity which results in the formation of specific intentions, or in the resolution to take precautionary measures, is naturally labelled 'thinking about what is involved in growing cabbages more than a foot in diameter'. And the person's grasp of the subject matter, that is, ability to think effectively about it, shows up here in linkages and patterns which are the same as, or analogous to, the linkages and patterns in belief-to-belief inference. It is this commonality of linkages and patterns which underpins the appearance of the same that-clauses in combination with the different propositional attitude verbs. If the commonalities did not exist our everyday use of propositional attitude vocabulary would not have the success it does. Hence the idea of grasp on a subject matter as a multifaceted ability which shows itself in many different kinds of cognitive state and performance is central to our conception of ourselves and our thinking.

We are now in a position to introduce co-cognition. Co-cognition is just a fancy name for the everyday notion of thinking about the same subject matter (where 'thinking' is understood in the wide sense specified two paragraphs ago). Those who co-cognise exercise the same underlying multifaceted ability to deal with some subject matter. So, for example, two persons M and N co-cognise when each has the same beliefs and interests and reasons to the same further belief. But also M at time t1 may co-cognise with herself at t2, in that at t2 she makes belief-to-belief inferences about some subject matter, while at t1 she entertained fantasy-to-fantasy development or intention-to-intention specification with the same contents. Or M and N may co-cognise if M actually believes what N entertains as mere fantasy, but each exercises the same grasp of the subject matter and so the same patterns and linkages are detectable in their thoughts.

The notion of co-cognition here introduced is a capacious one and many complexities and sub-varieties need to be considered. I remark here on just a few points particularly relevant in the present context. Ability to co-cognise is not an all-or-nothing matter. M and N may both have some grasp of a given subject matter, but M in a richer and more adequate way than N. N will then be capable of some co-cognition with M, but there will be other of M's thinking with which N cannot co-cognise. At one limit N may be able to co-cognise with M only in the very skeletal sense of grasping the logical form of M's thought, for example that M is thinking that all Fs are G, for some properties F and G. Here the only subject matters M and N share a grasp on – that is, the only concepts they both exercise – are those introduced by the word 'all' and by the predicate construction.

Co-cognition with another who has different beliefs can be easier or more difficult, depending on how much difference of outlook there is between the parties and in what respects. Relatedly entertaining and reasoning from a hypothesis or fantasy one does not believe can be easier or more difficult depending on how radical that counterfactual supposition is. Sometimes co-cognising with another is easy, for example where M and N share a great number of substantive general beliefs and differ only in some minor particular belief and its ramifications. But where M and N differ in large-scale features of their worldview, attempts at co-cognition may run less smoothly. For example, they may require the co-cogniser to switch off deeply ingrained habits of inference, which are associated with his or her entrenched beliefs. Such switching off can be exceedingly difficult.

Earlier I stressed that unless there were commonality of linkages and patterns of connection across different propositional attitudes we could not assume, as we clearly do, that different attitudes could be directed at the same content. But what these difficulties suggest is that it would be wrong to assume that the parallelisms involved are complete and exact, or that it is always easy to bring them into being. Roughly speaking, the more different another outlook is from our current one, the more difficulty there is in co-cognising with it. Clearly a fuller treatment of co-cognition would need to say much more about these extremely important issues and the related questions of what is involved in persons sharing concepts, or sharing grasp on a subject matter. We would also need to consider what, if anything, fills the gap when easy co-cognition fails. Are we forced to give up? Can we simply at that point abandon anything co-cognitive and successfully switch to pure theory instead? Do we have techniques for extending our co-cognitive range? What role might theoretical considerations play in such techniques? I cannot here deal with these extremely important topics. Consequently what follows fits best in the case of thinking about the thoughts of those who share our culture and outlook. Much more needs to be said about whatever understanding we can have of persons of radically different outlooks.

Consider now the following claim:

(A) It is an a priori truth that thinking about others' thoughts requires us, in usual and central cases, to think about the states of affairs which are the subject matter of those thoughts, namely to co-cognise with the person whose thoughts we seek to grasp.

Following the narrowing of focus noted in the first paragraph of this section, we shall concentrate on the particular application of (A) in which it speaks of one person's processes of reasoning where they are directed at working out the upshot of another person's processes of reasoning. It is obvious, truistic, that the target who starts by believing that p_1–p_n must, in the process of reasoning to the conclusion that q, think about the subject matter of those beliefs. What (A) says of this case is that someone else who endeavours to work out what the first person's reasoning will lead to must also think about the subject matter of the beliefs p_1–p_n and q.

Compare this with the rather different claim:

(B) It is an a posteriori truth that when we think about others' thoughts we sometimes 'unhook' some of our cognitive mechanisms so that they can run 'off-line' and then feed them with 'pretend' versions of the sorts of thought we attribute to the other.

(A) is the claim that co-cognition is important in our dealings with other minds. (B) is the claim that off-line simulation is the sub-personal process in which such co-cognition is realised. We shall return to (B) later.

Our next move must be to consider the relation of (A) to theory theory about the psychological and to ask whether (A) is plausible.

3. THEORY THEORY AND THOUGHTS AS AN INDEPENDENT SUBJECT MATTER

It is clear that (A) expresses some kind of simulationist claim. Moreover (A) is formulated entirely in commonsense and everyday terms. So if we continue to operate at this level of everyday notions, what is the claim to which (A) stands opposed? I suggest that it is the claim that thoughts about X form a separate subject matter which is independent of the subject matter X. I suggest also that this is one natural way of spelling out what is claimed by theory theory, in what I shall call its strong version. As evidence that some do understand 'theory theory' this way consider a boxological diagram offered by Stich and Nichols as a rendition of theory theory (1995b: 89). In this diagram a box called 'folk psychology' appears beside a box called 'folk physics' within the overall 'Beliefs' box. It is difficult to read this other than as a commitment to the idea that the body of information which underpins dealings with others' thoughts is independent of the body of information which underpins dealings with physical objects. If one were countenancing the possibility that in thinking about another's thoughts about physical objects a person would have to call upon his or her own knowledge of physical objects, it would be very strange to configure the diagram as Stich and Nichols do. So one claim of strong theory theory (as defined here) would be that grasp on the subject matter of vegetables is one thing and grasp on the subject matter of thoughts about vegetables is a quite different and independent thing.

Strong theory theory has a certain prima facie plausibility. We might well suppose that some thinkers (young children? autistics?) could have quite reasonable cognitive grasp of vegetables without much, if any, cognitive grasp of psychological states. So that way round, arguably, there is independence. And it might seem that the reverse holds also. Thoughts about vegetables are, after all, extremely different from vegetables. They do not grow in the ground but occur in people's minds or heads; their causes and effects (perceptions, feelings, actions, etc.) are quite different from those of vegetables (soil, rain, seeds, etc.). They are classified as beliefs or intentions and are assigned properties like being true or being fulfilled, while vegetables are classified as carrots or cabbages and assigned properties like having high vitamin C content or weighing two pounds. By concentrating on these sorts of observations we might persuade ourselves that thoughts about vegetables are as independent of vegetables as are stocks and shares.

What is right here is the stress on the fact that ability to think about thoughts requires grasp of such distinctive concepts as 'belief', 'intention', 'truth', 'fulfilment' and the like. But what the approach overlooks is the fact that thoughts represent aspects of the world. They are that in having which a person is aware of the world as containing vegetables or stocks and shares. In our everyday conception of thoughts, their possession of representational content is one of their most salient features. There is therefore a likelihood that some of the important features of particular thoughts, from our point of view in our everyday reflections on them, are connected with features of what they represent. Recognition of this suggests that the ability to think about thoughts might require both a grip on what is distinctive about thoughts as such and an ability to think about the subject matter of the thoughts, for the same sort of reason we found in the case of photographs.

Reflection on photographs might help us to see the important principles at issue here. Here what makes it possible for grasp on the subject matter X to be deployed as part of grasp on the subject matter of photographs of X is the usual success of photographs in accurately capturing the appearance of what they represent. But might it be the case that we do not, in fact, rely on this at all but instead produce our predictions about the appearance of photographs of X by calling upon an entirely separate and photograph-specific body of information? In certain cases, those where photographic accuracy fails, a good grasp of what photographs of X are like may indeed require possession of information which has nothing to do with what X is like but is specific to photographs of X. Perhaps turnips emit strange rays which produce black-and-white zigzags on any film exposed to them. More realistically, there are effects like the pink eyes which flash photographs often endow us with. But the idea that all competence in thinking about what photographs look like is sustained by such photograph-specific bodies of information is surely not worth serious contemplation. Among other difficulties, it postulates an immensely wasteful duplication of bodies of knowledge, and it fails to explain why someone acquiring knowledge about the appearance of a new kind of thing automatically acquires abilities to think about the appearance of photographs of that sort of thing.

In the case of thoughts, what we are interested in at the moment is not what they are like in themselves but rather their relations to other thoughts. Remember that our paradigm question is 'She believes p_1–p_n and is interested in whether q; what is her likely opinion?' So to underpin (A), viz., the claim that the reflection required for answering this question is, in part at least, reflection on the subject matter of her beliefs, what is needed is some analogous presupposition of success in thought. What would fit the bill is a presupposition that connections in thought tend to mirror connections between states of affairs. So when, for example, the (complex) state of affairs that p_1 and p_2 and ... p_n necessitates (or makes likely) that q, then believing that p_1–p_n tends to lead to concluding that q on the basis that p_1–p_n.

The idea that connections in thought follow connections between states of affairs is the idea that we are rational – in some sense of that term. The kind of rationality needed to justify (A) is, however, very weak. Underpinning (A) does not require that we be capable of achieving, let alone actually do achieve, such grandiose objectives as total consistency and completeness in our thoughts. Nor does it demand that our sense of what follows from what be illusion-free. The claim that we are rational in the sense needed to underpin (A) is consistent with acknowledging that we have built-in liabilities to certain kinds of inferential error. Nor does it require that we be capable of detecting all connections, including those holding in virtue of very complex and intricate features of the situations involved. All that (A) presupposes is that when trying to work out whether such and such follows from so and so what guides us in making these transitions in thought is something it is sensible to rely on. And it is sensible to rely on it if (for all we know) there is a good chance of its working and there is nothing better to call on. Commitment to our rationality (in some such minimal sense) is not a strong tendentious claim which empirical science could lead us to abandon. On the contrary, it is an extremely modest assumption which we cannot do without. We cannot do without it because it is presupposed by unavoidable kinds of common everyday thinking. We pose to ourselves questions – 'Have I got enough money left to buy this?' 'How many cups of coffee have I had so far today?' 'Does this objection refute that claim?' 'Would this chair fit into my sitting room?' 'How will my colleagues react to this proposal?' and so on. We take it for granted that where information we already possess implies an answer to such questions there is a good chance of our becoming aware of the information and its implications and so coming to knowledge of the answer. It is very obscure indeed how we would conduct our lives if we did not have this faith in our thinking abilities.

Given the assumption of such very minimal rationality, we can show why reliance on co-cognition is a sensible way to proceed in trying to grasp where another's reflections may lead. The other thinks that p_1-p_n and is wondering whether q. I would like to know what she will conclude. Her thoughts (I assume) will follow the connections between things. So I ask myself 'Would the obtaining of p_1-p_n necessitate or make likely the obtaining of q?' To answer this question I must myself think about the states of affairs in question, as the other is also doing, that is, I must co-cognize with the other. If I come to the answer that a state of affairs in which p_1-p_n would necessitate or make likely that q, then I shall expect the other to arrive at the belief that q.

This basic strategy can be supplemented and refined in all kinds of ways, in the light of knowledge of human propensity to error or quirks in a particular person's thinking, just as the basic strategy for predicting the appearance of photographs can be fine-tuned by knowledge of such things as the pink-eye effect. But acknowledging an important role for this kind of supplementation (and also for general grasp on psychological categories) is a far cry from acknowledging that strong theory theory could be right. For strong theory theory to be defensible we need to make plausible the idea that we actually grasp (even if only tacitly) some principles about how particular contentful thoughts are connected, principles which have nothing to do with connections between the states of affairs these thoughts are about, and that this grasp is our major resource in generating successful predictions of others' thoughts.

If you are sympathetic to the idea that X and photographs of X are not independent subject matters, I hope I have said enough to suggest that, for very similar reasons, X and thoughts about X also are not independent subject matters for us, and hence that strong theory theory is not a serious option. Clearly a great deal more needs to be said about the notion of rationality required for the elaboration of the co-cognition view and how it is related to other notions of rationality. There are also more arguments to be deployed in support of (A). But I shall leave those matters for the moment and press on with sketching the overall position. (Rationality is discussed further in Essays 8 and 12.)

4. CONDITIONALS

In the last section I claimed that one natural understanding of strong theory theory is as the idea that thoughts are an independent subject matter from the subject matter of what they are about. To strengthen that claim, and also to recommend further the idea that we are committed to the notion of grasp on a subject matter as a multifaceted ability, it will be useful to digress briefly into the topic of conditionals. The whole debate about simulation and the psychological is initiated by the plain fact that we are capable of arriving at new psychological judgements about others. It is also a plain fact that we can arrive at new conditional judgements, about states of affairs we do not believe to obtain and which may indeed not obtain. For the sake of having a label, let us call the subject matter of these judgements 'connections of possibilities'. How do we arrive at judgements about them?

One proposal is that we do so by employing the same grasp of subject matters as are manifested at other points in our thinking. Here is a co-cognitive proposal along these lines:

(A') It is an a priori truth that thinking about connections of possibilities requires us, in usual and central cases, to think about the states of affairs which are taken to be possible, i.e. to co-cognise with the kind of thinking we might do in belief-to-belief inferences about those states of affairs.

We could fill out (A') as follows. We arrive at a conditional belief, such as 'If p then q', by thinking about the state of affairs the antecedent specifies, that is, by exercising our grasp of that subject matter and seeing where it leads us. For example, we start by wondering 'What if p?' or we imagine or hypothesise that p. Any fruitful process of reflection initiated by such an attitude – that is, any pondering on 'What if p?' which results in the realisation 'If p then q' – will call on the ability to think about the subject matter of the state of affairs that p, just as much as would thinking initiated by the intention that p or the belief that p. Wondering what if, imagining, hypothesising and so on are attitudes importantly different from intending or believing, in that they play a different role in overall cognitive functioning. But we rightly see them as belonging to the same family, because the same cognitive abilities, the same grasp of subject matters, are exercised in them too.

To dispute (A') we would have to deny that when we think about a state of affairs as real and when we think about it as possible we think about the same thing, are occupied with the same subject matter. So to dispute (A') is to propose that when we think about what I have called 'connections of possibilities', as opposed to states of affairs taken as actual, what we are really concerned with is an independent subject matter, dealing with which calls upon its own independent information store and cognitive grasp. In this light consider the following quotation from Nichols et al.

One possibility is that the evaluation of conditionals depends on a body of meta-linguistic principles concerning entailment relations among sentences.... According to this meta-linguistic theory, we know, perhaps tacitly, that certain sentences follow from other sentences. And we can see, as a result, that if some sentences were true, other sentences would also be true. To clarify the nature of this account, let's consider an example. Most would take the following [conditional] to be true:

If Bill Clinton had lost the election, Hillary Clinton would not be the First Lady. On the current proposal, we evaluate this sentence in the following way. We know that the following sentences are true: 'The First Lady is the wife of the President'; 'Hillary Clinton is Bill Clinton's wife'; 'The loser of the election doesn't become President'. In addition, we know various entailment relations among sentences. Given our knowledge of the entailment relations, plus our knowledge of the true sentences, we reason that if 'Bill Clinton lost the election' were true, 'Hillary Clinton is not the First Lady' would also be true. This account... relies on a body of information about relations between sentences. (Nichols et al. 1996: 94–95)

This proposal, supposedly congenial to anti-simulationists, is offered in the context of an attempt to undermine a rival 'simulationist' proposal about knowledge of conditionals. The simulationist proposal to which it is opposed is formulated by Nichols et al. not as (A′) but rather as something akin to (B). So it is articulated in terms of taking inference mechanisms 'off-line', feeding them with 'pretend beliefs' and so forth. But if my construal of the geography of the debate is correct, then in the discussions up to now the two strands of concern with simulation have been run together. Hence there may be justification for seeing the proposal as, in part at least, offered as an attempted alternative to (A′), that is, to the co-cognitive account. What it postulates is just what we should expect on that reading, viz., that the thinking by which we arrive at conditional judgements is not concerned with non-linguistic states of affairs but rather has its own independent subject matter, namely sentences and the relations between them.

But what Nichols et al. suggest is not a viable alternative to the commonsense idea embodied in (A′). Their suggestion either leads to an infinite regress or requires admission of the possibility of co-cognitive (A′)-style thinking at least about sentences. And if we go the latter way it becomes unclear why we should confine the ability to these cases alone. To see this in more detail let us start from the fact that it would be absurd to credit us in advance with knowledge of every meta-linguistic conditional of the form 'If S1 were true then S2 would be true' for which we can come to a corresponding ground-level conditional belief. The proposal itself acknowledges this by speaking of our 'reasoning' to our belief in the idea that if 'Bill Clinton lost the election' were true then 'Hillary Clinton is not the First Lady' would also be true. So, according to the proposal, we are capable of forming new conditional beliefs of the form 'if S1 were true then S2 would be true'. How do we do this?

If we apply the proposal again, we get the suggestion that we do it by applying meta-linguistic knowledge about relations of implication between sentences about sentences. Something enables me to realise that if '"Bill Clinton lost the election" is true' were true, then '"Hillary Clinton is not the First Lady" is true' would be true. And how do we come to form this belief? By applying yet more meta-linguistic knowledge? This option is clearly quite hopeless since it leads to an infinite regress.

To halt the regress we have to say that, at some level, we know enough about sentences and what it takes for them to be true for us to be able to evaluate 'If S1 were true then S2 would be true' without needing to detour via consideration of further meta-linguistic states of affairs. But although it avoids the infinite regress, this hardly provides a more attractive position. It allows that we are able to think, without calling on further meta-linguistic knowledge, about the possibility that a certain sentence is true and that, through so thinking, we can see that if it were true then some other sentence would be true. In allowing this it has allowed the existence of the sort of attitude postulated by (A'), namely an ability to think about sentences which is not straightforwardly having either intentions or beliefs about them, but is rather hypothesising or wondering 'what if' about them. So it has acknowledged the truth of (A'), at least as far as our cognitive dealings with sentences are concerned. But at the same time it has insisted, in an entirely unmotivated way, that this ability to think about mere possibilities is confined to contemplating sentences and their properties.

Another difficulty with the proposal is that it can offer no account of our ability to arrive at conditional judgements about subject matters which we can represent to ourselves in language only by indexical phrases like 'this colour', 'that angle', 'this degree of viscosity' and the like. Also, if we are prepared to credit any non-language-using animals with ability to arrive at new conditional beliefs, the proposal can offer no story about how they do so.

The upshot of these reflections is that the proposal by Nichols et al. does not provide a viable alternative which does away with the need to allow for 'simulation', in the sense of co-cognition, in our account of our dealings with conditionals. The reflections reveal how deeply embedded is the assumption that we can deploy our grasp on a subject matter in attitudes such as wondering 'what if' – that is, in contemplating states of affairs as merely possible – as well as in beliefs and intentions. So the claim of (A') to articulate an important a priori insight into our ability to arrive at conditional judgements remains as strong as ever.

Acknowledging this, however, does not commit us to the idea that when we think about possibilities we take our inference mechanisms 'off-line' and feed them with 'pretend beliefs'. Nothing we have said so far requires us to suppose that hypothesising that p is having a 'pretend belief' that p – any more than recognising that grasp of a subject matter is exercised in developing intentions requires us to think that filling out intentions is a matter of having 'pretend beliefs'. To bring this out consider that we can formulate quite an ingenious and interesting hypothesis about intentions. It is this. When I form the high-level intention that p and wish to move on to further more detailed intentions, what I do (not consciously but only sub-personally, of course) is create a pretend belief that p which I feed into my theoretical inference mechanism, taken off-line; I then take some of the output pretend beliefs as the bases for the formation of my further more detailed intentions. For all I know, this story about sub-personal mechanisms of intention formation is correct. But the important point is that it is not something we are committed to merely in virtue of recognising that beliefs and intentions may have the same content, and hence that theoretical and practical inferences may exhibit analogous patterns.

We shall turn to consider the role of empirical hypotheses about sub-personal mechanisms in the next section. But first a brief comment on the word 'simulation'.

(A) and (A') deserve the label 'simulationist claims' if we take likeness or resemblance to be a sort of 'simulation'. So on (A') the thinking which goes on when we arrive at conditional beliefs resembles, and in that sense simulates, the thinking which goes on in reflection based on categorical beliefs. It resembles it in that it calls on the same grasp of the subject matter and results in thoughts which exhibit the same patterns and linkages. But unfortunately the word 'simulation' has strong associations with ideas such as 'non-genuine', 'pretence', 'mere model', 'bogus' and the like. And moreover the word has become firmly established in this debate from its use by Gordon in his seminal paper on the issue (Gordon 1986). I conjecture that these associations of the word have played a part in the way in which the co-cognition option has tended to become invisible and discussants have seemed to take for granted that the only way of spelling out 'simulationist' insights is to start talking about 'pretend' beliefs, 'off-line running' of systems and so on. In my early foray into the area (Heal 1986) I used the word 'replicate', which lacks the strong overtones of spuriousness and so forth that haunt 'simulation'. 'Co-cognition' is designed to have the same neutrality and hence to provide a vehicle for carrying on debate which has less built-in risk of distortion.

5. THE RELATION OF THE A PRIORI AND A POSTERIORI CLAIMS

Up to now our attention has been on (A). Now it is time to look more closely at (B) and to consider its relations to (A). (A) by itself cannot entail (B), given that the one is a priori and the other a posteriori. But given further assumptions, themselves empirical, (A) might well support (B). If, however, those further assumptions are themselves false, then (A) might be true and (B) false.

One of these further assumptions, a high-level and general one, I shall call 'the general systems hypothesis'. It says that a person's psychological life proceeds in virtue of the interrelated functioning of various systems (structures, mechanisms, devices, programmes) one of which (or some group of which) provides the primary location for each of the familiar kinds of state and operation spoken of in ordinary language – that is, memory, reasoning, emotion, imagination, decision, perceptions and so on. These systems have some properties and individuating conditions which can be specified in terms other than those of commonsense psychology.

Here, for example, is one familiar way of filling out the hypothesis, although doubtless others are possible. If we work from the top down, we may hope to first identify and specify properties of the systems in terms not identical with but close to those of ordinary language by laying out the functions which the systems contribute to overall operation of the person. Next we unpack this further by discovering (for instance) the computations the systems must perform to carry out their functions. Next we move to discover the particular algorithms, out of the many that would be adequate, which they actually employ to carry out those computations. And finally, perhaps, we may even find some neurophysiological complexes, whether dedicated bundles of neurones or distinctive patterns of weighting of connection between neurones or whatever, in which we can see the algorithm being implemented.

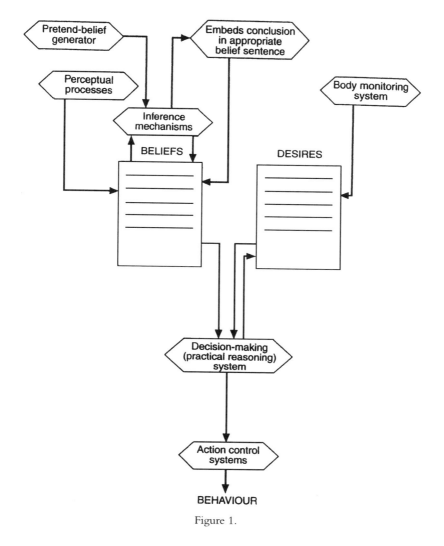

Figure 1.

A second and more specific assumption is also needed to make (A) support (B), namely the truth of specific version of the systems hypothesis. This is the version on which the actual sub-personal systems of thought consist of (at least) a belief store, a desire store, some theoretical inference machinery and some practical reasoning machinery, all existing in a particular configuration of potential causal relations, such as the one sketched in the 'boxological' representations of Stich and Nichols (e.g., 1995b: 96) and reproduced here as Figure 1.

If these two assumptions are true, then (A) supports (B). (A) tells us that the ability to think about another's thoughts calls upon and incorporates the ability to think about the subject matter of those thoughts. (B) offers us an account of some actual psychological systems and processes by which that dependence of abilities could be realised.

But are the further assumptions true? Some may think that the first is obviously acceptable and is itself, perhaps, pretty well towards the a priori end of the spectrum. This is because (so this thought goes) accepting the general systems hypothesis is part of what it is to be committed to realism about the psychological. If we do not insist that there is something properly natural and scientific (e.g., of a computational and ultimately of a neurophysiological kind) for mental states and processes to consist in, then either we have allowed in dualism, or we are countenancing a merely behavioural account of the truth conditions of psychological claims, or we have bowed out of realism altogether and are going for instrumentalism. We need not enter this debate here. It is enough to note that the vaguer we are about what kind of systems underpinning is needed for realism about the psychological, the more likely it is that the systems hypothesis is a priori but the less content it gets. Let us concede for the sake of the debate that the general systems hypothesis is true. Let us concentrate instead on the specific systems hypothesis.

It seems extremely plausible that it is empirical and that alternatives can be envisaged. I should like to reinforce this by sketching a systems account with a different architecture from that of (B). (B) assumes that inference is centrally a belief-to-belief matter, so that inference mechanisms operate only on beliefs, or on something which is similar enough to a belief to make the wheels of the mechanisms go round; hence the need for 'pretend beliefs' when some kind of thinking goes on which is patently not straight belief-to-belief inference. But perhaps in this respect the specific hypothesis is wrong, and inference mechanisms do not take beliefs as input but rather take items which represent or encode propositional contents without attached attitudes. Thus, working out relations of relevance, entailment, contradiction and the like between representations is one thing and done by one bit of mental machinery, while applying or withholding attitudes is a different matter, handled by some other part of the mental machinery. If this were so, then there would be no need for a person to generate a 'pretend' belief to input to her inference mechanisms when she thinks about another's beliefs. Moreover, she can input the content of the other's belief to those mechanisms without unhooking them or taking them 'off-line'. All she needs to do is input a content, perhaps tagging it as the content of the other's belief, note the output, and tag that too as the content of a probable further belief of the other. The overall machinery here is simpler than on (B), in that no devices are needed to take the inference mechanisms off-line or reconnect them. On the other hand, it is more complicated in that we need devices to keep track of which attitudes are adopted, and by which persons, to the various content-representations which are present. Both suggestions satisfy the general systems hypothesis that the personal-level story told in (A) be backed up by some account of how it could be realised. The decision between it and (B) will need to be made on empirical grounds.

It is doubtless apparent that the account just sketched was not randomly devised. It is a systems hypothesis where the machinery postulated runs more closely parallel to the psychological categories invoked in (A) than does the machinery of (B). But many other systems hypotheses are surely possible, for example ones invoking a much more modular view of the mind or ones incorporating more connectionist architectures, and so forth.

If the alternative sketched were empirically supported as against (B), then we would not be justified in postulating 'off-line' running of mental systems or 'pretend beliefs' to be fed into them. So 'simulationism', in one sense, would be refuted. But is strong theory theory thereby favoured? Not at all. Strong theory theory is nowhere in the running as an option in the imagined investigation. All that has been discredited is one hypothesis about how (A) is realised. My conjecture is that in the simulation debate hitherto some participants have been too little aware that the general systems hypothesis and its more specific (B) sub-version are presupposed by the formulations offered, and also too little aware that the sub-version itself is empirical and controversial. The effect of this has been to obscure the difference between (A) and (B) and to allow it to appear that there is only one reading of the simulation hypothesis, namely as an empirical rival to theory theory.

Another reason why we may have been so gripped by the idea that simulation and theory theory are empirical rivals is that the general 'simulation versus theory' contrast has been explained and illustrated by non-mental systems, for example by pointing to the use of model aircraft in wind tunnels. This ploy (which I have used myself) provides a vivid and effective way of making clear how we could have the ability to arrive at detailed and accurate predictions about some subject matter without possessing any sort of full theory of it. But the aircraft case, and others which are cited as well, are ones where it seems clear that it is at least possible that we should have a full theory and so be able to dispense with simulation. They are also cases where the idea that 'simulation' is something non-genuine, involving a kind of model or simulacrum, is prominent. These two ideas may be imported into the psychological case, where they combine with the assumption of the truth of the (B) sub-version of the systems hypothesis to push us in the direction of seeing the central question as being 'Should we accept (B) or theory theory as an account of our ability to predict?' But these three ideas (the feasibility of strong theory theory for the psychological, that 'simulated' must imply 'bogus' and that the (B) systems sub-version is the only option) are all seriously flawed. The result of operating with them in the background is that misconstrual of the overall shape of the debate which I have been concerned to expose and counter.

6. RESPONSE TO STICH AND NICHOLS

An earlier exchange between Stich and Nichols and myself focused in part on cognitive penetrability and whether arguments against simulationism (in whatever form) could be found by invoking this notion. Stich and Nichols have acknowledged the force of the points I urged against their earlier claims on this topic and have, in section 3 of their paper, elaborated further how the off-line simulation approach can allow for various kinds of cognitive penetration (Heal Essay 5; Stich and Nichols 1997). So I shall say nothing further on this issue. In section 2 of their paper, Stich and Nichols contend that 'the "simulation" label has become quite useless because 'simulations are not a theoretically interesting kind'. Having myself, in this essay, introduced more distinctions between meanings of 'simulation', I am hardly in a position to dispute this, or at least to dispute the very closely related claim that the debate cannot any longer fruitfully continue using only the general and undifferentiated term 'simulation'. I am in full agreement with Stich and Nichols that we must now move on to work with only more sharply defined ideas. We should, however, remember that it is no kind of criticism of proponents of simulation that they did not at the start of the debate anticipate all the possible complexities and distinctions which it would later prove useful to note. If they had not initiated the debate by calling on the general and schematic notion of simulation (and thus challenged the existing orthodoxy couched in terms of possession of some 'theory'), we would not have been put on the track of the more detailed and interesting ideas which are now coming into focus.

As I remarked in Section 1, in previous discussions I have hinted at some of the themes developed in the body of this essay but have not set them out fully, thus leaving myself open to various misunderstandings. Some such misunderstandings are manifested in Stich and Nichols' section 2, and we may note them just for the record. One distinction of which Stich and Nichols make much (claiming that proponents of simulation, including myself, have not given it adequate attention) is that between what they call 'actual-situation-simulation', in which the would-be predictor has or acquires the very same mental states as the person to be predicted, and 'pretence-driven-off-line-simulation', in which the predictor does not share the mental states of the one to be predicted but instead devises 'pretend' versions of them and feeds them into mental mechanisms run 'off-line'. They suggest that actual-situation-simulation is unproblematic and clearly does occur, whereas the feasibility and existence of pretence-driven-off-line-simulation are much more questionable. They also write, 'We're fairly confident that Heal thinks pretence-driven-off-line-simulation is the process underlying many cases in which we predict the thoughts or actions of other people' (1997: 304). Two points need making here. One is that I have never endorsed the off-line-simulation hypothesis and have always (quite deliberately) expressed my views without using the terminology of 'pretend beliefs', 'off-line running' and the like. The second is that the distinction of which Stich and Nichols make so much does not exist as far as the co-cognition approach is concerned. If the distinction has any analogue at the personal level it is the distinction between thinking about a subject matter in the mode of belief-to-belief inference and thinking about it in the mode of, for example, wondering 'what if?' The believer in co-cognition would not, however, acknowledge any contrast between an unproblematic similarity between two persons who both infer q from p and some supposed more problematic similarity between two persons when one infers q from p and the other wonders 'What if p?' and realises 'If p then q'. For the proponent of co-cognition, the existence of both kinds of similarity is entirely unproblematic; they are both plain examples of co-cognition.

In section 4 of their paper, Stich and Nichols criticise a suggestion from me that simulation should only confidently offer itself as the method by which one person anticipates another's mental states where those states are ones with content and where the contents are rationally or intelligibly linked. They take it that this is offered as an empirical conjecture that 'pretend states do not have the power to engage the mental mechanisms or processes that result in irrational outcomes', and they offer a boxological diagram designed to summarise what they take the suggestion to be (1997: 317). Construing the proposal this way, they are, not surprisingly, unenthusiastic about it.

I shall not here attempt to spell out the proposal in alternative terms or argue in its favour. I remark only that it was prefixed by the words, 'The kind of simulationism I would like to defend says that . . .'. That kind of simulationism is the co-cognition view and not the off-line simulation view. So whatever merits or defensibility the proposal has will be apparent only from the co-cognition perspective. Its content is not helpfully represented by their boxological diagram.

A posteriori and a priori studies of the mind need to go hand in hand. Investigations in psychology and neuroscience can reveal surprising facts about our mental lives and suggest to us hypotheses about the underpinnings or realisations of mental states and processes. It may also be that such empirical studies gradually feed back into and transform our conceptions of such states and processes and radically modify our self-image. But it is important that empirical study should at least start by accurately registering what our ideas now are and how deeply entrenched some of them appear to be. Certainly, philosophy of mind can benefit from more awareness of empirical findings. But equally, cognitive science and psychology could benefit by admitting some of the distinctions and observations assembled in the studies of philosophers.

7

Semantic Holism: Still a Good Buy

1. INTRODUCTION

Holism is an alluring and heady notion.[1] Many claims that this or that notion is 'holistic' have been made, and in particular the idea that semantic notions such as meaning or content are 'holistic' has seemed plausible to a good number of philosophers. It is not obvious, however, that they have all meant the same thing, and Fodor and Lepore, in *Holism: A Shopper's Guide*, have performed a useful service (Fodor and Lepore 1992). They offer an account of what holism is, together with an outline attack on it and an attempt to undermine the major arguments for it. There is, however, further clarification to undertake since, despite their best efforts, the exact content of the thesis remains in doubt. This is in part because Fodor and Lepore (sometimes with and sometimes without argument) proceed as if certain distinct positions are in fact equivalent. The upshot of this is that plausible versions of semantic holism are run together with implausible versions, and the innocent are made to suffer with the guilty.

The structure of the rest of this essay is as follows. The next section aims to disentangle various ways in which 'semantic holism' may be understood and to explain how some of them seem to get run together by Fodor and Lepore. Section 3 is primarily ad hominem. It starts from ideas which Fodor and Lepore themselves introduce under the heading 'the primacy of belief' and suggests that their attempt to undermine arguments for holism by this route backfires. Section 4 pursues one of the themes of Section 3 and offers a positive argument for the first element of what I claim to be

---

1. I am grateful to Jonathan Cohen for comments on an earlier version of this paper (Cohen 1999). Some points from my reply to him (Heal 1999) are incorporated into this revision.

the most plausible version of semantic holism, an argument centring on the familiar idea that the notion of thought is essentially linked to that of a rational thinker. Section 5 offers some thoughts about how to defend the other element in that holism.

The holism I wish to defend is, prima facie, unambitious. It is nevertheless worth bringing it into focus and seeking to secure it, because doing so is the foundation for further important enterprises. Moreover, it is less anodyne than it looks as it threatens to bring with it unsettling consequences, although these will not be discussed here.[2]

2. WHAT IS HOLISM?

What is semantic holism? Before we consider this question directly, let us clarify some terminological points. I shall, as do Fodor and Lepore, use 'semantic holism', 'meaning holism' and 'content holism' interchangeably to refer to the central idea which interests us. I shall, however, concern myself for the most part with thoughts and not with all items, psychological and linguistic alike, to which representational content can be attributed. Also, I shall narrow the focus by concentrating on whole thoughts with contents suitable to be reported in that-clauses. Semantic holism, then, as we shall construe it has as its central thrust something like this: if an individual thought has a certain content, then this is bound up with or involves the nature of some collection of thoughts of which it is an element.

One way of spelling this out offers us a two-part thesis:

(1a) We cannot make sense of there being just one thought. If there is any thought, then there must be quite a number of different thoughts attributable to the same thinker.
(1b) The presence in a set of thoughts of one with a given content imposes some constraints on the contents of the rest of the set.

The prima facie unambitious thesis of which I spoke above is the conjunction of these. But now here is another thesis which can also be labelled 'semantic holism'.

(2) 'Only whole languages or whole theories or whole belief systems really have meanings, so that the meanings of smaller units are merely derivative'.

---

2. Some of these consequences and possible ways of avoiding them are explored in Heal 1989.

This is a familiar idea, largely because of Quine's influence on our way of conceiving of these issues. But leaving aside his verificationist route to (2), let us ask whether (2) follows from (1). Certainly we must allow that if (1) is true then meaningful items exist only in sets. But is there an argument from this to the idea that only the whole set 'really' has meaning? There is no obvious or direct route. In fact, far from (1) entailing (2), it looks rather as if (2) is in tension with (1), and, given the apparent consistency of (1), this suggests non-entailment of (2) by (1).

An initial tension between (1) and (2) arises from the use of the word 'really' in (2) in combination with talk of 'content' in (1b). If we read 'really have meanings' in (2) in such a way that talk of the meaning of the smaller units is seen as a misleading and dispensable idiom, then (1) is, in its most obvious reading, false, since it seems to use 'content' or 'meaning' in some substantive sense in application to individual thoughts. But perhaps this drastic reading of 'really have meanings' is not what is intended, and claim (2) would be better put in terms of a contrast between 'primary' and 'derivative' meaning. Let us imagine it so reworded. Now we can put succinctly a difficulty for attempting to derive even this recast (2) from (1). It is that (1) carries no commitment to the idea of the whole as the primary meaning bearer. It is consistent with (1) to suppose it is equally true that if a whole is to have its meaning then it must be a collection of elements, each with an appropriate part-style meaning. On such a view we would have mutual dependence without priority either way.

In the light of this it would seem wise to set (2) to one side. Clearly it imports a substantial extra element into our conception of holism over and above those introduced by (1) and it would be better, in investigating the content and plausibility of holism, to avoid taking on commitment to defending such an extra element.

Finally here is a third claim:

(3) The meaning an individual thought has depends upon the whole collection (i.e., theory or set of capacities) in which it occurs, in such a way that any change in the whole collection (the addition or removal of an element or the substitution of one element for another) changes the content of every thought in it.

Prima facie this is much stronger than (1). It entails it (at least if we assume that a singleton thought cannot constitute a theory or collection of capacities), but it gives a strong and distinctive reading to the notion of 'constraint' invoked in (1b). The upshot is something which can be seen immediately to have unwelcome consequences. It implies, for example, that two people who have different theories of the world cannot share any beliefs. Hence, as Fodor and Lepore point out, all kinds of everyday notions – such as piecemeal acquisition of a theory or people having changing views on the same subject matter and so on – come under threat (1992: 8ff.). These startling and unwelcome consequences are the prime reason why Fodor at least, of our two authors, is hostile to holism.

But which of these claims, (1), (2) or (3), do Fodor and Lepore in fact mean by 'semantic holism'? There is textual evidence to support all three readings. Thus (2) is directly quoted from page x, where it is given as an account of what meaning 'holism' says. However (3) is clearly what is doing the work when the unpalatable consequences outlined above are deduced directly from something called 'holism' (1992: 8ff.). There is strong evidence also in favour of (1), or even perhaps just (1a). Thus we find: 'This book is largely about whether semantic properties are anatomic. We take this to be a relatively precise way of asking one of the questions that philosophers have meant to raise under the rubric of semantic holism' (1992: 4). What we are to understand by 'anatomic' is explained in the glossary: 'Anatomic property: A property is anatomic just in case if anything has it, then at least one other thing does' (1992: 257). Supporting this reading we also have the glossary entry: 'Holistic property: A property is holistic just in case if anything has it, then lots of things do' (1992: 258).

How may we explain this rather confusing situation? It seems likely that (2) is on the scene partly because of Quinean influences and partly also because there may be a route to it from (3). This issue will not be discussed further. The more important question for our purposes is why Fodor and Lepore take themselves to be entitled to shuttle between (1) and (3) as though there could be no important difference. The answer is to be found in a discussion of where Fodor and Lepore in effect allow that there might be an understanding of 'holism' where it is linked with what they call 'weak anatomism' and on which it does not support (3) (1992: 27ff.). Weak anatomism, as they there explain it, is the view that for any given content, for example the content that p, it cannot be assigned to a thought unless the thought is part of some appropriate set; but accepting this is taken to involve no commitment to the idea that all appropriate sets must contain certain common elements. Fodor and Lepore distinguish this from 'strong anatomism', the view that if a given thought is to be the thought that p, then there must be other specific contents, say that q and that r, also present in the set. Thus weak anatomism is (1), while strong anatomism is (1a) together with a version of (1b) which spells out 'constraint' in this particular manner. (Fodor and Lepore credit the distinction of weak and strong anatomism to Boghossian, Loewer and Maudlin, without however giving any bibliographical references. I have argued elsewhere that it is an important contrast [Heal 1989: chap. 5].)

Weak anatomism, however, seems to Fodor and Lepore to be a position they need not bother with. They claim that (1a) only seems plausible to philosophers because they accept strong anatomism (1992: 29). And they then argue that strong anatomism entails (3), given rejection of a clear analytic/synthetic distinction. So against a background which endorses strong anatomism but rejects the distinction, they take themselves to be entitled to call indifferently upon formulations like (1a) and formulations like (3) in their subsequent discussion.

Their argument, put briefly, goes as follows. Suppose you accept some strong anatomistic premise, for example you find it enormously plausible that a person cannot believe that something is a cat without believing that it is an animal. In other words, you take it that a person does not have our concept 'cat' unless he or she knows that cats are animals. Presumably you will allow that other beliefs also will be required. What, for example, about having eyes? Would one really understand 'cat' unless one believed that cats have eyes? And, in fact, isn't it also part of the idea of a cat that it should see well at night? And perhaps one doesn't understand 'night' without believing that it alternates with day and is caused by the change in the relative positions of the earth and sun? So now it transpires that a person cannot understand 'cat' without knowing about the earth, sun, and so forth. This conclusion is certainly unpalatable, but where are we to stop the transitions into it? We speak colloquially of 'my idea of a cat', meaning all the things I hold true of cats, and in this sense (slightly stretched) it is part of my idea of a cat that it is an animal living on a planet, which rotates on its axis about a star and thus experiences day and night. The problem is to sieve out, from such an extended 'idea of a cat' the elements which are to be 'the' concept of a cat. It is not at all clear that there is any principled way of doing it. Thus, if we start on this line of thought, we seem likely to end up with the conclusion that no one understands 'cat' as I do unless he or she shares all my beliefs. And now (3) threatens.

One way of resisting this result is to seek to defend the analytic/synthetic distinction and, relatedly, to elaborate some 'molecularist' view about meaning, intermediate between atomism and holism in version (3) (Dummett has attempted this [1975], and Peacocke also thinks such an approach promising [1992].) But we shall not consider the viability of this, asking instead how we should respond to the argument if we are sympathetic to the idea that the sieving cannot be done in a non-arbitrary way.

The other available move is to refuse the very first step onto the slippery slope, namely the insistence that, for any given content that p, there are some other specific contents which a thinker must entertain. Instead we could say that there is no limit to the mistakes people can make or the connections they can overlook, especially if circumstances conspire to lead them in the wrong direction. In saying this we do not have to deny that there are necessary truths, or even that some of them are accessible a priori. We only have to deny that these facts have the supposed psychological consequences about unbreakable connections between thoughts.

But if we say this, we may have warded off (3) but we have certainly also lost one argument in favour of (1). Why should we not at this point go atomist, as Fodor would like, and say that the thought that something is a cat can occur quite by itself? Let us start from some considerations urged by Fodor and Lepore in their discussion of belief (1992: chap. 4).

3. HOLISM AND BELIEF

They begin here by conceding holism for beliefs. By this they mean that both (1a) and (1b) hold for beliefs, viz., that beliefs must come in sets and that the contents must satisfy constraints of rational coherence. (They presumably do not mean that (3) holds for beliefs, otherwise they would have conceded what Fodor at least most wishes to deny. Here is further evidence of the need to pay attention to the difference between (1) and (3).) This holism obtains because what it is for something to be a belief is functionally defined in terms of role in inference and such like. But, say Fodor and Lepore, this is all to do with beliefs and not with content-bearing states as such. Hence it does not bear on meaning holism.

It's not implausible that the essential properties of beliefs constrain their functional roles vis à vis other mental states . . . ; whereas, plausibly, the conditions for a mental representation to be semantically evaluable constrain . . . its causal relations to things-in-the-world. . . . [A] mental representation's having the content that it does needn't be supposed to depend on its having the functional role that it does – or, indeed, on its having any functional role at all. (1992: 124)

So mental representations can exist even though there are no representations with the functional role of belief? This is what is needed if the conditions on beliefs are not to generate conditions on content. Of course we must agree with Fodor and Lepore that not every mental representation is a belief. So mental representations will not directly inherit conditions from beliefs in virtue of being beliefs. But if they can only exist as parts of sets which do include beliefs, and beliefs are subject to holistic constraints, then holism for content does follow.

Fodor and Lepore do present one argument designed to suggest that there could be mental life without beliefs (1992: 119–120). They suggest that a creature could have desires and be moved by them to act without having beliefs. For example, dehydration might trigger a state which in its turn directly triggered intake of liquid, without the creature having further states which are beliefs about the utility of the behaviour. The case is meant to undermine the idea that beliefs are always essential to the explanation of action.

Let us concede the coherence of a simple creature in which some state directly triggers drinking without any guidance by further information-bearing states. And let us concede also the propriety of calling such a state 'desire for liquid'. Does the case show what is required? It does not. Fodor and Lepore have mislocated the most fundamental role of belief vis-à-vis desire and action. That role is not to guide action appropriately, through information about ends and means, but to lead to cessation of action by feedback when the goal is achieved. Whatever case there is for calling the inner state of the simple creature 'desire for liquid' operates just as strongly to justify calling the change which ingestion of the liquid produces 'belief in the presence of liquid'. Note that even if we allow this to be the sum total of a mental life, then the holistic claim (1) would be vindicated – albeit in a rather minimal manner – since there are here two content-bearing states and there is a constraint on their relations, namely that they are a desire and a belief with the same content.

If we allow the above considerations to establish that there is no mental life without belief can Fodor and Lepore attempt to avoid holism by withdrawing their concession that holism is true of belief? They can and they do (1992: 134). Their idea here is that, even if it is built into the definition of 'belief' that beliefs are holistic, it is a contingent matter that actual behaviour-guiding states satisfy that definition. There could be creatures who have contentful and behaviour-controlling states which do not satisfy holistic constraints. Either the states come singly or the content of one state exerts no constraining influence on the content of the others.

To assess this let us consider the question of what is added to 'representation' by 'mental'. From a naturalistic perspective it may seem that it adds little. We see that the world contains a great variety of complex persisting structures such as plants, animals and machines. Some of their states can be seen as 'representing' external features (in the sense that they have causal/nomological links to those features) and may be described in intensional sentences. The representing powers of such persisting structures differ in many ways, for example, the kinds and numbers of features they respond to, whether such features can be distant in space and time, whether the representations causally influence each other and whether these patterns of interaction are isomorphic to the patterns of rational inference and so forth. But which of these representations are mental and why?

One thing it is enormously plausible to insist on is that representations are mental only if they can contribute to the explanation of behaviour. A 'representation' occurring in a causal dead end, so that, however the rest of the mind is disposed, it cannot have influence on initiating, controlling or inhibiting behaviour, is not mental. But, having admitted this, need we impose any further constraints on those sets of representations which are allowed to constitute minds? (Fodor does, of course, have further constraints he would like to impose, for example, about the nature of the causal nomological connections. But they do not bear on this issue so we shall not consider them.) In particular, need we say that satisfaction of normative constraints of 'rationality' (broadly construed) is required of any set of representations properly to be called mental? Fodor and Lepore claim that there is no good reason to do so (1992: chaps. 4 and 5). They attack a number of arguments from Davidson (1984) and Dennett (1979 and 1987) which are supposed to lead to that conclusion. And if the arguments fail then, Fodor and Lepore imply, for all we can see, minds are just black boxes containing behaviour-controlling representations, and what they are like is entirely up for empirical investigation. If Fodor and Lepore are right, then we have no reason not to allow that any old jumble of representations occurring in a persisting structure and causing its behaviour can and do constitute the mind of that structure.

4. WHY THOUGHTS HANG TOGETHER

In this section and the next I wish to offer arguments, which support (1a) and (1b), respectively, and which jointly suggest reasons for being unhappy with the black-box conception of mind just sketched.

Let us start by introducing a new notion, namely that of what I shall call a 'subject'. A subject is a unified locus of cognitive virtues, which, starting from an exiguous base, gradually builds up a more and more detailed and elaborated view of its world and of its potential for action in it, so that its interactions with that world become by degrees more effectively attuned to it. 'Cognitive virtues' are to be construed broadly to include the abilities to perceive veridically, to remember accurately, to evaluate sensitively, to reason validly and to choose sensibly. To say that a subject is unified is to say that the cognitive states which the subject arrives at by the exercise of one ability are available to affect appropriately the manner in which the other abilities are exercised. So the state of the subject at any given time is to be seen as the result of the joint exercise of the abilities over time, on the world in which the subject initially found him- or herself situated.

A caution before we proceed further. Subjects are, by definition, 'rational', in some sense of that word. They have cognitive virtues. But it is important not to read too much into the notion of a subject. Consider three golfers. The first is Super Golfer with amazing powers. She is able to hole in one, however long the fairway and however awkwardly contoured the green. The second is Moderate Golfer. She knows more or less where the hole is and has some capacity to control the direction and strength of the shot, but is liable to errors of both conception and execution. Moderate Golfer will, probably, get the ball in the hole in the end if she has enough time, although it may well take her many shots. Our third player is Totally Incompetent Golfer. Her strokes are quite randomly related to the distance and direction of the hole and only with extraordinary luck will she get her ball into the hole.

If we take arriving at a true belief or a sensible intention to be analogous (for our current purposes) to getting the ball in the hole, then to be a subject a being requires to be the cognitive equivalent of Moderate Golfer, not of Super Golfer. Being a subject does not require faultless perception or reasoning. To possess cognitive virtues, and so to be rational, in the sense intended here, is not to be cognitively perfect. Hence many recent empirical studies which show our liability to various systematic forms of perceptual, memory or inferential error provide no evidence against the idea that we are subjects. If a thinker's cognitive powers are unified and she has different routes to judgement on the same subject matter, then the tendency of the exercise of the powers will be to self-correction and so to improvement of overall cognitive position, unless the initial endowment of perception, memory and reasoning abilities functions quite randomly or with persistent perversity. And the crucial factor in making some being a subject is that its efforts to think about things, that is, its exercising of its cognitive abilities, tend in the direction of better cognitive grip on its world and its projects.

With the notion of a subject in hand there are two claims which I should like to defend. The first is that the activity of a subject issues in representational states which satisfy (1b), but in a manner which does not license strong anatomism or threaten commitment to (3). The second is that the notion of thought is intimately linked with that of a subject.

As to the first claim, if a subject has a number of thoughts, the presence of one with a given content will constrain the others in the following way. Their content must be such that we can see how the whole set containing the given element could be the outcome of the interacting competences of a subject. So the set must not contain too many gross contradictions in belief (on pain of undermining the ascription of unity and ability to reason) and it must represent fairly accurately at least some of the items surrounding the subject (on pain of denying the subject perceptual contact with the world and intelligible epistemological anchorage for his or her worldview).

But what this underpins is (1b) rather than strong anatomism. Thus it allows that a subject could think 'this is a cat' without thinking 'this is an animal', because it builds in the possibility that a subject's abilities may be exercised in unlucky circumstances which lead him or her to excusable but bizarre views. For example, a subject might learn the word 'cat' in the normal way and then become convinced (on perhaps not totally absurd grounds) that cats were cunning Martian robots sent to spy on humans. In this situation there are enough of the ordinary views about cats still in place to make the set an appropriate setting for 'cat' beliefs, that is, to make the use of the word 'cat' in reporting the subject's beliefs appropriate, for most purposes at least.

Another issue is of considerable importance at this point, although we lack space to pursue it properly. It is that, very plausibly, attribution of content to thoughts is context-relative, in something like the way in which attribution of flatness to a field is context-relative. A field may rightly be called 'flat' if one is contemplating landing a helicopter on it when the same field would wrongly be called 'flat' if one were thinking of playing croquet on it. Similarly, a person may properly be credited with the belief 'this is a cat' in the context of one enquiry but not in the context of another. This is a possibility extremely uncongenial to Fodor, because the kind of cognitive science he would like to see arguably requires impersonal, non-context-relative, predicates.

Reverting to our main line of concern, let us consider why we might suppose that the notion of a subject is particularly closely connected with that of thought. Davidson and Dennett can of course be seen as urging its centrality. Thus Davidson claims that interpretation of others must go forward under the guidance of the Principle of Charity, namely, of ascribing error to others as far as possible only when it is rationally explicable. Dennett's view is that attribution of thoughts to a creature involves taking up the intentional stance towards it; and a creature is an appropriate object towards which to take the stance if its behaviour approximates to that of a subject. Dennett further argues that we are justified in taking up the intentional stance to other humans and animals because we see that evolution can be expected to produce such creatures. In disputing these claims and related ones Fodor and Lepore are in effect launching a sustained attack on the idea that the notion of a subject has any role to play in the philosophy of mind or philosophy of psychology.

The prima facie force of this attack is, I suggest, made greater by the fact that all the participants in the debate present their considerations as having to do with the use of psychological notions in third-person applications. The initial claims of Davidson and Dennett have the form 'When you look at another human animal you should use these and these notions and strategies in predicting, understanding, etc.' This very naturally invites from Fodor and Lepore the riposte 'Why should I approach any objects in the natural world with this conceptual baggage?'

The commitment, which all parties share, to searching for insight into psychological notions by considering primarily their third-person use is the legacy of abandonment of Cartesian introspectionism. But in this particular case by staying so resolutely third-personal we may have missed a trick. I do not mean by this that I can introspectively acquire a clear and distinct idea that I am a subject. The suggestion is rather that the centrality of the notion of a subject for thought, and hence for content, is most directly apparent when we take a first-person viewpoint.[3] I cannot but take it for granted that I am a subject. This assumption is one which underpins all my investigating, planning, deliberating and reflecting, from the perception and memory guided organisation of everyday life to more obviously intellectual enterprises. Mental life is active in that we are constantly making choices (where to look, what facts to mull over, which line of argument to try to strengthen . . .), and thus we launch ourselves

---

3. How it then becomes central for the second- and third-person cases also is considered in Essays 3 and 12.

on cognitive enterprises which will, we hope, result in the formation of the right beliefs or decisions. But it is only if I am a subject that these activities will be non-accidentally successful. If my looking is not likely to result in seeing what is there, or mulling over the argument to result in my grasping its validity or detecting its flaw, what is the point of looking or mulling?

It is worth pausing to consider this issue at a little more length. The central claim above is that taking oneself to be a subject is a precondition of an active, purposeful mental life. The argument for this is a generalisation of some considerations about intention. Consider an agent who chooses to do X with the aim of bringing about a state of affairs S. It is inconsistent for the agent to combine this with belief that doing X is not in any degree likely to bring about S. An agent who has such a belief may indeed feel impelled to do X and may desire S. But the belief in the lack of connection between doing X and S ought to drain the doing of X of any linkage with the aim of securing S. Insofar as it does not, the agent has an inconsistent outlook. What this shows is that intentional action has a belief-like aspect. It involves seeing the action undertaken as a suitable vehicle for achieving the end envisaged. It is a corollary of this belief-like aspect of intending that an agent who cannot give up the aim of seeking to secure S and also cannot give up trying to do so by doing X also cannot give up taking it that doing X is likely to produce S.

Consider now our own situation. We cannot but seek cognitive improvement in the form of more and better articulated information about what concerns us. The only idea we have of how to achieve it gives a central place to such activities as looking and pondering. Hence we cannot but take it that these activities are likely to contribute to what we desire. But taking it that looking and pondering are likely to produce cognitive improvement is taking it that we are subjects. Hence as long as we pursue active mental lives, namely engage in such things as looking and pondering with a view to improving our cognitive states, we cannot but take ourselves to be subjects.

To say this is not to deny that true beliefs and sensible intentions can sometimes come about not because of the cognitive virtue of the thinker but because of luck. A thinker may proceed irrationally in a particular case and still end up with a true belief or sensible intention. So it is not the case that it is only if I am a subject that I can have a successful and purposeful cognitive life. For all we have seen, it may be possible (in some sense of 'possible') for there to be a Totally Incompetent Thinker who nevertheless, through some run of extraordinary luck, forms mainly true beliefs and sensible intentions. But this does not show that we can do without the presumption that we are subjects, that is, are cognitively speaking at least the equivalent of Moderate Golfer. As we have seen, my intentional activities of thinking have a belief-like aspect. So they connect with some self-conception which presents those activities to me as a way of achieving my cognitive aims. But conceiving of myself as an extraordinarily lucky but totally incompetent thinker is not a self-conception which will fit this role. An agent is one who takes it that securing what she wants is dependent on her exercise of her own powers so that what she does has a real tendency to produce what she wants. To think of myself as totally incompetent in some area is, in effect, to cease to think of myself as a potential agent in that area. (A similar view is urged, but in connection with bodily actions only, by Robins [1986].)

These reflections do not aim to demonstate that the assumption that I am a subject can be shown to be correct by some formal proof. Nor is the assumption open to empirical proof or disproof. In undertaking any investigation into the success of my cognitive efforts and the reasons for it, I take for granted such facts as that I am capable of noting and remembering the results of experiments, drawing warranted conclusions from them and so forth. Empirical investigation can show me what kind of subject I am, the strengths and limitations of my cognitive abilities, but cannot either strengthen or weaken the assumption that I am a subject.

The suggestion is, rather, that the assumption underpins the way I conduct my life in the sense that it is a framework principle or hinge in the sense outlined by Wittgenstein in *On Certainty*. I can contemplate the possibility that I am a Fodorean jumble of representations, subject to perceptual illusion and inferential blunders, lacking that unity and critical self-awareness which would enable me to improve my cognitive functioning. But what can I do with this thought? Absolutely nothing. To attempt to take it seriously is to precipitate myself into a frictionless limbo, where the wheels of thought spin round but can get no purchase. Of course I can in a mundane way accumulate evidence that particular bits of my cognitive functioning are prone to error (my hearing is going, I make arithmetical mistakes . . .). But in identifying these and deciding what to do about them (get a hearing aid, calculator . . .) I again take for granted my effectiveness as a subject.

So we have no option but to take it that we are subjects. And thinking is, I suggest, centrally an activity we attribute to ourselves insofar as we conceive of ourselves as subjects. So thoughts, bearers of underived content, are centrally the states of subjects when they operate cognitively.

When we ask whether other animals or computers can think, what we want to know is whether what they do is sufficiently like what we do to be called 'thinking'. We are not concerned with whether they have internal states which have causal/nomological links with the environment and explain their behaviour. The answer to this is obvious already. What we want to know is whether they are like us in being, perhaps in some stretched or thin sense, subjects.

Fodor may insist, in a Humpty Dumpty–like way, that by 'the study of thoughts' he means only the study of bundles of representations, defined entirely naturalistically. And that study undoubtedly exists. But failing some demonstration that the notion of a subject is incoherent (or not even a useful heuristic tool), he is not entitled to hijack the phrase from its more obvious and historically sanctioned application, in which it picks out the study of activities of subjects and how they might be empirically manifested. And if this latter is what we are engaged in, then semantic holism is the order of the day.

At least this is what we may say if we are convinced what the full thesis (1) holds of the states of subjects. But earlier we set on one side the question of supporting (1a). And it is to this dropped thread that we should now return.

5. WHY THOUGHTS COME IN GROUPS

If a subject has many thoughts, then they must cohere. But why must a subject have a multiplicity of thoughts? Stress on the necessary rationality of thought may not give us an answer here, because rationality is centrally a notion which underpins permissions and prohibitions but not positive instructions. So perhaps (1a) needs a different kind of support from that appropriate to (1b). The suggestion I shall make is that it is general metaphysical considerations about the interconnections of thought, complexity, dispositions and the basis of dispositions which will help us here.

A certain extremely general thesis is common to an immense range of views about the nature of thought, from Fodorean naturalism to views of a dualist character, or ones that stress the normative elements in thought. This thesis is that for a creature to have a concept is for it to have a certain disposition (or ability), namely to get into a state – that is, actually to have a thought – under certain circumstances. Let us accept this, and let us also take it that dispositions need some kind of basis, so that a creature which has an ability at a time has it in virtue of certain other, for example, structural, features which it possesses at that time. We may then think that the state of mind of a creature at a time is specified by listing what dispositions it has and which are currently being activated; this in turn, is all imagined to be fixed by, or anchored in, the instantaneous non-dispositional state.

Section 4 was vague about the origins and initial capacities of subjects. But it is generally agreed that 100 percent empiricism is unintelligible, and that any thinking thing must start its career with some kind of mental structure, which we can construe as possession of at least proto-concepts. So why should this initial structure not be very rich? Consider the following scenario: Athena, equipped with many conceptual capacities, springs from the head of Zeus; just one set of capacities is activated, so she thinks '2 + 2 = 4'; then she is unfortunately run over by a bus and never thinks anything else. The highly schematised picture of the last paragraph does not seem to rule this out.

But there are reasons for considerable uneasiness with it. What kind of possibility are we supposed to be contemplating here? If the laws of our world are in force, then the instantaneous appearance of highly structured creatures is impossible. The only way of getting such a creature, one with a structure intricate enough to support the dispositions required for thought, is by slow growth. Thus, by the time there is enough complexity of potential interaction with the world for attribution of one particular thought to be comfortable, whatever behaviour supports that attribution will occur in an ongoing stream of varied interactions with the world which will surely also ground other thought attributions.

Alternatively, someone may try to make capital from the idea of more remote possible worlds in which this-worldly scientific laws do not hold. But now the difficulty is that there is no reason to suppose that the specification of a structure at an instant will pin down those dispositions we need to justify attribution of thought. We have cut the imagined structures free from their usual causes and effects, and so have no grounds for saying that a structure is such that if it comes to exist then so and so will ensue. We can make sense of the Athena fantasy only by imagining the laws both in force and also (conveniently) suspended for just the event of her appearance. But this is the kind of undisciplined thought experiment from which nothing about any interesting kind of possibility follows.

Another way of putting what is, I think, the same root argument is this. It is living animals in this world which are central candidates for being thinkers, and extremely simple (e.g., merely one-celled) living creatures do not have thoughts. So for thought we need a complex living creature and, given the general nature of our world (the variety of substances and shapes in it, the materials of which bodies are made, the survival needs of organisms, etc.), there is no way that such a creature can exist without interacting with the world in a variety of skilful and effective ways, ways which will ground many thought attributions if they ground any at all. And it will not do for a sceptic about the analytic/synthetic distinction (like Fodor) to protest that this is merely a nomological necessity and has not shown us anything deep about the concept of thought. If someone wishes to indulge in science fiction about instantaneous creation of complex objects (or in other speculations about the existence of non-material thinkers, like angels), then the onus is on him or her to show that the fantasy is of any importance.

8

Other Minds, Rationality and Analogy

1. INTRODUCTION

We are often in the position of knowing something about another's state of mind and wanting to know more. For example, I may know of my friend Maria (hereafter 'M') that she believes that p_1, p_2 ... and p_n, and has set herself to reflect on whether q; I would like to know what conclusion she has reached. Or I know something about her projects and wonder what particular moves she will take to fulfil them. Or I know that she will shortly receive certain information and wonder how she will feel about it. Or I know that she had certain visual experiences and wonder what kinds of afterimages, if any, they produced. Quite often, also, when we are curious in these sorts of ways about others' mental states we can come up with an answer. How do we do it?

Psychological states are extremely various, as are also the kinds of interactions they have with each other. I myself am extremely doubtful that there is any one story to be told about how we proceed in all cases. So the purpose of this essay is not to answer in full generality the question of how we form views on others' thoughts, but only to explore how we may articulate one particular story about how we do it in some cases, namely the cases I mentioned first, where what interests me is what M has concluded about whether q, in the light of her other beliefs.

One view about how I satisfy my curiosity in this case is that I apply a theory (perhaps tacitly known) about the workings of minds. This theory tells me that beliefs p_1–p_n, given interest in whether q, are likely to cause belief that q. This combines with my knowledge about M to deliver the conclusion that she believes that q. A very different sort of answer is that I set my own thought processes to engage with the same subject matter

131

as M engages with, viz., I think about the states of affairs that p_1-p_n and their relation with the state of affairs that q. This thinking leads me to entertain (in some distinctive mode) the thought that q, upon which I then attribute to M the belief that q. The first answer would be given by one who favours the so-called theory theory and the second by a proponent of what is often called the 'simulation theory'. For reasons I shall not rehearse here (but see Essay 6), I prefer the label 'co-cognition' to 'simulation' and will mainly use it in what follows.

The concern of this essay is not to defend one of these approaches as against the other, since that has been done elsewhere. Rather, I shall assume sympathy with the co-cognitive approach, as an account of at least some cases, and ask how that account can defensibly be articulated. There are opposing views on this among those who have debated the feasibility of the co-cognitive strategy. Some see the approach as a version of the argument from analogy and take it to be a positive virtue that it does not require acceptance of any linkage between the notions of thought and rationality (Goldman 1995a). Others, however (of whom I am one), take it to be a natural ally of a rationality-presupposing view (Moran 1994). The aim of this essay is to defend further the coherence and attraction of some position of this latter type. I shall try to show that powerful-seeming arguments in favour of the analogy view can be neutralised and that the rationality-presupposing position need not require us to accept an unrealistic idealisation of ourselves. My claim, in brief, is that the view which stresses analogy both underestimates the cognitive capacities with which we can credit ourselves and overestimates our similarity to each other.

2. TWO CONSTRUALS OF CO-COGNITIVE REASONING

Nearly all those who discuss the co-cognition idea are agreed that, if the co-cognitive story is correct for at least some cases, then there exists in those cases a certain temporal structure in the process of arriving at a new judgement about another's thoughts. The structure, schematically presented and in its simplest form, is this:

At t_1: I judge that M believes that p_1-p_n and is interested in whether q.
At t_2: I entertain reflectively the contents p_1-p_n.
At t_3: This reflection leads to my entertaining the content that q.
At t_4: I conclude that M believes that q.

A central difference between co-cognition approaches and theory theory approaches is brought out in this narrative. It is the insistence that what mediates between my states at t_1 and at t_4 is not my thinking about M's thoughts, deploying a theory about thoughts, but rather my thinking about the subject matter of M's thoughts.

The narrative, however, does not show why going through this sequence is a defensible way of arriving at beliefs about others' thoughts. Considered as a piece of reasoning the sequence described lacks logical articulation. My entertaining at t_3 the content that q, as an outcome of the reflective process initiated at t_2, is just blankly juxtaposed with my acquiring at t_4 a conviction about M. If challenged, what reasons might I give in support of that conviction? Nothing said in this narrative gives a clear answer to this question. Perhaps some further content which supplies an articulation is actually present in my mind, in some more or less explicit form? It is, however, a notoriously tricky matter to define tacit belief and to assemble empirical evidence for it. And even if we found evidence of some tacit commitments, the question of their truth would still arise. So I shall not start by pursuing this line. Rather we shall approach the issue of how to understand co-cognition by another route.

Let us proceed for the moment as if there were no further content entertained by me as I arrive at my belief about M in the way described. By innate propensity and/or social training, I just am set up so as to go through sequences of this form. If we are externalists about knowledge this does not threaten the idea that in doing this we function as we should and thereby arrive at knowledge. All that is required for the sequences to be commendable and knowledge-producing is that going through them reliably produces true beliefs. When, however, we become aware of what we are doing, epistemological conscience requires us to ask whether and why this kind of sequence is a reliable producer of true beliefs. The reliability depends upon certain things being so, but what are those things? We need to know the answer to this question if we are to be convinced that the method is indeed defensible or to consider how it might be improved. The appraisals required by a responsible externalism push us in the direction of making our reasonings more defensible from an internalist point of view.

The first step in such a reflective appraisal will be to provide a commentary on the narrative, bringing out possible structures of the events considered as an information-processing sequence. This commentary will first consider what information is available to me at each stage, through already acknowledged good routes of information acquisition. Then it will ask how that information bears on the final conclusion. And from that it will consider what further requires to be the case if transition from the available information to the conclusion is to be truth-preserving. To look at things this way is, in effect, to ask what plausible further content would, if explicitly present at various points, fill out the sequence so that it became a valid piece of articulated reasoning.

What I start with is clearly the information about M credited to me at t_1. What is the function of the reflection between t_2 and t_3? The answer must be that it is to make available to me some further information which is not yet to hand at t_1. What is this information about? One option is that it is about me. The fact is that for me the reflection between t_2 and t_3 leads to the thought that q; the information that this occurs is available to me by the acknowledged channel (however it works) of self-awareness.

There are various different cases here which need distinguishing. If I myself believe that $p_1–p_n$ then, very probably, I shall at t_3 actually come to believe that q on the basis that $p_1–p_n$ and it is this fact about my actual beliefs which will come to hand. But if I do not share M's initial beliefs, then the position is instead that my non-believingly entertaining the thought that $p_1–p_n$ leads me on to some non-belief entertaining that q. We shall, for the purposes of this discussion, take it that, even in this second case, it is information about my own propensities to belief which becomes available to me at t_3 through self-awareness. (This is, for example, because I rightly assume that developments of thought in my imagination parallel those in my serious inferences. The many interesting issues about imagination and belief which arise here we shall sweep under the carpet, since, although important in other contexts for the development of the co-cognition account, they are irrelevant to our main concerns.)

The upshot of taking things this way is that we see that at t_3 I have two premises in hand, namely the information about M from which I started, and the information about me which I have just acquired. What then needs to be the case if the desired shape of conclusion about M is to be rightly inferred from these premises? It is clear that what is required is that M and I be alike in mental functioning, in particular in propensities to belief acquisition.

In the light of all this, here is one reconstruction. What it presents is an argument which, as a self-conscious co-cognitive reasoner, I might offer if challenged to provide grounds for my conclusion about M's belief.

Schema I

(1) M believes that $p_1–p_n$ and is interested in whether q.
(2) If I were to believe that $p_1–p_n$ and were interested in whether q, then I would believe that q.

(3) M and I are alike in mental functioning.
So
(4) M believes that q.

But this is not the only reconstruction possible, not the only way in which I might defend my conclusion. The other reconstruction starts from a second option, namely that the information which becomes available to me at t_3 is not about myself but about the world, for example about an entailment holding between the states of affairs that p_1–p_n and that q. Now the needed further assumption, if the move to the conclusion at t_4 is to be truth-preserving in this and similar cases, is that M's transitions in thought reflect relations of entailment. So the second reconstruction goes like this:

Schema II

(1) M believes that p_1–p_n and is interested in whether q.
(2') That p_1–p_n entail that q.
(3') M is such that, given belief in the premises of an entailment and interest in the conclusion, she will come to believe the conclusion.
So
(4) M believes that q.

Each of these reconstructions is schematic in that it can be filled in with different contents in the p_1–p_n and q slots. Each is also schematic in another way, in that it can be taken as representative of a family of arguments which can be derived by elaborating and mutually adjusting the premises in various ways. For example, we can get different versions of Schema I by including further conditions in premise (1) ('M is F and believes p_1–p_n') while also including mention of F in the antecedent of (2) ('If I were F and believed p_1–p_n . . .'). We could get a different version of Schema II by changing (2') to 'That p_1–p_n obviously entail that q' and (3') to 'M is such that, given belief in the premises of an obvious entailment and interest in the conclusion, she will come to believe the conclusion'. Many other variations are possible.

The families of arguments summarised in Schemata I and II provide, I suggest, the only two ways of building a logical bridge between (1) and (4). What I acquire at t_3, which forms the second premise of the explicit argument, must either be information about myself (e.g., my propensities to thought) or about the world apart from myself (e.g., relations of entailment). If the information is about me, then the further premise which allows derivation of a conclusion about M must be about some

135

relation of appropriate similarity between me and M. If, on the other hand, the information is not essentially about me but is about the world, then the only shape of a third premise which will do the job of underpinning the final attribution to M is some claim about M's cognitive abilities vis à vis that aspect of the world, viz., that she possesses some cognitive competence in that direction.

Does the possibility of systematic perversity undermine this conclusion? The following reasoning fits Schema II and might seem to attribute no positive cognitive abilities to M: 'M believes that p_1–p_n. The right conclusion from p_1–p_n is that q. M is perverse (or contrary or counter-suggestible). Therefore M will believe that not q'. But the ability to come consistently to a perverse conclusion is different from just getting muddled and coming randomly to true and false conclusions. To be reliably perverse requires one to have some grip on the real structure of the issues, in order to avoid, occasionally, falling into the correct conclusion.

An implication of this is that if we want a reconstruction of the co-cognitive route to views about others' thinking which does not build in any favourable assumptions whatsoever about their cognitive capacities then we must stick with Schema I. Conversely, if we are prepared to countenance a premise like (3′) then we can avoid having co-cognitive reasoning turn out, on self-conscious reconstruction, to be a version of argument from analogy. There is, however, no way of reconstructing the reasoning on which it both avoids any sort of rationality assumption and also avoids being a version of the argument from analogy. If on reflection I am not prepared to endorse arguing from how it is with me to how it is with the other, and am also unwilling to credit the other with any positive cognitive competence, then I am left with no way of explaining why the described co-cognitive method of forming beliefs about others (i.e., moving through the sequence from t_1 to t_4) is defensible. The sequence now appears to be merely some strange mumbo jumbo I go through, the upshot of which I have no right to endorse. There is, then, difficulty in endorsing a co-cognitive methodology if one rejects both a rationality assumption and also argument from analogy with one's own case. No difficulty arises, however, in combining the assumption that others are like me, with the view that one way in which we are alike is in being, at least to some extent, rational.

How does this conclusion relate to the ingenious views advanced by Gordon (1995b, 1996)? He seems to wish to reject a rationality assumption and yet also to deny that co-cognitive methods of arriving at views about others involve any inference from how it is with me to how it is with the other. According to the argument presented above, this is not a coherent position. But it may be that the appearance of conflict between my claims and Gordon's is misleading. Gordon's views, on their most natural interpretation, are about the content which is explicitly represented within the co-cognitive reasoning process, about the vehicles in which that content is carried and about the temporal sequence of occurrences which constitute the co-cognitive derivation. It may be that everything he says about this is correct. If so, we can agree with him that no conscious inference from me to M need occur when I arrive co-cognitively at some judgement about M's beliefs and also no conscious judgement on M's competence. All of this, however, is compatible with saying that a reflective survey of the process, asking what is required if it is to be defensible as a route of knowledge acquisition, will reveal the need for further content, along the lines of one or other reconstruction sketched above.

But there is also another, and perhaps more questionable strand, in Gordon's thought. He is concerned to emphasise that there is a difference between imaginative enterprises directed to finding out what I (JH) would do if so and so, and imaginative enterprises in which I identify with M and so try to think what M is likely to do if so and so. It is the second kind of enterprise which is central to his theory of how we think about other minds, and he seems, at some points, to suggest that once this is clear, the pressure to suppose that such thinking involves a version of the argument from analogy is removed, even when we are taking for granted that no rationality presupposition can be made.

This however is not the case. The contrast in imaginative enterprises is indeed important. But it only makes less obvious, and pushes into a different place in the structure, the need for the inference from myself to the other if a rationality assumption is not allowed. Suppose I realise, on reflection, that what I am doing in thinking about M's thoughts is, as Gordon suggests, imaginatively identifying with M and then attributing to M the thoughts which arise in me when I so identify. What justifies me in taking the outcome seriously as a correct representation of M? As soon as this question is raised, it is clear that there is an issue as to whether my would-be identification with M is successful. Is the thinking which I engage in, qua identifying myself with M, actually like M's thinking? Unless I can reassure myself that it is, then the fact that I engage in the second rather than the first imaginative enterprise is of no help in defending my right to my final judgement about M. And if I reassure myself that I succeed in making myself like M when I identify with her, then the final attribution to her will be reflectively justified by this likeness, together with appeal to how it actually went with me during the imaginative identification.

So the upshot of the discussion so far is that we have two candidates as reconstructions of the shape of co-cognitive reasoning. Each presents an explicit argument in which a co-cognitive element is embedded, but the settings of the co-cognitions, that is, of the reflections which occur between t_2 and t_3, are different on the two stories. For anything we have seen so far, both of these candidates are defensible and might be proposed as the right reconstruction in particular appropriate cases. It seems to me that this is the correct view and that we do use, sometimes explicitly and sometimes less so, both forms of argument.

There are cases where only Schema I seems sensible. For example, if I want to know through some sort of simulation what kind of afterimages another will experience following a particular kind of visual confrontation, then I will have to put myself through the same visual experience and then infer from what happens to me. It also seems plainly to be the case that we sometimes recall our own experiences to help us gain insight into what others are feeling or thinking. But the point I want to stress is that it would not be right to extrapolate from these cases to the claim that only Schema I is defensible or is used.

Some, however, have supposed that only instances of arguments in the family of Schema I should be endorsed as having any hope of being both sound and valid. It is urged that the co-cognitive approach has an advantage over the views associated with Davidson or Dennett in that it can explain how we make judgements about others' thoughts quite independently of any presupposition of rationality. The assumptions behind this preference for Schema I seem to be that it is an empirical matter how rational we are (or, indeed, whether we are rational at all), and that we can be more certain that we are like each other than that we have any degree of rationality.

It is this view and the assumptions on which it rests which we need now to assess. In the next section we shall consider some general and high-level arguments which might be offered against or in favour of the two schemata.

3. THREE INCONCLUSIVE ARGUMENTS

(A) First we shall consider how well arguing in accordance with Schema I escapes the classic worries about argument by analogy. The old and familiar version of the argument is associated with the dualist idea of each person

having introspective access to private items, which cannot (conceptually) be displayed to anyone else. It claims to offer a route to knowledge of both the existence and also the nature of others' private items. Given the initial assumption of privacy, the route offered cannot but seem a wild and irresponsible generalisation from one case. So the classic argument has both metaphysical and epistemological elements which are extremely suspect.

The version of argument from analogy which we are now considering can be freed entirely from these difficulties. To do so we must start by rejecting both dualism and the related radical privacy of the mental and take it instead that mental states are a part of the public natural world and are manifested in the observable complex behaviour of the human body. (One version of such an outlook is our familiar functionalism, but there are other versions too.) Now we add that commonsense observation and scientific investigation alike show us that human beings are extremely similar in their bodily and psychological functioning. Given the first of these points, we do not need any argument from analogy to convince us of the existence of other minds. From the second I can see that reflecting on how things are in my own case can be of use in suggesting particular detailed judgements about how they are for others, because I have good grounds for thinking that, over a wide range of mental states and their linkages, what goes for me goes for others too.

This use of analogy need not be bound up with views about self-knowledge (e.g., ones postulating a distinctive introspectible quale for each mental state), which some find objectionable. It can be combined with whatever view of self-knowledge we prefer, for example, with the idea that self-knowledge is the result of applying 'ascent routines' or is the result of the brain operating some self-scanning procedures or whatever. All that we require is that people do, by some means or other, have knowledge of (at least a good range of) their own mental states and their linkages. This it would be hard to deny.

So there is nothing wrong in principle with reasoning of the form exhibited in Schema I. But its escape from the difficulties of the classic argument from analogy depends upon its locating itself in a different epistemological context. It must not present itself as operating in a setting of sceptical doubt about my ability to know of the existence and nature of others' thoughts. Rather it must assume a context of established facts about such things.

(B) Having established the defensibility of arguing by Schema I, let us now consider an entirely general argument for thinking that it must be

preferred to Schema II. The plain fact, it might be said, is that I and M are two distinct persons. Suppose that M reflects that p_1–p_n and arrives at some new thought; I also entertain the thoughts that p_1–p_n and arrive at some new thought. I now attribute to M the thought I arrive at. Surely this can deliver a truth about M only if M and I are alike. Cognitive similarity between myself and M is thus a requirement of the success of any co-cognitive procedure. Hence, it seems, Schema I must capture what is going on, from the rational reconstruction point of view.

This is a tempting but fallacious line of thought. Crucial to seeing this is grasping the distinction between what can figure when considering the practical question about whether to undertake some thinking and what can figure as a premise in that thinking itself. Suppose I put to myself the question 'Shall I try and work out the answer to this arithmetic problem?' In answering this I need to take as explicit premise some view about my arithmetical abilities. If I know myself to be a duffer at arithmetic then I should conclude that it is a waste of time to attempt the problem. But if I do take it that I can do arithmetic and move on to attempt the sum, then the premises on which I rely in giving the answer are the arithmetical facts, not facts about my cognitive competence: $(6 \times 4) + (11 \times 3) = 57$ because $6 \times 4 = 24$, $11 \times 3 = 33$ and $24 + 33 = 57$, and not because I can do arithmetic. To suppose myself to be competent to do arithmetic is to suppose that I can form a view about the answer to the sum, taking as premises the arithmetically relevant facts. It is not to suppose that I can form a view, taking as premise the claim that I am competent to form a view. A presupposition of its being sensible to undertake a sort of thinking must not be taken as a premise of the thinking itself.

Matters run parallel if we consider a particular piece of reasoning, proceeding explicitly according to Schema II, where I come to believe (2′) as a result of some reflection between t_2 and t_3. It is indeed true that, if I step back and consider what is going on, I will see that I can come to have confidence in (2′) only because of the thinking which I have done myself, and that this thinking must be my exercise of the same competence which I attribute to M. Thus, in reasoning according to Schema II, I am committed to taking M and myself to be similar in being able to think effectively about this subject matter (just as when I set out to do arithmetic I am committed to taking myself to be competent to work out the sum). To acknowledge this is, however, quite different from supposing that Schema I presents the only possible explicit reconstruction of co-cognitive reasoning.

We should not let ourselves be confused by the facts that the overt subject matter of premise (2′) in Schema II is a cognitive competence (namely M's) and that the presupposition implicit in supposing I can reason according to the schema also concerns a cognitive competence (namely mine). Muddling the subject matter of thought with a presupposition of thinking as an activity is just as erroneous here as in the arithmetical case. Resistance to the fallacious move might also be strengthened by reminding ourselves that nothing could show that reasoning by Schema II is really reasoning by Schema I. Arguments which fit Schema II are clearly valid as they stand, and hence no extra premise about likeness between myself and M could be needed.

(C) A third general argument might be presented, this time in favour of Schema II. Let us take it that I start by supposing that my reasoning is defensible according to Schema I. So I conceive of the thinking which I do between t_2 and t_3 as a kind of experiment on myself, where observation of the outcome will allow me to make an inference to how it is with M. Now M's thinking about p_1-p_n is directed to finding out whether those premises support the conclusion that q. She is not just idly letting associations of ideas float through her mind but endeavouring to find out what is really the case. It follows that any thinking I do which is to have a defensible claim to be relevantly analogous to hers must also be directed in the same way. Idle associating by me is not similar enough to what she is doing to be a believable candidate for something which will produce a properly similar outcome. I myself must do truth-directed thinking, with comparable effort and seriousness to hers. These facts are often obscured by the way the co-cognitive ideas are presented in some of the 'simulationist' literature, by use of notions like 'pretend beliefs' and the 'off-line running' of mental systems. Such idioms give the erroneous impression that co-cognitive thinking, on a Schema I view, could be a detached enterprise where I need not put in any cognitive effort or take any responsibility for the outcome.

Hence, if I share her starting beliefs I will end up with some further real belief on my own part, for example that q. And if I do not share her starting beliefs, I will at least come actually to believe something about connections in the world, for example that the claims p_1-p_n entail that q. There is thus no getting at the information about me which is to figure as premise (2) in a Schema I argument without also equipping myself with information suitable to figure as premise (2′) in a Schema II argument. Moreover, in supposing that I can do such a thing as find out whether the claims p_1-p_n entail that q, I show that I credit myself with some cognitive abilities in this direction. There is no reason to be less respectful of M's cognitive powers; after all, the assumption, on Schema I, is precisely that we are similar. The upshot is that whenever I might reason according to Schema I, I will also be in a position to reason according to Schema II. Why, then, should I prefer to reconstruct things according to Schema I and not Schema II, especially since use of Schema I seems to require me to put in an extra step of information processing, namely the one where I move from information about the world to information about my beliefs? (Considerations somewhat like these are also advanced by Moran [1994].)

There is an obvious answer to this question, which brings us to the central appeal of Schema I, namely our acknowledged fallibility as reasoners. It has always been apparent that human beings are prone to errors in reasoning and to being taken in by fallacies. Recent research has brought to light many hitherto unrecognised weaknesses and has suggested that we share built-in propensities to cognitive illusions in connection with notions as simple and fundamental as quantification (Stich 1990; Stein 1996). Hence it seems that, even if I do come to a view about some entailment, as a result of my thinking between t_2 and t_3, I can and should, when I come to consider M's thought, distance myself from that belief and reason as follows: 'I may be wrong here, so I should not rely on this entailment as a premise. But even if I am wrong, still M and I are alike. So if I have made a mistake M is likely to have made the same one. So probably M believes that q.'

4. RATIONALITY

Should this answer persuade us that Schema II reasoning is always irresponsible and that Schema I reasoning is always to be preferred? It should not. Its appeal depends in part upon invocation of an overly demanding sense of 'rationality' and in part upon an improperly selective use of sceptical moves. This section will try to make good these criticisms and to show that Schema II reasoning is just as defensible as Schema I reasoning. The next section will consider our similarities and differences as thinkers and will bring out that there are various kinds of cases in which only Schema II reasoning could plausibly be deployed.

Approaches in the philosophy of mind which suggest an a priori link between thought and rationality (e.g., those of Davidson and Dennett) have suffered a bad press through leaving vague the notion of rationality involved and/or allowing the notion to be spelled out, implicitly or explicitly, in extremely demanding terms according to which, for example, rationality requires thoroughgoing consistency and completeness in belief. But, as remarked earlier in Section 2, willingness to use arguments from the family of Schema II is not bound up with commitment to any such unrealistically demanding notion. I reason according to Schema II if I credit M with ability to see obvious entailments, to add up short columns of figures, to avoid clearly evident fallacies, to follow rules of inference in which she has been trained and the like. Hence we must not rule out Schema II on the grounds that it builds in some absurdly idealised requirement. It does no such thing. All it requires is that I be willing to attribute to M whatever degree of competence in thinking is, in the light of the empirical evidence, properly to be credited to her. For anything we have seen, this could be either limited or quite extensive. It is not true that empirical studies have shown that we are entirely unable to reason validly and hence that attributions of any competence to oneself or another are suspect. A more realistic view of these studies sees them as doing for our reasoning ability what studies of visual limitations and illusions do for our sense of sight, namely revealing to us the strengths and weaknesses of the faculty, what kinds of pitfalls we should look out for when exercising it, where mechanical aids might be particularly useful and the like.

The case against Schema II reasoning, then, cannot rest upon particular, empirically backed, claims of cognitive incompetence, because these specific and evidenced claims only cover a small part of the territory and leave Schema II reasoning still widely available. Can it rest upon a general observation of our fallibility? If so, it must be proper to reason as follows: Reflection leads me to conclude that the claims p_1-p_n entail that q; but I could be wrong in this because human beings are fallible; so I should withdraw my willingness to rely on this entailment as a premise and ought to retreat to the safer ground of saying that it seems to me that the entailment holds (and hence that if I were to believe that p_1-p_n and were interested in whether q then I would believe that q). A proper epistemic caution thus leads me to trade in premise (2′) of a Schema II argument for premise (2) of a Schema I argument.

The problem with this way of recommending Schema I is that if the policy of retreat in face of the reminder of fallibility is followed on all occasions it will also deprive me of the other premises of the Schema I argument. At first I confidently judge that M believes that p_1-p_n. But (I realise) I could be wrong. So I had better trade in that premise for the more secure alternative that it seems to me that M believes that p_1-p_n. Likewise I initially take it that M and I are alike (on the basis of the many past occasions I remember on which we have thought or acted alike). But I might be wrong about this too, since my memory might deceive me or I might be reasoning incorrectly from the facts I do remember. So I had better trade in this claim as well and replace it with the weaker but more secure one that it seems to me that M and I are alike. This process of retreat ends me up in a bad place, where I am blocked from further inferences. The revised and more secure premises are so weak that they fail to engage with each other.

It is possible resist this erosion of our ability to think fruitfully while still recommending Schema I over Schema II only if there are good reasons for taking the sceptical retreat to be mandatory in the case of the entailment claim but not mandatory in the case of the claim about M's beliefs or about M's similarity to me. But what could these reasons be? Why should I be more seriously sceptical about my ability to detect logical relations than about my other cognitive abilities? Moreover, there will be many cases in which my route to my views about M's beliefs or about M's similarity to me have required me to reason according to the very kinds of entailment patterns which I am now (supposedly) taking to be doubtful.

In summary, then, awareness of our continuing human fallibility cannot bar me from Schema II reasoning in general. Such awareness ought to make me alert for counter-evidence and willing to hear opposing points of view. But this is an attitude I should bring to any judgement in any circumstance. It affects Schema I reasoning just as much as Schema II reasoning and provides no systematic consideration in favour of preferring the former to the latter.

5. SIMILARITIES AND DIFFERENCES

How similar are we to each other? In certain basic propensities (visual capacities, liability to bodily pain, preference for being warm and dry over cold and wet, pleasure in good food, tendency to fall for the gambler's fallacy ...) most of us probably do resemble each other to a great extent. But in many other respects we are often very unlike. The cases we have considered so far focus on possible differences in factual beliefs adopted. But persons may also clearly differ in the following general ways: (i) inference strategies they have been trained in; (ii) amount of experience they have had in dealing with various subject matters; (iii) degree of logical acumen they can call on; (iv) natural inventiveness and ability to come up with useful new ideas; (v) tastes, interests and so on. When dealing with a particular problem people may also differ in (vi) the time they have available for thinking about it and (vii) the degree of stress they are under when thinking of the problem. This is just a start. The list of possible differences could surely be extended further.

How do we cope when faced with the problem of anticipating the behaviour and thoughts of others who are unlike us in these kinds of ways? Are we completely stymied? Sometimes we are. For example, if the other is more ingenious and sharper than I, then I shall not be able to anticipate his or her future thoughts. I shall just have to wait and see what appears. But on other occasions we can cope quite effectively.

Here is an example. I am observing an inexperienced chess enthusiast playing with a wilier opponent who has set a trap for him. I can appreciate the trap, but I can see also that the inexperienced player will not do so and will think (falsely), 'Move such and such is part of a winning strategy for me'. Here the inexperienced player and I differ considerably in the degree of practice we have had in playing chess and in our ability to think up moves and see their consequences. Nevertheless I successfully anticipate his judgement.

How do I arrive at my successful predictions in this case? We cannot suppose that my success is the result of my going through the simple co-cognitive sequence described in Section 2 where I take on in imagination the other's beliefs about the chess situation and reason from them to the conclusion 'This is a winning strategy for me'. Starting from the given premises about the chess situation I would not come to this conclusion be-cause of my different level of understanding of the game. It is not plausible either to suppose that my success in prediction is the result of my reverting to use of pure theory. The arguments against the possibility of pure theory remain as compelling as ever. It seems, then, that I am somehow factoring in the differences between the other and myself and allowing them to in-fluence the outcome of a process which, however, still has a co-cognitive element at its core. But am I doing it according to Schema I or Schema II?

What operating according to Schema I requires is that I treat the dif-ferences in skill and experience as I treat the differences in belief, namely as factors of which I must produce some sort of replica in myself. I am to perform a kind of experiment on myself in which I set up my own mental state to be as like that of the other as I can manage and then engage in the thinking. It is the upshot of this which entitles me to the judgement 'If I were less experienced and faced with this chess position then I would come to believe so and so'.

But this story about what goes on does not fit well in the case in question. With the inexperienced chess player, in order to re-create his thinking with this kind of closeness what I would need to do is to shut down the part of my mind which generates and intelligently appraises the strategies which he is not yet capable of generating and appraising. But how am I thus to render myself temporarily uninventive or uncritical? Shutting down capacities is not something we can do at will or by engaging in some imaginative enterprise, since what it is to possess them is precisely to have certain thoughts strike one or come to one spontaneously upon the presentation of certain problems. Certainly I can refrain from spending time in following up certain lines of thought in detail, but I cannot prevent them suggesting themselves to me, or prevent myself from seeing that they open up promising avenues. It is clear, then, that such shutting down is not what I, as the more experienced player, would do in this case. Rather, my strategy is to use my capacity in the chess situation as presented to generate a rich appreciation of the options available and then to cull from this range those which I judge to be too advanced, leaving only some limited range of obviously attractive moves as ones the inexperienced player might choose.

Operating such a culling procedure is a quite different matter from setting myself up so that the complex options do not present themselves. It is nevertheless a co-cognitive and not a purely theoretical strategy which I am following. Reflection upon the chess situation, using chess knowledge, is central to what I do. It is, however, Schema II and not Schema I which provides the framework for an operation with this structure. In this sort of case the reflection between t_2 and t_3 presents me, not just with one opinion about the existence of an entailment, but rather with a richer picture of the logical structure of the problem space and the various kinds of moves which can be made within it, how easy each of them is to find and the like. I then choose among them those which I think most likely to be hit on by the inexperienced chess player. In so doing I am certainly not taking it that he is unable to think about chess, and I would not label him 'irrational'. Rather, I have a view about the particular current shape of his capacity to think about chess which leads me to the type of cull I make and hence to my prediction. In upshot, then, the most economical description of what goes on is that it is the Schema II style of thinking, guided or supplemented by theory.

The story just sketched can be applied, mutatis mutandis, in a very wide range of cases in which others differ from me in the kinds of ways mentioned at the start of this section. On the other hand, it may be that something more on the Schema I model is possible in some of these cases. Perhaps emotional factors can be 'simulated' in such a way that they can be incorporated into a Schema I exercise. I would like to emphasise again how varied psychological states and processes are, how much they differ in whether they can be 'simulated' and how varied are our interests in thinking about them. No one story is going to cover every case from routine anticipations of where other pedestrians in the street may step to complex thought about how a colleague might develop some long-term plan in academic politics, or from quick and cool calculation on how to defeat an opponent in chess to time-consuming and imaginatively engaged concern with those suffering from some trauma. We should not rush to generalise, but should be prepared for a picture in which elements of theory interact with co-cognitive elements in many complex mixtures.

AFTERNOTE: GOOD BAD REASONING

In introducing Schema II in Section 2 of this essay I refer to the possibility of modifying it from the first bold and simple formulation to take account of the fact that people are far from ideally rational. The only variant of Schema II there discussed is replacing 'entails' with 'obviously entails' in premises $(2')$ and $(3')$ to accommodate the fact that there are inferences too intricate for us to grasp. But other variants will be needed if we are to accommodate the prediction of the inexperienced chess player discussed in Section 5, since it does not conform to any version of Schema II yet made explicit. The player's conclusion – 'Such and such a move is part of a winning strategy for me' – is not entailed, let alone obviously entailed, by the available premises about the positions of the pieces on the board and the rules of the game.[1] So to deal with the case we would need a version of Schema II which does not speak of actual entailment but of some other relation of premise and conclusion.

Is there a modification of Schema II which shows that it can encompass this case? One definitive feature of Schema II reasoning is that the information which the predictor gets into clear focus at t_3 is not about his or her own psychology but about the world apart from the predictor, for example about connections of states of affairs or propositions. The other mark of Schema II reasoning is that the target to be predicted is credited with some degree of cognitive competence in dealing with that aspect of the world. Both of these marks seem to be present in the envisaged situation, which suggests that we should be able to find some version of Schema II to accommodate it. But how exactly should it be formulated?

1. I am grateful to Timothy Williamson for drawing these issues to my attention.

The inexperienced player was specified to have the ability to explore some of the possibilities which his position allows. What leads to his error is his inability to spot some of them and hence to assume that the range of options is smaller than it is. But we can see, on reflection, that his making this assumption does not in itself show him irrational. Thinking is a practical activity which takes time and resources. Hence it is sensible for a thinker to assume that what presents itself to him is what there is, unless he has specific reason to think that he is likely to go wrong in the case in hand. So concluding that such and such a move is a good one is the rational thing for the inexperienced player to do, given his resources and the upshot of his (real but not extensive) exercise of his skills in recognising and appraising moves. We may put matters (somewhat schematically) thus. The player comes to believe some premises ('These and those moves are possible; they have such and such strengths and weaknesses; these considerations are all the relevant considerations') which together do entail his conclusion. Two of these premises are true and the third is false. Nevertheless, his accepting the third is something which is itself rationally defensible. (We should acknowledge that certain ways of filling in the situation might make us less sympathetic to the novice. For example, if he is allowed to know that chess is an ancient and immensely complex game, then he should not be so willing to trust to his own powers. But let us imagine him to be ignorant of the history and reputation of the game.)

What we have here is a case of what we might call 'good bad reasoning', that is, reasoning which is creditable, shows an intellect working in a way we can respect, but which nevertheless results in endorsement of an invalid inference.[2] And I suggest that there are numerous other cases of the same general kind, which can therefore be seen as falling under Schema II. Consider, for example, the gambler's fallacy. Here a thinker notes a real similarity between predicting that a tossed coin will fall heads up a tenth time after a run of nine heads and predicting in advance a run of ten heads. In both cases, if what is predicted comes to pass then something very unlikely will have happened. A mistake will, however, arise if the thinker takes this similarity to have a significance – viz., of licensing the inference to the unlikelihood of another head – which it does not have. But it may not be irrational for the thinker to take it to have that significance when he has only limited resources for thought and lack of reason to question first impressions.

2. Thanks to Tom Baldwin for suggesting the phrase.

It is worth noting that there are two ways in which a person may come to a right prediction about the views of another who is still in the grip of the gambler's fallacy. One is the comparatively subtle use of Schema II outlined above, on which one who has seen through the fallacy may predict the conclusion of one who has not. But another is the use of the simplest version of Schema II by a predictor who has not yet seen through the fallacy. Does the fact that neither party has seen through the fallacy mean that Schema I must be more appropriate here as a reconstruction? Not at all. All it means is that the Schema II reasoning, when reconstructed, will have false premises at both (2′) (that the erroneous inference is valid) and at (3′) (that the other is capable of detecting the truth here). The predictor arrives at a correct conclusion because the errors in these premises cancel each other out, not because she is reasoning soundly according to Schema I.

So the suggestion is that prediction of various kinds of invalid reasoning can be fitted under Schema II. Making an invalid inference often arises from the exercise of the same skills as underpin valid inference, namely of noting relevant facts and being sensitive to what they suggest. Becoming aware of such things, in the absence of awareness of other relevant factors, may lead to a person having the impression that one thing follows from another when it does not. And, given limitations on our resources, it is not practically irrational to rely on such impressions. A way of encapsulating this briefly might be to speak of 'prima facie implications'. Schema II would then have a version which uses premises at (2′) of the form 'Such and such prima facie implies so and so' and records at (3′) that M is capable of recognising prima facie implications.

Prima facie implication is a person-relative notion, and what prima facie implications a person finds in a premise or set of premises will depend in part on general features of human psychology and in part on distinctive features of cultural or individual history. So in thinking about what good bad reasoning a person might engage in we need to equip ourselves with empirical data about humans in general and this person in particular. But it would be a mistake to infer that this is a point in favour of Schema I. Rather, what we have are considerations in favour of developing a notion of rationality which allows that people may all be rational and engage in creditable reasoning even when they vary considerably in their actual thinking abilities (see Essay 12).

Let me conclude by repeating that it is no part of my case that there is one and only one way in which we do or ought to arrive co-cognitively at opinions about others' thoughts. Doubtless there are cases which turn out to be most defensible if reconstructed as reasoning according to Schema I as well as those which turn out best if reconstructed as reasoning according to Schema II. And perhaps there are cases where it is indeterminate which reconstruction would be best – or where elements of both need to be called upon.

Part Three

Indexical Predicates and Their Applications

9

Indexical Predicates and Their Uses

1. INTRODUCTION

The central aim of this essay is to set out and defend the idea that in-dexicality may be a feature not only of referring expressions but also of predicate expressions. Section 2 examines the notions of reference, predi-cation and indexicality, and explains how they will be understood in what follows. Section 3 asks, on this basis, what an indexical predicate or predi-cate component would look like. It also asks whether we can identify any in English and suggests that we can find at least one specimen. Section 4 argues that the phenomenon is more widespread than might at first ap-pear. Finally, Section 5 considers ramifications of the idea, among them some of the uses to which indexical predication may be put and some of the reasons why it may be important for us. I hint at the end of this section at what seems to me potentially one of the most interesting applications, namely in giving an account of the means by which we represent items which are themselves representational. So, I suggest, the idea of indexical predication holds out the possibility of illuminating the structure of indi-rect speech reports and of our thoughts about others' thoughts. But full development of these ideas lies beyond the scope of this essay.

I do not seek to provide at any point a full formal treatment of the idea of indexical predication. The aim is rather to make plausible the claim that there is here a real linguistic phenomenon. I believe that we can be reasonably sure of the broad outlines of it and that it would merit treatment in any of the many formal frameworks which are available. I shall have to call at various points upon certain syntactic, semantic and metaphysical notions, but I hope to keep these as uncontentious and non-committal as possible.

Once we have the idea of indexical predication in hand we may see it as hinted at or implicit in a number of existing discussions. Thus Quine's notion of deferred ostension is perhaps relevant (Quine 1969: 41). And we may see moves towards the idea in some existing treatments of indirect speech (McFetridge 1976; Brandom 1994: 534–539). But it has not been labelled and explored as such and deserves a more focused treatment.

2. REFERENCE, PREDICATION AND INDEXICALITY

Could there be indexical predication? To clarify this question we need to remind ourselves of some central facts about the contrast between reference and predication and about indexicality. We shall need also to consider some complexities in the notions, but let us start with the generally accepted ideas.

Referring expressions are ones which (purport to) pick out particular things. Proper names, like 'Napoleon', 'Jumbo' or 'Everest', are central examples. Predicates are expressions which can be used to characterise, describe or relate particulars so picked out. Paradigm cases are '____ sings', '____ is red', '____ loves ____', '____ laughs rudely', '____ is an elephant' and '____ is a large grey elephant'. Neither names nor predicates on their own constitute complete sentences or can be used to say anything true or false, but each predicate expression contains, so to speak, a number of name-shaped holes, and when these are filled in with an appropriate number of referring expressions the result is a particularly basic sort of sentence. Predicates can be simple, as with '____ sings', but many of them (as in the later examples above) consist of suitably structured complexes put together from predicate-building devices, including at least verbs, adjectives, nouns and adverbs. I shall call these devices 'predicate components'.

Let us now consider indexicality. It is a necessary condition for a sentence type to be indexical that its tokens make different claims depending upon the context in which they are uttered and hence, in many cases, will vary in truth value. It is a necessary condition for an expression to be indexical that sentence types in which it occurs have tokens which, because of its presence, are thus capable of making different claims. Are these necessary conditions also sufficient for indexicality of sentence type or expression type? Certainly in some usages it is taken that the conditions are sufficient. I would like to suggest, however, that there are two kinds of context dependence, and that there is some justification in the precedents of usage and implicit understanding for confining the label 'indexical'

154

to the second, and hence taking the conditions to be necessary but not sufficient.

Let us consider first the idea of a word type being associated with a family or range of specific semantic roles rather than with just one such role. We may think of this as a kind of licensed, systematic ambiguity. There is a good deal of plausibility in seeing things this way in connection with many predicates (Unger 1984; Lewis 1983: 233–249; Travis 1989). 'Flat' is a familiar example. If I produce a token of 'The top of Ilkley Moor is flat' when we are considering places for landing a rescue helicopter, the remark may well be true. But if we consider another token of this same type, said when what is at issue is an interestingly different venue for a game of croquet, then it would be false. So it seems that different claims are being made. What explains this variation in the content and so in the truth value of the tokens? The suggestion is that a speaker can use 'flat' to effect a variety of different characterisations and is effecting different ones on the two occasions. So the hearer will need to determine which specific characterisation is offered by a token utterance in the light of mutual knowledge of interests and facts.

This phenomenon is not confined to predicates. It can be exhibited by proper names such as 'Smith' or 'Miranda'. Both of these are types which are elements of a familiar repertoire of referring devices called on by speakers in our linguistic community, where we know that each type has more than one bearer. (Indeed, with a family name, such as 'Smith', it is part of its conventional role that it should be applicable to all the persons in a certain group, namely the members of a family.) Yet an individual token of such a name can be used as a referring expression, as when I say, 'Smith has gone up to town today'. Of whom do I speak, supposing that there are several persons of that name known to both of us? Context will, with luck, make this clear to the hearer; and, as with 'flat', it is mutual knowledge of interests and facts which will do the job (Cohen 1980).

However 'Smith' is surely not an example which would leap to mind if one were asked to provide a specimen of an indexical referring expression. Its mode of operation is significantly different from that of the familiar paradigms of indexicals such as 'I', 'here' and 'that'. The key contrast is this. In the case of 'Smith', as far as the type expression is concerned, the rule which speaker and hearer bring to a context and which constrains them in that context, is the entirely vague and general requirement that speaker and hearer are each to proceed in a way which will enable the one to speak intelligibly and the other to understand, in the light of their mutual knowledge. In the cases of 'I', 'here', 'that' and the like, by contrast, there is, for each word, a much more determinate rule governing the type, a rule which is grasped in advance, is part of the meaning conventions of the language and which links context and referent in a specific manner. For example, in the case of 'I' the rule is that it refers to whoever uttered it. This rule operates and fixes a referent for 'I' independent of any mutual knowledge possessed by speaker and hearer, other than their shared knowledge of the language.

When we reflect on such rules, we see that tokens of type words governed by them derive specific semantic role 'from their context' in a richer sense than do words like 'Smith'. Tokens of 'I', 'here' and 'that' get their semantic role from their context in the sense that, for each type, the rule governing its use leads us from a token and its context to an item of some category present in the context, where association with such an item is enough to enable the token to play the semantic role appropriate to its syntactic type. The semantic role of a referring expression is to pick out a particular, the state of which is what fixes the truth or falsity of utterances in which the referring expression occurs. So if a referring expression comes to be associated with some particular, which can in virtue of the association be assigned the job of so contributing to the truth or falsity of sentences, then the expression is thereby kitted out to play its role. On that model of the role of a referring expression, we can see how 'I' works: the rule governing it supplies a function from a token and context to a particular and directs us to take that particular to be the one the state of which is relevant to the truth or falsity of the whole utterance. So that token of 'I' comes to refer to that particular.

It is cases of this sort of context dependence which provide the paradigms of our notion of indexicality; and the etymological origin of the term links it to the idea of pointing. Both of these things suggest that many philosophers' implicit conception of indexicality is better captured by this second kind of context dependence, with its idea of a rule by which we latch on to some element in the context, than by the entirely general notion of context dependence. Whatever the rights and wrongs of this verbal point, it is the second kind of context dependence which I shall, in what follows, mean by 'indexicality'. 'Context' here does not mean just the immediate surroundings of an utterance; we can refer indexically to objects which are very distant spatially ('that galaxy') or no longer existent ('my last duchess'). Moreover, the mutual knowledge possessed by speaker and hearer can be an important feature of context and the scope of its potentially relevant content cannot be limited. So to be sure of specifying adequately the context of a token we need to specify every fact about the world in which it occurs. The vast bulk of such facts will in practice be irrelevant to context-dependent interpretation of the token; but we cannot in principle rule out any as necessarily so. (Some complications are noted by Lewis 1983: 226ff.)

If the idea of indexical predication is to be so much as intelligible then we must be able to say about predication things analogous to the things just said about reference. So we need, first, that a token predicate or predicate component be enabled to play its semantic role if it gets to be associated with some worldly correlate. Second, we need that such correlates belong to a category of things which are capable of being present in a context. And, third, we need that there could be a determinate rule taking us from token and context to some specific such correlate. If all this were the case, then we could have the following situation. A token indexical predicate or predicate component is uttered; the rule governing it associates it with a worldly correlate of a certain category from its actual context; in virtue of this association it is equipped to play its semantic role, that is, equipped to contribute to describing or characterizing some particular; so, finally, the indexical is then suited to be linked with some referring expression and thereby to contribute to making a complete claim.

Let us run an example to illustrate the schema. We start from a context in which Mary sings. Let us now grant that the possible claim 'Mary sings' would be true, if it were made, partly in virtue of the presence in the context of something which is the worldly correlate of the possible predicate token '____ sings'. Suppose that I were then to utter an indexical predicate token which gets to be associated with that worldly correlate – that is, with whatever it is which would make the use of a token of '____ sings' contribute a true description of Mary – and that I then use this indexical predicate to make a complete sentence by linking it to the name 'Joan'. What I have now done is say of Joan what would have been said of Mary by 'Mary sings'. Again, suppose a context in which Mary laughs rudely and so the worldly correlate of a possible token of 'rudely' is present. If I can now get some indexical predicate component to be associated with that worldly correlate then I can place it suitably in a sentence to say that Anthony belched rudely.

I suggest that there is nothing seriously controversial in this story, although the talk of 'worldly correlates' may make some uneasy. The story does indeed commit us to realism in some form; we are taking it that subject and predicate in a token utterance each contributes something distinctive to the determinate truth conditions of the claim, and that what makes an individual utterance true is something in the world independent of that utterance. But the story is neutral on the many further disputes about how this very skeletal realism should be spelled out. For example, it does not commit us to the idea that the objects and resemblances we discern in the world can be understood independently of our capacities and interests. Equally, it does not commit us to any particular conception of the nature of the worldly correlates of predicates or predicate components, and we can elaborate the outlook in terms of a variety of very different semantic and metaphysical theories. For example, we could say (in a familiar and traditional way) that the worldly correlate of a predicate is a universal, and then the presence of a worldly correlate in a context would amount to the universal being instantiated. But we could say instead that the worldly correlate we need is a set of tropes, which is present if a member is present. Some may think that both of these stories seriously underestimate the radical semantic difference between reference and predication. They might prefer to say that the correlate is a function from particulars to truth values. Its being present in a context would then need to be construed as the presence of an object delivering the value true. And yet other theories are possible. It is not a commitment of this story that every token of a given word type, for example '____ sings' or 'rudely', must have the same worldly correlate. The theory offered here is compatible with the neo-Wittgensteinian semantic view favoured, for example, by Travis (1989), on which the variability of contribution which we earlier recognised in 'flat' is ubiquitous. What is necessary for the theory to work is only that it be at least possible to say the same thing of Mary and of Joan, namely, that it is not ruled out that the same predicate correlate be present in two situations. Similarly, we can tell many different stories about the worldly correlates of predicate components. Perhaps they too correlate with universals; or perhaps their link is with entities of other categories such as activities, manners, kinds, degrees and the like; or perhaps they are correlated with functions of some suitable sort and so forth.[1]

In what follows I shall talk of properties as the worldly correlates of whole predicates, and of such things as activities, manners, kinds and so

1. Philosophers have not paid as much attention to predicate components as perhaps they should have. One line, found, for example, in some of Davidson's work (Davidson 1980: essays 6–9), seeks to flatten out many of the apparent differences by enriching the repertoire of kinds of particulars referred to and calling on the formal framework of predicate calculus. It aims to present predicate components, as far as possible, as different idioms for kinds of simple predication. Other approaches invoke an apparatus of possible worlds and functions defined in terms of them (e.g., Lewis 1983: 189–233). Wiggins (1984, 1986) offers an interestingly different view.

forth as the correlates of predicate components; these idioms are familiar, convenient and make for brevity of expression. But I do not intend my use of the idioms to signal commitment to any particular metaphysics. The crucial commitment is simply to realism, to the idea that token expressions make specific contributions to truth conditions while actual truth or falsity is determined by the world. The claim is that some version of the schematic story which we need in order to defend the possibility of indexical predicates and predicate components can be set up in all of the frameworks which are serious contenders as accounts of the semantics and metaphysics of predicates. So we ought to accept that indexical predicates and predicate components might exist. But do they? Let us consider further what they would actually look like and whether we can find any in English.

3. INDEXICAL PREDICATES

To be an indexical predicate or predicate component an expression must satisfy three conditions:

(1) Syntactically it plays the role and exhibits the combinatorial possibilities appropriate to its category; thus, if it is a complete predicate, it will combine with a referring expression to yield a sentence; if an adverb, it will combine with a verb to yield another verb, and so forth.
(2) Its inclusion in a sentence must render that sentence context-dependent, that is, such that different tokens uttered in different contexts may make different claims and so become capable of varying in truth value.
(3) This context dependence is not the upshot of licensed systematic ambiguity but is due rather to the expression having its semantic role in virtue of some rule assigning to it as worldly correlate some item of a suitable category present in the context.

I further stipulate that a whole predicate is indexical if it is either a simple unitary predicate and is indexical or is constructed from components at least one of which is indexical.

Are there any indexical predicates, given the three conditions and this stipulation? Certain examples may immediately suggest themselves, but unfortunately they are extremely uninteresting. We only have to take a relational predicate and fill in one of the gaps with an indexical pronoun to arrive at such phrases as '_____ sat on this', '_____ loves you' and the like, which can now be regarded as indexical monadic predicates. If indexical predication is to be an interestingly new topic we shall need to clarify matters so as to eliminate these cases. They result from allowing referring expressions to be taken as predicate components for purposes of condition (1). So what we need to do is to tighten up the sense of 'predicate component' so as to exclude referring expressions. Let us take it that this is done and that (1)–(3) are to be understood accordingly. (As we shall see later, this stipulation is less clear and less helpful than might be supposed. But let it stand for the moment.)

There are still expressions which prima facie satisfy the conditions as now clarified, and which do not represent anything interesting or hitherto unremarked, namely the phrases '____ is present', '____ is distant' and the like. These do not enlarge our ideas on indexicality because we have been trained to see them as having an underlying logical form similar to that of '____ sat on this' or '____ loves you'. If I say 'Mary is present', what I do is relate her to another particular, viz., a place. This way of looking at things commits us to including places and times in the class of particulars, along with concrete items like mountains, plants, people and so on. In treating 'here' and 'now' as referring expressions, as the usual accounts of indexicality encourage us to do, we are already committed to that.[2]

I do not propose to dispute here the defensibility of these familiar moves. But what the cases show is that in order to define an interesting notion of indexical predicate, that is, one which takes us beyond what is already very familiar, we shall need to understand the notions of 'referring expression' and 'predicate component', as defined through some idea of logical form, and the related idea of some perspicuous improved language, rather than through English grammar. So we need to be open to the idea that what components a predicate has may not be immediately apparent on the surface but may come to light only given reflection and analysis; and also to the converse idea that surface complexity may be mere idiomatic flummery concealing a simpler underlying form. The notion of logical form invoked here will need clarification. We shall return to the matter in Section 4. For the moment, let us press on.

To advance matters, let us stipulatively introduce an indexical verb and consider its functioning. For example, consider the verb 'to brev'. It works like this. If I say 'Joan brevs' while pointing at Mary who sings,

2. For example, Kaplan (1989: 489) speaks explicitly of 'the adverbs "here", "now", "to-morrow", "yesterday", the adjectives "actual", "present" and others' as being among the expressions he aims to study; but this does not prevent him from passing immediately to talk of their 'referents', and then to a discussion in which it is taken for granted that what goes for 'I', 'you', 'that' and the like will go for these 'adverbs' and 'adjectives' also.

then what I say is true if, and only if, Joan also sings. But if I instead point to Anthony, who is laughing, then my utterance is true if and only if Joan is laughing. Or to put matters more generally, if one combines this verb with the name 'A', to produce the sentence 'A brevs' while pointing to someone performing an action, where that performance is the salient fact about them, then the utterance is true if and only if A performs an action of that same type, whatever it is.

It is clear, however, that English does not have any unitary indexical verbs of this kind. We do indeed have 'proverbs', that is, dummy verb forms which can stand in for any verb, for purposes of both lazy anaphora and quantificational moves, as noted by Grover et al. (1975). 'Do' has this role. We can say, for example, 'Mary sang and then Joan did' or 'Whatever Mary did, Bill did'. In playing these two roles proverbs operate in interesting parallel to two of the familiar uses of pronouns. So I can say, 'Mary got up and then she went to the window' where 'she' refers to Mary because of its linguistic context; and I can also say, 'Every girl thought she would win' where 'she' is bound by 'every girl'. Pronouns like these also have a third free-standing demonstrative role, as in 'She went to the window' where 'she' is used demonstratively and refers to Mary because of its non-linguistic context. The proverb 'do', however, does not have a third additional role analogous to this. I cannot say 'Joan did' as a free-standing sentence and have my utterance convey that Joan sang, in virtue of its connection with something going on in the extra-linguistic environment, for example Mary's singing. So the proverb 'do' does not play the imagined role of 'brev', but it is this latter role that we need for indexical predication. In addition to proverbs, Grover et al. (1975: 86) also point to the presence in English of a proadjective, namely 'such'. The same, however, is unfortunately true of it, namely that it has no natural indexical role. 'Mary is such' just standing on its own does not make sense.

We strike luckier, however, if we turn to adverbs. It is entirely possible and natural for me to say 'John sang thus' and then sing out of tune, or point to someone else doing so. This is a performance by which, in context, I can claim that John sang out of tune. If a different manner of performance were salient in my singing, for example if what were notable was that I sang in operatic fashion or very low and quietly, then I would have made a different claim about John, a claim which might well have had a different truth value. Similarly, I may say, 'Amanda placed the vase so', accompanying it by a particular sort of performance of vase placing, thereby indicating that Amanda placed the vase in that way. Again a different accompanying sort of placing would have led to the making of a different claim, and hence possibly a different truth value.[3]

Grammatically these words are adverbs, that is, devices for helping to build predicates; there is little intuitive attraction in the idea that 'thus' and 'so' are part of the referential apparatus of English; on the contrary, it seems obvious that they are part of the apparatus for characterising and describing. The possible variation in claim made, and so in truth value, between the tokens of these types is clearly due to the presence of the words 'thus' or 'so'. There is, however, no plausibility in the idea that these words are like 'flat', in being, so to speak, systematically ambiguous; rather it seems evident that what we have here is indexicality. So the three conditions we set out at the start of the section are here satisfied, and there does exist at least one sort of natural-language indexical predicate component with which we can construct indexical predicates.

The actual cases of 'thus' and 'so' show the real existence of indexical expressions which play the role of a certain sort of adverb. We saw above that we can imagine a possible indexical verb ('to brev'). The imagining can readily extend to encompass other kinds of possible predicate components. We could have an indexical sortal noun, 'a nuon'. It is to be used like this: if I say 'Jumbo is a nuon' while pointing to a python, then I am saying that Jumbo is a python, while if I say it while pointing to an elephant, then I am saying he is an elephant. Similarly we may coherently sketch uses for indexical adjectives.

I do not here mean to make any commitment to the idea that the very broad categories of verb, adverb, noun and adjective are in fact sufficient for purposes of syntactic or semantic theory. The categories may have significant subdivisions. There are many different kinds of verb (transitive, intransitive, etc.) and of adjectives (attributive, non-attributive, etc.) as well as different kinds of noun, adverb and so forth. Being non-committal on what categories of expression we recognise is part of being non-committal about what formal framework or frameworks are useful in seeking to understand natural language. The general point is that for many of the prima facie distinct and significant identifiable categories, we can imagine an indexical member of that category, namely one which syntactically fits the same slot but which makes its semantic contribution in virtue of some

---

3. Jespersen (1933: 159) remarks: 'Corresponding to *this* and *that* we have the two "pronominal adverbs" *thus* and *so*. *Thus* has a stronger demonstrative force than *so*, and generally indicates manner, = "in this way", either with a back reference or pointing to what follows.' I am grateful to Alex Oliver for drawing this passage from Jespersen to my attention.

rule associating a token of it with some item in the context, suitable to be the worldly correlate of a token of that category.

The sad fact, however, is that we do not have such expressions. So what do we do when they would be useful? For example, what do I do if I want to convey that Jumbo is not an elephant but a python, do not know the words 'elephant' or 'python' but do have a python and an elephant handy? I say, 'Jumbo belongs not to this species but to that', pointing first at the elephant and then at the python. Reflection swiftly brings to light many idioms of the same general kind, by which we make good the lack of the imagined indexicals. We have, for example, the predicates '___ has this property', '___ engages in that activity', '___ stands in that relation to ___', and many other expressions like 'to that degree', 'in that respect', 'of that size' and so forth. Indeed, we are extremely free with our use of this kind of device, namely the introduction of an apparent demonstrative term coupled with the name of some category (often preceded by a preposition) into places which can also be occupied by familiar predicate components.[4]

What I now want to suggest is that, for certain important and interesting purposes, we should group these phrases together with 'thus' and 'so', and that a defensible label for the whole grouping is 'indexical predicates and indexical predicate components'. The suggestion is that predicates consisting of or including these phrases should be recognised as indexical predicates.

This may well seem wrong, since although it is clear enough that 'Mary has this property' is indexical, one may wish to urge that the indexicality stems from the presence of the referring phrase 'this property'. The predicate '___ has this property' then fails to satisfy conditions (1)–(3) as laid down earlier; it seems to be just another case of that familiar kind of indexicality we had in '___ sits on this' or '___ is present.'

We are, however, committed to classifying expressions by logical form and not by surface form, in some sense of that slippery expression 'logical form'. So we need to return again to consider what this means and its implications for these cases.

4. PREDICATION AND LOGICAL FORM

Let us set aside indexicality for a while. Philosophers have long thought that one way of making our metaphysics clearer to ourselves is by a priori

---

4. These are, or have some close resemblance to, examples of what Quine calls 'deferred ostension'. He writes that this occurs 'when we explain the abstract singular term "green" or "alpha" by pointing at grass or a Greek inscription' (Quine 1969: 41).

reflection on our language and by attempting to devise a perspicuous formal language which is ideal for the purpose of revealing to us the metaphysical structure which we take the world to have. What we are metaphysically committed to is what is required to make our kind of language (not one with our particular stock of words, but rather one with our categories of words) capable of expressing truths. We obtain light on our metaphysical commitments by articulating the kind of contribution to truth conditions made by different sorts of words and the nature and shape of semantic connection with the world which each possesses. The metaphysically helpful formal language is a perspicuous one where the syntax and semantics are well understood and run hand in hand. Reflection on it, and in particular on the nature of the axioms which capture the semantic role of its elements, will then make the fundamental categories of our world articulation available to us.

Translating natural-language sentences into such a formal language is one of the things philosophers have meant by talk of 'logical form'. And it is this sense of 'logical form' we need in considering the kinds of questions raised earlier, namely whether there can be indexical predicate expressions which have the same semantic role as non-indexical expressions, in that they have the same worldly correlates and contribute the same thing to truth conditions in virtue of having these correlates. (Other notions of logical form arise in other enterprises, for example that of seeking to codify and facilitate inference, or that of seeking to capture some psychological structures underlying sentence production or comprehension. Let us set these on one side.)[5] Our current idea of logical form is vague and programmatic, but even in a sketchy state it can help us because it can plausibly guide us in making judgements about what sentences have the same form, even if it does not tell us what that form is.

Consider the sentences 'Mary is wise' and 'Mary has the property of wisdom'. It is clear that they are equivalent in some strong sense. It is not just that they have the same truth value, or even that they necessarily have the same truth value, although both these things are so. It is rather that the second sentence is proposed, by those who favour it, precisely as a way of unpacking what the first says, so as to reveal its metaphysical commitments and hence the structure of the world, insofar as it is captured by that sentence.

Notoriously, philosophers react differently to the availability of expressions apparently referring to properties and the like. Some welcome and

---

5. Sainsbury (1991: chap. 6) provides a useful discussion of the variety of uses of 'logical form'.

promote this sort of talk and all that seems to go with it. They regard the second locution as analysing a genuine complexity implicit in the first and are happy to countenance a wide variety of uses of referring expressions for non-particulars, including some which cannot be eliminated by translation back into familiar predications. Other philosophers are wary of seeming reference to such entities. They insist that such reference is only allowable when it can be eliminated by translation back into an idiom in which only particulars are referred to. These sceptics are just as much committed to the equivalence as the believers, but they preserve it in another way, not by recognising an analysis but by seeing a logical construct.

The issue of whether such entities as universals or properties should be countenanced (and if so which of them and in what sense they are real) depends upon the answers to many questions; for example, whether all useful references to them can be paraphrased away, what explanatory roles they can play, what identity questions can be pressed with regard to them and so forth.[6] Fortunately we do not need to adjudicate these issues here. It is enough for our purposes to point out that both parties to the dispute recognise the need to preserve and explain the equivalence.

Consider, in the light of this, 'Mary is wise', 'Mary has the property of wisdom' and 'Mary loves Harold'. How should we group these as to their logical form, in the sense of 'logical form' we are now using? One might say that the first is a monadic predication and the other two dyadic, and hence the second and third go together. But in the light of the equivalence noted above, this is not required and might be thought implausible. One very good explanation of the equivalence is precisely that 'Mary is wise' and 'Mary has the property of wisdom' have the same form. The two familiar philosophical stances sketched above do make this assumption, and it is an assumption which, for the purposes of this discussion, I shall endorse.

If we are the first kind of philosopher and favour properties and the like, then our ideal language will abound in terms referring to such objects. 'Mary is wise' will figure for us only as an explicitly introduced abbreviation for 'Mary has the property of wisdom', and so the two sentences will have the same form, namely one suitable for reporting the instantiation relation as holding between a particular and a monadic property. 'Mary loves Harold', by contrast, will be revealed as interestingly

6. Oliver (1996: esp. sections 15, 21 and 22) offers a helpful summary of and comment on some possible positions on these issues.

165

different because it has a form suitable for reporting the instantiation of a relation by an ordered pair of particulars. On the other hand, if we are sceptics about non-particulars, then our ideal language will contain no terms referring to them and mention of the property of wisdom will be introduced explicitly as a logical construct always translatable away. So 'Mary is wise' and 'Mary has the property of wisdom' will again have the same form, namely that of being the combination of name with a one-place predicate. And again 'Mary loves Harold' will come out as having a contrasted form, being the combination of two names with a two-place predicate.

In light of this, what should we say about the relations between 'Mary laughed rudely' and 'Mary laughed in a rude way', or 'Joan is building a house' and 'Joan is engaged in the activity of building a house', or 'Jumbo is an elephant' and 'Jumbo belongs to the elephant kind'? It seems clear that the same considerations apply to them. The sentences in each pair are equivalent, and the more elaborate version is endorsed by some as a way of unpacking what seems to them to be implicit in the simpler version. The same kinds of debate about whether this is revealing or merely obfuscating can be gone through in these cases too, and there is the same plausibility in saying that, whatever forms these sentences have, in each pair the members have the same form.

Back now to indexicals. The general moral clearly transfers to a language containing indexical predicates or predicate components. So either 'John sings thus' is an abbreviated version of what is better revealed in 'John sings in this manner' or the latter is a puffed up and potentially misleading version of the former. Whichever way we go they have the same logical form, in the sense of 'logical form' we are concerned with. Similarly for the equivalence between 'A brevs' and 'A is engaged in this activity', or 'A is a nuon' and 'A belongs to this kind'; except that in these latter cases the shorter versions are lacking in our actual language. So if we are sceptics about non-particulars we shall have to say that our language is unfortunately misleading in offering us nothing but puffed up forms. The interesting outcome of taking this option is that we end up being entitled to say that expressions like '____ has this property', 'to that degree', 'of this kind' are indexical predicates or indexical predicate components, and that the predicates they constitute or help to build satisfy conditions (1)–(3); the seeming presence of a referring expression is just a misleading surface feature of notation.

What happens to the notion of indexical predicate, as defined by (1)–(3), if we take the other option and allow in non-particulars? Our original rough-and-ready characterisation of a predicate combined a syntactic with a semantic criterion; a predicate was to be an expression which both contained a name-shaped hole or holes and also was used to characterise or relate. One way of putting the upshot of accepting non-particulars, and seeing predicates and their components as referring to them, is that on the syntactic criterion there are far fewer predicates than we thought and they will all have extremely thin, structural meanings. They will be such things as '_____ instantiates _____' or '_____ engages in _____' and what they will do is prevent the sentence from being a mere list of names. The entire substantive characterising and relating role will be shifted to the referring expressions.

We could acquiesce in this restriction of 'predicate'. In the sense of 'predicate' which then emerges I do not wish to say that there could be indexical predicates. I suggest, however, that there is no great violence to the intuitive notion we express by 'predicate' in refusing this syntactically driven option and in saying instead that the semantic role of describing, characterising and relating is an important defining feature of predicates. This then entitles us to use the labels 'indexical predicate' and 'indexical predicate component' with the same extension as does the sceptic about non-particulars. On this tack, in order to get our definition in line with our intended extension, we shall need to modify our account of 'predicate component', allowing referring expressions in appropriate contexts to be predicate components provided that they refer to the right kind of item, namely properties, qualities, activities, degrees, manners, kinds and so forth.

Thus whether we favour or reject non-particulars we may define the same class of indexical expressions; it will include '_____ does this', '_____ has this property', 'thus', 'so', 'in this manner', 'this kind', 'that activity' and so forth and so on. It is this class which I shall henceforth mean by 'indexical predicates and predicate components'.

5. MORE ASPECTS OF INDEXICAL PREDICATION

The previous section supplied an outline of indexical predication and the linguistic devices by which we accomplish it. I turn now to some further reflections on the phenomenon.

For ease of exposition I shall adopt the following convention. When invoking particular occurrences of indexical claims, I shall indicate the indexically picked-out item, whatever category it belongs to, by placing, at an appropriate place and in curly brackets, some linguistic expression which will enable it to be identified. For example, 'That cat {Tabitha} is friendly' can be used to speak of an utterance of 'That cat is friendly' said when Tabitha is the cat indicated. 'My curtains have this property {being red}' indicates an utterance of 'My curtains have this property' when being red is the property which the utterance and context together fix upon. 'Mary laughed thus {rudely}' is appropriate for an utterance of 'Mary laughed thus' when laughing rudely is the way of laughing singled out. In what follows I shall, for brevity, talk primarily of properties, but what is said goes mutatis mutandis for relations, manners, activities, kinds and so forth.

We should sharply distinguish indexical predication from the equally usable but quite different device of getting across a property possessed by some particular by explicitly likening it to some other particular. For example, I may say, 'My curtains are the same colour as this piece of material' while pointing to a red piece of material. This remark, in a context where someone can determine the colour of the cloth, will in practice serve to convey the information that the curtains are red. The indexical here is the familiar referring indexical which serves to pick out the second term of a relation between concrete particulars. It functions quite differently from the earlier '_____ have this property', the role of which semantically is to fix on some property present in the context rather than to fix on the particular in virtue of which the property is present. A property will be suitable related to the context, and the phrase containing 'this property' will latch on to it, precisely because it is instantiated in some item in the context. In such a case it may well also be possible to transmit the information conveyed by the indexical predication with an explicit relational claim reporting a similarity, but the semantics of the two kinds of claim are quite different.

Consider 'My curtains have this property {being red}' and contrast it with 'My curtains are the same colour as this piece of material {piece of red material}'. Most obviously the first, the indexical predication, involves no reference to the item in which the property is in fact in-stantiated, unlike the second, the familiar indexical reference. Hence the truth of what is said in the indexical predication does not entail the existence of that item. Further, the modal status of the two remarks may be different. It might be the case that the first is necessary. Those particular curtains cannot but be red, their material being essential to their identity and the material being naturally red and totally resistant to any dye. But it might not be the case that these very curtains have to be the same colour as the specimen, because the specimen, unlike the curtains, might take other dyes. A third contrast is that the two claims may behave differently when embedded in psychological contexts. So Beatrice might know that my curtains have this property {being red} without knowing that they are the same colour as this piece of material {piece of red material}. This will be the case if she is aware of the redness of the specimen from seeing it through a small hole, without being able to tell whether the redness is a property of a well-lit piece of material or a fine sunset sky. Conversely, Beatrice might know that my curtains are the same colour as this piece of material {piece of red material} without knowing that they have this property {being red}. This will be so if she has been reliably informed that the curtains and the piece of material are like-coloured and can identify the piece of material by feeling it inside a bag but does not know its colour.

When we use referring indexicals such as 'this' or 'that' there may be unclarity about what we refer to unless the context makes one particular object salient. If I simply point in a certain direction and say, 'That is very beautiful', there may be many items to which I could be referring, a cupboard, the array of ornaments in a cupboard, a particular one of the ornaments, a gleam of light on an ornament and so on. Sometimes the context of previous remarks, known interests and the like will suffice to show which of the potentially demonstrated items is in fact meant, but sometimes I shall need to use a noun to supplement the demonstrative, as in 'that cupboard', 'that array', 'that vase', 'that reflection' and so forth. Similar potential difficulties beset indexical predication and can be resolved in similar ways. A given object will have many properties. So if I just point to the object and say, 'A has that property', a great deal of unclarity may be left, but I can, if need be, remove it by specifying what sort of aspect of the object I wish attended to, by introducing phrases like 'that size', 'this shape', 'this colour', 'this exact shade', 'this surface texture' and so forth.

Both kinds of indexical engagement with the world are liable to the same sorts of breakdown, for example when there are too many worldly correlates of the indicated type present in the indicated location, or when there is no worldly correlate of the right type. Further, with both indexical reference and indexical predication the semantic rule for the type, that is, the rule which takes us from context and token to worldly correlate, is often not mechanically applicable but will need to be applied intelligently in the light of shared information about the context. Thus potential or actual misunderstandings can be removed by speaker and hearer calling either on pragmatic considerations or on moves of further specification or on both together.

The thrust of the last two paragraphs has been to emphasise the similarities of indexical reference and indexical predication, with respect to the way in which semantic and pragmatic factors may interact in fixing content for particular token utterances, with respect to the kinds of misunderstanding and breakdown which are possible and with respect to the kinds of moves we can make to forestall them. But there will also doubtless be differences in the exact way the interaction of semantic and pragmatic work out in detail in the two cases.

Referring indexicals can be divided into demonstratives and pure indexicals. Demonstratives, for example 'that leaf', are incomplete without the addition of something like a gesture of pointing. They serve to enable reference to one out of many items presented simultaneously in some perceptual array and thus require supplementation by something like a gesture. By contrast, pure indexicals, like 'here', 'now' and 'I', do not require the addition of anything analogous to pointing because the rules governing them (that they refer to the place, time and agent of the remark or thought) are of such a shape that there is (in normal situations) no possible indeterminacy. Any utterance or thought has only one place, time and agent, and so reference to them is secured without need for further clarificatory devices. The referent of a pure indexical may also, if it is the kind of thing capable of being an object of perception, be perceptually presented to the person who refers to it. For example, a person using 'here' may perceive the place she refers to at the same time that she refers to it. But the point about a pure indexical is that it secures its reference without benefit of demonstration and whether the item is perceived or not.

It seems at least theoretically possible that an analogous distinction can be made with indexical predications. The kinds we have considered so far are all demonstrative. The properties we attribute with their use are the kinds of properties of which we become aware in perception. Singling out one property from the many presented simultaneously in perception, for example by demonstrating a particular which has it, is required if the predication is to work. We should not, however, leap to the conclusion that all indexical predication is demonstrative. Perhaps there is pure indexical predication, by which we attribute properties in ways which do not depend upon instances being presented to us perceptually. I shall not here pursue this idea further, but it is worth mentioning, as it might prove to be of importance if we move on to exploit the idea of indexical predication in explaining features of our representations of representations, that is, our thought and talk about others' thought and talk.

Perry, Kaplan and others have made us aware that indexical reference is not merely a convenient but dispensable device for picking out items for which we lack context-independent names (Perry 1979; Kaplan 1989; Mellor 1991). Rather it is an essential element in our thought, integral to the content of those perceptual and action-controlling representations through which we are most immediately connected to our environments. Lack of conscious indexical referring thoughts would be lack of a sense of oneself as a perceiving, acting and spatio-temporally located being. At an even more primitive level, an animal with any serious level of spatial awareness or ability to initiate forward-looking and flexibly developing actions needs indexical thoughts (or proto-thoughts) in which the concepts (or proto-concepts) 'here', 'there', 'now', 'soon' and the like are exercised. Moreover, the character (in Kaplan's sense) of particular kinds of indexical reference, for example whether I think of a person as 'that person' or as 'I', connects with the distinctive psychological and epistemological roles of thoughts in which such references occur.

Are there analogous things to be said about indexical predication, about the indexical thoughts, which are expressed by indexically predicative utterances? I offer here a few sketchy remarks on these potentially complex topics. I am assuming in what follows that there is a parallelism between the linguistic and the psychological. Both linguistic items and psychological states can represent states of affairs; and both do so in virtue of being put together, in parallel ways, from elements (words, concepts) about which the same kind of semantic and logico-syntactic remarks can be made, for example that they refer, are predicatival, are indexical and so on.

What is distinctive of the psychological role of indexical predicatival thought about some feature is the way in which the feature itself is available to enter into determining the connections of that thought with other thoughts and actions. Consider a person who judges 'The curtains I am going to get are this colour {subtle and unusual shade of red}'. As long as the shade is perceptually present and available for indexical identification then actions and judgements concerned with matching, harmonious contrast and so forth clearly can occur. They can occur even if the thinker lacks an accurate and individuating non-indexical representation of the colour, even if she has no name for it, and poor ability to recognise and match it in its absence. Her abilities with the colour when it is present are the result of a constant sensitive interplay between her and the object in which the colour is exhibited; there will be a kind of constant experimenting with the colour, through which its nature and connections will reveal themselves. By contrast, possession of a certain sort of individuating and non-indexical representation of the colour would allow actions and judgements concerned with matching, contrast and so on to occur without any further glances at the specimen.[7] Such non-indexical grasp could well include quasi-theoretical specifications of the relations of the colour with other colours ('Orange does not go with purple', etc.), or information from which such judgements could be derived.

It may seem from this that to have a need to represent properties indexically is a cognitive weakness. If we had perfect pitch, had better ways of conceptualising and remembering subtle shades of colour or complex shapes, then we would not require indexical representations of such properties in order to handle problems about matching, contrast, harmony and so forth. But this may be too quick. Not to have in one's life a role for indexical representations of sounds, colours, shapes, textures and so on is either to have already discriminated and labelled all the perceptual richness and subtlety of the world (a tall order, even for minds vastly more powerful than ours) or to be blind to that richness, operating with a 'painting by numbers' kind of sensitivity in which everything is slotted into a limited and unchangeable number of categories and one is not open to discovery of new harmonies, kinds of relation and the like.

Moreover, it is not only with clearly observational properties like colour that ability to think indexically is important. Theoretical speculations begin with awareness of some interesting phenomenon, the nature of which we can, initially at least, merely gesture at with phrases like 'that funny property', 'this unfamiliar process', 'that strange kind of object' and so forth. Certainly we rightly feel a pressure to move on from such merely indexical grip to something more distanced. Only a non- or less indexical representation of such natural scientific phenomena will provide us with theoretical insight, and so with ability to reason about the connections of the property with other properties and to think fruitfully about it in its absence. So only such a representation will provide a systematic and flexibly applicable ability to predict and explain the occurrences of the property and the effects such occurrences may have. But if we lacked capacity for and willingness to use indexical predications we would be incapable of open-minded revisions and extensions of our repertoire of

7. It may be that at least part of the debate over so-called non-conceptual content in perception would be more helpfully conceived as a debate about the indexical nature of some representations (McDowell 1994: chap. 3).

172

predicatival notions. Moreover, we would be incapable of the initial iden-tifications ('being magnetic is this property') which enable us to do the experiments and observations in the light of which we build and improve our non-indexical grip.

Indexical predication is, arguably, not as fundamental as indexical refer-ence. For example, we do not have to credit all animals with it (although some of them may be capable of a form of it). We can at least imag-ine simple creatures which have only an innate and limited repertoire of features they can recognise and no ability to improve and make more complicated their representations of them. However, thought without in-dexical predicatival content lacks something central to human thought, namely the sense of ourselves not only as placed in an extended spatio-temporal world but also as placed in a world containing an immense range of aspects, features and kinds, on which our present grasp is partial and incomplete.

Finally, I would like to make some speculative remarks about yet further interesting applications of the notion of indexical predication. One way of conveying in speech the nature of another person's speech would be to call on the resources of indexical predication. For example, to report one of Galileo's much discussed remarks I could call upon an utterance of (to put it quickly and crudely) the following shape: 'Galileo spoke thus: the earth moves'. The token utterance of 'the earth moves' serves as the specimen from which the character I wish to attribute to Galileo's speech is to be identified, but it is not itself something to which I refer. (Consider again the difference between 'My curtains have this property {being red}' and 'My curtains are the same colour as this piece of material {piece of red material}'.) it seems plausible that by pursuing this line of thought we might arrive at an account of the nature of indirect speech which would have all the advantages of Davidson's well-known paratactic proposal (Davidson 1968) while avoiding many of the difficulties to which it gives rise (see Essay 10). Another, and very closely related, speculation sees a link between so-called simulationist approaches in philosophy of mind and proposals about the indexical nature of some of our vehicles of representation. A central simulationist theme is that in thinking about another's thought I must myself entertain a thought of the same nature as that which I ascribe to the other. So it may be that the idea of indexical predication can provide a framework of concepts, distinctions and the like, in terms of which some simulationist claims and their various versions can helpfully be articulated (see Essay 11).

10

On Speaking Thus: The Semantics of Indirect Discourse

1. INTRODUCTION

This essay applies to the elucidation of indirect discourse an idea which has already been defended elsewhere: that of indexical predication (see Essay 9). The resulting view has, I suggest, the advantages of Davidson's proposal in "On Saying That" without its disadvantages (Davidson 1984: essay 7, first published 1968). Indeed, if Davidson had revised this earlier proposal about indirect speech in the light of the ideas sketched in "Quotation", the upshot would resemble what is suggested here (Davidson 1984: essay 6, first published 1979; Rumfitt 1993: 431–432). Davidson's earlier proposal is that the 'that' of indirect discourse refers indexically to the particular utterance which follows it. The alternative view to be defended here is that a that-clause refers indexically to some non-particular item of which the particular utterance is an instance.[1]

The essay, however, does not focus on the nature and identity conditions of these non-particulars or on the project of providing some formal theory of indirect discourse, although it offers just a little on these topics in the final section. Rather, as the title suggests, the aim is to approach the study of reports of speech through the idea of indexical predication and thereby to situate indirect discourse in a wider context. Doing so brings out motivations for the general view which would still be operative even if some particular implementation is found unacceptable.

---

1. Other authors have offered accounts of indirect speech which share this general orientation. They include Bigelow (1975), Rumfitt (1993) and Brandom (1994: chap. 8, esp. 534–539). Rumfitt acknowledges impetus for his thoughts from McFetridge (1976). Sellars is on to the same idea (1963: 161–164). Altham also suggests related thoughts (1979).

Section 2 summarises the main relevant ideas about indexical predication. Section 3 brings out the usefulness of indexical predication in connection with talking about intricate and skilful human activities. Sections 4 through 8 apply this general thought to the case of language, examining the role of notations and the differences between direct and indirect speech reports. Finally, Section 9 returns to the issue of formalisation and the nature of the non-particulars to which that-clauses refer.

2. INDEXICAL PREDICATION

The kind of indexical expressions on which philosophers and logicians have concentrated are expressions for referring indexically to particulars, that is, spatio-temporally located individuals such as chunks of matter, mountains, trees, people, countries and so on. But we also have expressions which are indexical and the role of which is not to refer to such particulars but rather to characterise or describe them.

These expressions work by latching on to something in the context of utterance. This 'something' is the sort of thing which can be the semantic correlate of a predicate, for example a characteristic exhibited by some particular in that context. One example in English is 'thus', as used in such remarks as

(1) She sat thus

followed by the speaker sitting in a distinctive manner, say stiffly and upright. The 'thus' latches on to the manner of the subsequent sitting and the whole performance has the truth condition that she sat stiffly and upright. Another example is:

(2) My curtains are coloured thus

followed by the exhibition of a piece of material of a certain colour, the whole performance serving to characterise my curtains with respect to their colour. A further case is:

(3) My curtains are this colour

similarly followed by the exhibition of a piece of material of a certain colour. (2) and (3) are to be contrasted with

(4) My curtains are the same colour as this piece of material.

(4) uses indexical reference to a particular to help inform someone about the colour of my curtains, and its logical and epistemological character

175

are therefore significantly different from those of (2) and (3). For example, it entails the existence of the piece of material to which the curtains are compared while (2) and (3) do not (see Essay 9).

Grouping (2) with (3) brings out that the central feature of indexical predication (as here defined) is that it involves the use of an indexical expression which is not to refer to a particular but rather to characterise or describe. Indexical predication may, consistently with this, be effected through indexical reference to a non-particular, for example a colour, property, kind, action, number and so on. If non-particulars exist then particulars will be instances (tokens, specimens, members, etc.) of them. Hence we can, by deferred ostension, identify a non-particular via a particular which is an instance of it. This is what we present ourselves as doing in (3), where the piece of material serves as a vehicle by employment of which its colour may be identified and then attributed to my curtains.

I shall, in what follows, assume that we may countenance non-particulars and can refer to them. Nominalists may prefer not to countenance them. It is then up to them to explain away, by paraphrase or in some other fashion, the seeming commitment to non-particulars embodied in such phrases as 'the property of wisdom', 'the number 2' or 'this colour'. For example, the paraphrase route to defusing apparent commitment to non-particulars might well seek to present (3) as merely a puffed-up and misleading version of (2). Whether or not this strategy works, indexical predication is still with us. Moreover, if the arguments of Sections 3 and onwards are persuasive, the view that it is central in indirect speech remains defensible. How a nominalist presentation of the insight would proceed depends upon the kind of nominalism in question and the sorts of apparatus it allows itself. (Nominalists should not, however, proceed by reviving Davidson's proposal from "On Saying That". For reasons why this is not a good move see Section 6 below.) Since defence of nominalism is no part of my brief, I shall not pursue these issues.

3. SOME USES FOR INDEXICAL PREDICATIVE LOCUTIONS

Indexical predicative expressions are useful linguistic tools in situations where a person wishes to characterise an item and where it is easier to produce a specimen which has the character to be attributed than to produce some non-indexical specification of that character. This could be for reasons which are particular to an individual speaker, for example her ignorance of some ordinary word. More interestingly, it could be for reasons which affect all of us, as in the case of specifying finely discriminated shades of colour. We can tell them apart when confronted with them and have preferences about which to put on our walls, but cannot remember them clearly enough for non-indexical names like 'pale peach' or 'summer dawn' to be, by themselves, an adequate vehicle for talking of them. So on many occasions when we want to talk about colours we need the help of fabric specimens and shade cards. Another reason for using indexical predicative expressions could be that adequate non-indexical means of characterisation have not yet been invented. Or perhaps they have been invented but are cumbersome.

Dance movements illustrate this last point. We have a rough-and-ready everyday vocabulary – 'leap', 'twirl', 'waltz' and so forth – and ballet enthusiasts have a more specialised vocabulary – 'entrechat', 'plié' and the like. But even with this supplement we lack vocabulary to record all the detailed aspects of movements which are important to dancers. Only recently has a reasonably adequate dance notation been developed for classical ballet, but it is little known and laborious to use. (For more on the development of dance notations, see the interesting account by Guest [1984].) Hence the detailed choreography of the great ballets has been (and in practice still is) passed down by older dancers to the next generation, in a teaching process calling on indexical predicative devices ('One does it thus . . .'; 'At this point you do this movement . . .', etc.).

We possess many sorts of intricate know-how, in exercising which we show ourselves to be, in some sense, aware of features of our own and others' performances, while at the same time we are unable to specify explicitly the structures and patterns we are responding to and producing. Such performances are a subject matter for which non-indexical characterisation either does not exist or is likely to be cumbersome and unhelpful for certain purposes. By contrast, in these cases indexical characterisations will be found to be easily produced and helpful.

Another example may help us to see the plausibility and ramifications of this. Imagine a group of people who have considerable musical skills. Children growing up in their culture hear, and then learn to take part in, structured musical exchanges in which one person devises and sings a short tune to which another person then responds with a complementary phrase. An observer may work out that certain constraints, for example of consistency of key, rhythm or the like, are observed in all performances. She may also see that other rules (about relation of key, similarity of rhythm, etc.) govern the acceptability of a response to an original performance. The fact that such rules might be discovered by an observer is quite consistent with the performers themselves having no non-indexical descriptions for the particular features of key or rhythm which their actual performances show them to be, in some sense, aware of and responding to.

If members of this community want to talk about their own and others' musical performances the only recourse they have, but one which lies to hand very naturally, is indexical predication. So they can say things like 'Wasn't it fine when she sang [thus]: {dum deedly dum} in response to his singing [thus]: {la lala la}?' or 'I sang {diddly tweedle} because he sang {fa la la la la}'. Phrases like 'Dum deedly dum' and such are, of course, place holders here for bits of actual singing. When representing indexical predications I shall use curly brackets to provide a space within which appears some linguistic stand-in which should enable the reader to grasp what predication is being made and/or what sort of vehicle is carrying it.

Our musical practices are different from the ones sketched, but not in ways which have us better placed than the imagined people to do without indexical specifications of music. For us, as for them, indexical methods of describing music, by humming, singing, playing an instrument or whatever, are the ones we call upon when we get into particular detailed kinds of discussion about works or performances. We say, for example, 'He sang thus: ...', and we sing or hum or play as he did. Or perhaps we say 'He sang *this*: ...', and we sing or hum or play the tune which he sang.

The appearance of indexicals like 'this' and nouns like 'tune', with the syntax we give them, underpins the possibility of a whole range of kinds of remark and enquiry. We introduce names for familiar tunes ("Pop Goes the Weasel", etc.), predicate things of tunes, quantify over them, count them and make identity claims about them. The use of 'this' rather than 'thus' connects with our focusing upon some features in which performances match rather than others, viz., tune–relevant matters rather than others such as absolute volume, or beauty of tone. So when 'this' is in operation it may be contrasted with 'thus'; we may say 'she sang this ... thus ...', indicating indexically first the tune and then the manner of singing. 'Thus' is, however, flexible enough to be used on occasion to encompass the whole range of aspects of singing, including tune–relevant ones.

What counts as 'singing the same tune' is highly context-sensitive. Performances might be classed as 'of the same tune' in some circumstances and not in others. Variation in such things as time signature, presence of syncopation, degree of decoratedness and whether major or minor can sometimes be relevant and sometimes not. If a composer is offering variations on a theme one might well say, 'Now the tune comes again, in a minor key', but if a teacher asks one child to sing the same tune as another, then the minor version would probably not count as the same.

The context relativity of our judgements about tune identity lends no support to nominalism. The moral is rather that expressions for picking out tunes have an indeterminacy of reference, which is in practice resolved by context. Hence there is no such thing as the one true "Pop Goes the Weasel". Rather, that name is associated with a whole family of different equivalence relations between performances, some more and some less demanding. Hence it is used to refer to different tune-like abstract entities on different occasions.

Others' verbal performances, our responses to them and our interests in reporting, commenting on and explaining them present important parallels to the musical case. Understanding a language involves grasp on how sounds may be put together to make words, how words may be put together to make sentences and how the semantic properties of sentences are (wholly or partly) determined by semantic properties of words and constructions. There are also constraints on how to carry on conversations. Whether one linguistic performance is an appropriate response to another depends upon relations between their semantic properties. Clearly we cannot press these analogies between music and language too far, but some central and relevant points of comparison seem to stand. They are that in speaking a language (*a*) we exercise a skill in producing and responding to complex structured items, (*b*) there are principles governing the construction and properties of these things, (*c*) we show that we are in some sense aware of these principles and properties by our skilful performances, but (*d*) we cannot state the principles or specify the properties explicitly.

The obvious conclusion to draw from this is that reporting of others' speech is another area in which the natural resources to call on are those of indexical predication. But before exploring this we shall consider how notations work. Some grip on this is necessary to get a clear view of certain potentially confusing differences between kinds of speech report.

4. NOTATIONS AND DESCRIPTIONS

If and when a notation is devised it will provide a non-indexical way of specifying performances. But notated records, for example for music, are not likely wholly to replace indexical descriptions in the sorts of talk about skilful performances we imagined earlier.

One reason for this is that the notation is cumbersome. Another is that a notated specification of a performance does not itself provide description in terms of the higher-level features which are relevant to judgement and appreciation of music. A notation is more or less adequate depending on whether it records more or less of the data from which such higher-level features can be reconstructed. But, however adequate it is, the information it supplies needs processing to deliver the verdicts and appreciations which interest us. For most of us the only way of moving from a notated record to an appreciation is via a reconstruction – that is, having the music played, or at least imagining it. We need the indexical representation to engage with in order to exercise our skills of discrimination and response.

Spoken language and written notations of it present a parallel with, but also a difference from, the musical case. The parallel is that the phonetic character of spoken language can be recorded by a written notation but can often be conveyed more easily and usefully by indexical means. The difference is that language is important to us not only for its phonetic properties but also for its semantic properties (in a broad sense of 'semantic'). Semantic properties are not supervenient on phonetic ones but depend upon the existence of a set of practices – conventionally sustained and different for each language – which give uttered sounds a role in the lives of speakers, as they interact with their world and each other.

So notating uttered sounds does not, by itself, notate significance. We have only a very few non-indexical descriptions of semantic properties (e.g., phrases like 'expresses Pythagoras' theorem', 'is a command', 'is a universal claim' and the like), and we have no notation for semantics. Hence our prime recourse in conveying information about the semantic properties of others' speech must be indexical. The discussion of Sections 6–8 will seek to substantiate this claim by looking at actual cases.

Clarity on a further point about written language will be helpful for avoiding confusion in what follows. Our alphabetic writing provides both a notation for spoken sounds and also an alternative means of expression, possessing semantic properties in its own right. Although in our writing these functions go together, they do not necessarily go together. To see them separated consider (a) phonetic symbols as used by linguists to represent accurately the subtleties of pronunciation, dialect and so on, and (b) Chinese characters. The phonetic symbols have no semantics of their own and are purely a notational device. The Chinese characters, by contrast, are a self-standing semantic system but have no one phonetic interpretation. They have been used to write many radically different spoken languages – for example, Korean and Japanese as well as Mandarin – and when they have a phonetic role, the correlation is with the sound having the same meaning in the spoken language of the user of the characters.

Our own written letters can be used both to notate speakable nonsense syllables ('slithy toves') and also to communicate, as I am doing now by writing this essay. A reader does not have to convert this essay to sounds heard in imagination in order to understand it. I spell this out because it is important at a couple of points in what follows. We shall concentrate on reports of spoken remarks to avoid the multiplication of complexities.

5. WAYS OF REPORTING SPEECH

Consider now Galileo's well-known spoken remark 'Eppur, si muove'. Here are some possible reports of it.

(5) 'Galileo said, "Aypoor see mwovay"'.

Please take (5) to be written. There is nothing indexical going on here. Phonetic features of Galileo's speaking are specified via the non-indexical device of a notation.

(6) 'Galileo maintained Galileo's hypothesis'. (Let us suppose that we have given the name 'Galileo's Hypothesis' to the view that the Earth moves – on the model of 'Pythagoras' Theorem', 'Goldbach's Conjecture' and so forth.)

This is a report which concentrates on conveying information about the semantic properties of Galileo's utterance. Again there is nothing indexical. We employ a non-indexical label for what Galileo stated. (Compare 'He sang "Pop Goes the Weasel"'.)

(7a) 'Galileo said, "Aypoor see mwovay"'.

By contrast with (5), you are to imagine this spoken. So my writing here 'Aypoor . . . etc.' is what I do in order to give you as good an idea as I can of the sounds uttered by the person giving the report which I specify in (7a). The person who gives the report does not use written letters; he or she just utters sounds. I might have reported the same spoken remark about Galileo by writing it down as

(7b) 'Galileo said, "Eppur si muove"'.

This report, the one presented to you by (7a) and (7b), concentrates on conveying information about the sounds Galileo uttered. This is a classic case of a so-called direct speech report.

(8) 'Galileo said, "All the same, it does move"'.

This kind of case is not much commented on, but has points of interest. We shall return to it in Section 7 below.

(9a) 'Galileo said that the Earth moves'.
(9b) 'Galileo said that it moves'.

We have here classic indirect speech reports. They consist of what linguists call the matrix sentence, 'Galileo said...', completed by the complementiser 'that' and the complement sentence 'the Earth moves' or 'it moves'.

Let us now leave (5) and (6) aside and concentrate on reports of the shapes of (7), (8) and (9).

6. DIRECT SPEECH REPORTS

Reports like (7) are what spring to mind when 'direct speech' is mentioned. Such reports are thought of as aimed primarily at conveying the words uttered. Neither reporter nor hearer need understand the words reportedly spoken. Meaning is relevant, but only obliquely because the reporter needs enough grip on the reported language to identify the phonemes in it. (If one is aware of the importance of tone in spoken Chinese and of one's inability to identify and reproduce it, then one knows that one's attempts at direct reports of spoken Chinese could be disastrous failures.) It is characteristic of direct reports that the matrix sentence and the complement sentence may be in different languages, although of course they need not be.

If you were at all persuaded by the earlier account of reports of musical performances you should be sympathetic to the idea of seeing direct speech reports as functioning in the same way. In both cases performers have skills of a high order in producing complex sound sequences but little explicit know-that about the rules for doing it. With an ear attuned to English or Italian, a person can reproduce sequences of phonemes which she has heard without being able to say much about what these phonemes are or the rules for their combination. By such reproduction she can indexically describe the nature of another's speech performance. In the analogous written reports of written communication, this sort of context is one in which quotation marks are called for. So quotation marks are an indexical device, roughly similar to 'thus' or 'this', and the quoted sentence is the specimen from which the attributed character is to be identified.

Davidson, in effect, offers this account of reports like (7). He writes:

On my theory, which we may call the *demonstrative theory* of quotation, the inscription inside [the quotation marks] does not refer to anything at all, nor is it part of any expression that does. Rather it is the quotation marks that do all the referring, and they help to refer to a shape by pointing out something that has it. . . . The singular term is the quotation marks, which may be read . . . the expression with the shape pictured here. (Davidson 1984: essay 6, 90)

In this piece (first published in 1979) Davidson does not insist that the quotation marks refer to the particular inscription they enclose. An 'expression' as he means it here is a non-particular, an abstract entity which has instances or tokens.

This account is preferable to one constructed to run parallel to Davidson's own earlier account of indirect speech, outlined in the famous "On saying that" (Davidson 1984: essay 7; first published 1968). That earlier model, if applied here, would read the quotation marks as referring to the token words occurring within them or to the act of uttering those words. It would attribute to Galileo a relation, saying, to a particular utterance produced by me. What does it take for Galileo to say my utterance? Following the earlier Davidson we would elucidate this informally by saying that my utterance needs to samesay some utterance of Galileo's, that is, there needs to be some utterance of Galileo's which matches, in some specified way, the utterance produced by me. This theory is subject to a variety of familiar and powerful criticisms, for example by Blackburn (1975), McFetridge (1976) and Schiffer (1987: 131–133). (Lepore and Loewer [1989] have ingenious responses to some of these criticisms. But however ingenious they are, the initial implausibility of the earlier account remains and an alternative looks desirable.) I shall not rehearse these earlier criticisms here but will add one further point against the account.

An account of this shape might seem a neat idea to someone with nominalist sympathies. It accommodates the indexicality which is plausibly present in speech reports while countenancing only nominalistically acceptable entities. But we can now see that, given the concept of indexical predication, the move is unmotivated even for a nominalist. Nominalism may be defensible, but if so this will be in virtue of the discovery of some general ways of defusing the ontological commitment of apparent reference to non-particulars. There are many seeming references to non-particulars, for example in 'Socrates has the property of wisdom' or '$2 + 2 = 4$', which the nominalist cannot with any plausibility dispose of by proposing particulars for the problematic expressions to refer to.

The apparent reference in these cases must be dealt with by other kinds of moves such as deflationary translation. If these moves work, then they will work also for the apparent non-particulars which we invoke in spelling out the indexical predications of direct speech. If they do not work, then we had better bite on the bullet and cease to be nominalists.

This is a moral which we should carry forward as we turn to discuss reports which are not concerned only with words uttered as phonemes but also with significance. Nominalists should not shrink from recognising (seeming) reference to non-particulars. Rather they should look for general strategies for blocking untoward consequences of such reference.

7. REPORTING MEANING

Significance or semantic character is what knowing a language enables one to appreciate. Without such knowledge one hears a mere jumble of noises; with it one hears a meaning-laden performance. Knowledge of a language involves grasp on semantic properties of words (their referents and perhaps senses as well) and how the semantic properties of sentences are determined by those of words and constructions. It includes an ability to appreciate the contribution of connectives, tenses, quantifiers, modal expressions and other constructions, together with awareness of the difference between indexical and non-indexical expressions, sensitivity to the way the truth conditions of some sentences depend on context and the like. Appreciation of the inferential potential of an utterance is also part of the grasp of its semantic character.

Knowledge of the significance of linguistic utterances will also include more than these truth- and inference-related matters. For example, it will include grasp of kinds of speech act, rhetorical devices, the emotional force of certain words or tones of voice, the restrictions of social role in who may use certain vocabulary and many other similar matters. So one who hears and understands a meaning-laden performance has know-how in dealing with a great range of significant features of the kind gestured at above.

Suppose that you wish to report upon a linguistic performance and that the aim is to put your hearer in a position to appreciate as much as possible of the significance of the remark. Given that you have a know-how of producing utterances and appreciating them but only limited know-that about exactly what you are producing or responding to, the sensible thing is to indicate the character of the original remark by producing one like it in as many of the significance-relevant aspects as you can deal with or are important to you. In other words, it is natural and sensible to call upon the resources of indexical predication.

So, for example, you say, 'He said, "This is a bit of bad situation"', and in delivering the quote you reproduce his slightly humorous understated tone of voice. This puts your audience in a position to appreciate the truth conditional content of what was said, also the particular words or concepts via which that content was conveyed, the speaker's attitude to the content and possibly other things as well. Or you say, 'She said, "No way am *I* going to take the rap for *you*"', reproducing the furious tone of voice and putting in the emphasis on the 'I' and the 'you'.

You might also, however, to save time and because the rhetorical flourishes are not of importance to you or your hearer, report this last remark by saying in a neutral tone, 'She said, "I am not going to take the blame for you"'. This possibility shows us that significance-conveying indexical reporting can be extremely flexible. The person doing the reporting may choose to preserve or discard, in her indexically used specimen, whatever features of the original seem important. Another example of the same flexibility is preservation of the tone and indexical character of the original while translating it from one language to another. This is what underpins the possibility of reporting Galileo as in (8).

Reports of the shape of (7) or (8) may take either 'thus' or 'this' inserted between the speech verb and the indexically used specimen. As with music, the use of 'this' tends to narrow down the kind of match we invoke and keys us in to the possibility of using the apparatus of reference and quantification. The earlier remarks about the context relativity of identity, however, clearly apply here, and the method of reporting is immensely flexible. One person might say the same as another for some purposes and not others. (See Clark and Gerrig 1991 for a similar view of direct speech reports.) We shall return to this in Section 9.

Are (8) and these other examples cases of direct or indirect speech reports? The examples can evoke conflicting intuitions since they involve the idiom of quotation, and yet in them we focus on meaning and not just words uttered. Philosophical usage is not clear enough here to mandate an answer. For the sake of having some labels, I shall call them 'semantic direct reports' as opposed to 'phonetic direct reports', which are the more familiar sort of direct speech reports.

In summary, the claim so far is this. Indexical predicative reporting of others' speech is extremely likely to occur because, in both its phonetic and semantic aspects, speaking is an activity about which we have a great deal of know-how but not much know-that. Examination of particular kinds of report, viz., those like (7) and (8), bears out this view.

8. INDIRECT SPEECH REPORTS

How, then, are classic indirect speech reports, namely ones in which 'that' as a complementiser is either present or would be acceptable, different from semantic direct reports? How do remarks like (9) contrast with those like (8)?

Immediately apparent differences are the lack of quotation marks (in written versions) and the need for 'that' (if anything) rather than 'thus' or 'this' as a link word. There is no 'thus' version of indirect speech. Its idioms are firmly locked into a set of practices involving referential and quantificational talk – for example, predicating being interesting of what someone said, asking whether it was identical with what someone else said, asking how many things she said and so on.

The literature brings other differences to our attention. With direct speech reports the context for working out the reference of any indexicals in the complement sentence is the context of the original remark, while with indirect speech the relevant context is that of the matrix sentence. So where the original remark, said to me by A, is 'You are a fool', my indirect report of this will be 'A said that I was a fool' (McDowell 1980; Brandom 1984; Sainsbury 1997). Because the context relevant to interpreting indexicals in indirect speech is that of the matrix and not of the original, it will only be in certain special circumstances that we can recover from the complement which indexical was used in the original. The concern of the reporter, with respect to indexicals, is usually to match the referent they contributed to the original utterance rather than to convey information about how the referent was specified.

Another difference is that in direct speech reports there is no syntactic or semantic interaction between the words of the matrix sentence and the words of the complement sentence, while with indirect speech there are some limited possibilities of interaction. Thus with direct speech if the original speaker says 'I am F', then the pronoun 'I' appears also in the report ('Tom said, "I am F"'), while in indirect speech we have instead 'Tom said that he was F', where 'he' is, plausibly, taken as having an anaphoric relation back to 'Tom'. In direct speech we have 'Every boy said, "I am a nice fellow"', while in indirect speech we have 'Every boy said that he was a nice fellow', where 'he' is now most naturally seen as a variable, bound by 'every boy'. Higginbotham brings out forcefully the difficulties this sort of case raises for a paratactic account of indirect speech, that is, an account which claims that the complement sentence has no syntactic or semantic interaction with the matrix sentence (Higginbotham 1986). A paratactic account of direct speech reports is defensible, but not of indirect speech reports.

Do these differences show that indirect speech reports do not call upon the resources of indexical predication? There are powerful reasons for resisting this idea. The complement sentence, even if no longer to be seen as completely self-contained, still has most of the structure and elements of a self-contained sentence. It has its own subject, which can have adjectives and subordinate clauses attached; its verb can have the full range of modal and tensed features and can be modified by the full range of adverbs; it can contain the whole gamut of complexity offered by deployment of quantifiers and sentential connectives (Givon, 1980). It is all this which enables it to convey the presence of matching complexity and structure in the reported remark. Hence all the arguments set out earlier, the arguments for supposing that acts exhibiting complex know-how need to be reported indexically, retain their full force. Our strategy, then, should be to hang on to the indexical account as far as we can and to seek to integrate it with the facts about interaction noted above.

The change in context of evaluation of indexical referring expressions presents no difficulties. As we have seen, a semantic direct report may shift the language used ('Galileo said, "All the same, it does move"' rather than 'Galileo said, "Eppur, si muove"'). It is sensible to do this if the hearer understands the language of the reporter but not that of the original remark. Calling on the resources of the context of the report and not of the original will have analogous advantages in connection with referring indexicals, since the hearer will have the resources to interpret any referring indexicals in the context of report but may lack the corresponding knowledge (who was being addressed, where and when) about the original remark. So we may see the facts about referring indexicals as broadly of the same kind as the facts about possible shifts in language. Both are examples of just the sort of flexibility we would expect in indexical predications.

What of the fact that pronouns in the complement sentence can relate anaphorically to expressions in the matrix sentence, or be bound by quantifiers in the matrix? To deal with these issues, we need to become just slightly more technical. Consider, to start, with 'Tom says that he is a nice fellow'. (We shall concentrate on the reading on which this is heard as reporting Tom talking about himself. The other reading on which he

187

is talking of some other person is irrelevant to our concerns here.) On the indexical predicatival account, this claims of Tom that he says something sharing significant semantic features with the complement. If the anaphoric linkage exists, then one significant semantic feature of the complement will be that it contains an expression referring to Tom; another significant feature will be that this term is the subject of a predicate meaning 'is a nice fellow'. So, if the report is true, Tom uttered something referring to himself ('I' or 'Tom' or some other phrase) as subject of a predicate meaning 'is a nice fellow'. This interpretation, recommended to us by applying the strategy of reading the whole as an indexical predication together with seeing 'he' as anaphorically dependent on 'Tom', gives us exactly what we want.

What of Higginbotham's example: 'Every boy [says] that he is a nice fellow' (Higginbotham 1986: 39; for ease of exposition, I modify the example by changing the verb from 'believe' to 'say')? It is natural to take this remark as a generalisation, of which 'Tom says that he is a nice fellow' is an instance. Given this, we should interpret the remark as claiming that each boy has the property which 'Tom says that he is a nice fellow' attributes to Tom, namely the property of producing some utterance in which an expression referring to him, the boy who speaks, is subject and an expression meaning 'is a nice fellow' is predicate. (For this way of understanding pronouns as bound variables, see Evans 1985.) Again this seems, intuitively, to be just what we want.

On this treatment of the example there is no one sentence which has the same informational content as what each boy says, since each boy said a different thing. If we think of the indexical predication account as requiring us to identify such a sentence then indeed it fails in this case. However we need not think the account demands this. To allow quantification to reach inside complement sentences is precisely to allow ourselves to construct indirect speech reports which need interpreting not on this simple model but rather in the more complex way outlined in the previous paragraph, where our understanding of indexical predication is allowed to interact with our understanding of quantification. On the view sketched, the existence of some syntactic and semantic integration of the complement sentence into the matrix sentence in indirect speech is a significant difference from direct speech. But this fact does not make direct and indirect speech reports the radically different sorts of animals which they are sometimes supposed to be.

The account proposed is close in spirit to Davidson's. It preserves his idea that the vehicles of our reports of others' speech are indexically used sentences. It offers a similar explanation of opacity, namely that there is no guarantee that replacement of a term in the complement sentence by a co-referential term will preserve all the significance-related features of the utterance which the original term contributed. It also stresses 'semantic innocence', that is, that words in the complement sentence do not acquire different meanings (senses, references or whatever) in virtue of appearing in that role. They play their role in complement sentences in virtue of having their ordinary meanings, whatever they are. If they did not have their ordinary meanings in complement sentences, then their presence there could not serve to characterise indexically the meaning of the utterance which is reported.

But the view offered here differs from Davidson's in abandoning insistence on the wholly paratactic status of complement sentences. It differs also in stressing that the indexicality is predicatival. It thereby avoids all the difficulties which arise for Davidson's proposal from taking the 'that' to refer to the following token sentence or utterance. These points are linked. If the indexicality involves reference to a particular we need some particular to be pointed at. It will then seem plausible that this entity must be outside and independent of the matrix sentence. Hence we are pushed in the direction of a paratactic account which cannot accommodate the interaction of matrix and complement. But if we conceive of the indexicality as predicatival then there is, as we have just seen, no reason why it cannot function in tandem with further features of matrix and complement (e.g., quantificational linking) to allow the expression of complex claims like the one about the boys and their remarks.[2]

9. PROPOSITIONS AND FORMALISATION

What are the implications of the approach outlined here for the logical form of indirect speech reports, for the notion of a proposition and for the possibility of a formal semantics of indirect discourse? In this final section I offer some sketchy and speculative remarks on these topics.

One implication of the theory offered here is that token that-clauses can properly be taken to refer to non-particulars. We reject nominalism

---

2. Hornsby (1977) explores the possibility of defending a Davidsonian paratactic account by taking the referent of the 'that' to be an open sentence, where pronouns in the complement are not bound by elements in the matrix. Rumfitt (1993) also takes himself to be defending a paratactic account and cites Hornsby's suggestion with approval. But if the proposal outlined here is correct, we need not take the heroic course this seems to require of denying the apparent interaction between matrix and complement.

and hence are hospitable to many kinds of entities. We recognise tunes (entities which can be hummed or sung or composed or listened to or . . .) and colours (which may be exhibited or seen or mixed or . . .) and entities specified by that-clauses (which may be asserted or believed or proved or entailed or . . .). Let us follow tradition and call these last things 'propositions'. So a particular utterance of 'Galileo said that the Earth moves' reports a relation between Galileo and some proposition picked out by the token that-clause.

The suggestion of this essay is that the combination of the 'that' of indirect discourse with the clause which follows it functions roughly like 'this [tune] {dum di dum di deedly dum}' or 'that [colour] {a ripe tomato}'. In all three cases we have an indexical expression suitable to refer to a non-particular, and associated with it we have some particular (the token complement sentence, the singing, the tomato). The particular provides the vehicle through which the required non-particular is present in the situation in such a way that it can be referred to. The upshot of referring to it and relating it to some particular, as in a whole sentence like 'She sang [this] {dum di dum di deedly dum}' or 'Galileo said [that] {the Earth moves}'), is that she and Galileo are thereby described or characterised, that is, some indexical predication is effected.

Pursuit of the parallel with tunes will help to make clearer one aspect of this proposal, namely the context relativity in the reference of that-clauses. (What follows concerns the identity criteria of propositions. It takes no stand on the more metaphysical issue of what sort of thing have these identity criteria, namely what sort of thing a 'proposition' is. Some, for example, might want to identify a proposition with a set of synonymous utterances or with an ordered pair of an individual and a property, or with a set of possible worlds. This essay takes no stand on the propriety or otherwise of these suggestions. For an interesting discussion of the difficulties of such identificatory moves see Moore 1999.) Let us return to some of the ideas of the end of Section 3. I suggested there that there is no one tune entity picked out by all tokens of 'this [tune] {dum di dum di deedly dum}'. Rather different tokens may pick out different entities, depending on whether 'being of the same tune' requires performances to match only in basic melodic outline or also in other features such as degree of decoratedness, time signature and so forth. This implies that 'tune' is not a sortal which brings clear-cut identity criteria with it. Rather, it is associated with a family of more specific sortals, and we understand from context which of these more specific notions is being invoked on any occasion. The general notion 'tune' puts limits on what could be relevant to whether two performances are 'of the same tune'. We discard interest in certain things when we move from 'sings thus: {dum di . . .}' to 'sings this: {dum di . . .}'. For example, absolute pitch and beauty of tone in singing are not relevant to tune identity, although they could be relevant to the accuracy of an indexical description of a singing introduced by 'thus'. On the other hand, such factors as the relative pitch, length and loudness of notes, and higher-level features which can be defined from these, are just the sort of things which are potentially relevant to tune identity. But which are actually important is fixed by the interests of speaker and hearer. Roughly speaking, talk of 'tunes' invites us to concentrate on musical structure and possibilities of musical development and to ignore idiosyncratic details of performance. But within that general framework it leaves much unspecified.

I would like to suggest that 'proposition' is in the same boat. The shift from 'spoke thus' to 'said that' invites us to concentrate on some aspects of utterances and to ignore others, but leaves a great deal of flexibility as to which among the potentially relevant features are actually given weight on any particular occasion. It is clear that indirect speech reports may be sensitive to (at least) such matters as the referents of the words used, their standard inferential links, their indexical character and the logical structure of the remark as a whole. On the other hand, exactly which such features are of importance may vary from occasion to occasion.

There is disagreement over what kinds of features may be recorded in indirect speech, and so be relevant to the truth of indirect speech reports. Hand claims that a variety of stylistic devices, such as exclamations, topicalisation and preposing, can be preserved in direct speech reports but not in indirect speech reports (Hand 1991). So, for example, 'Tom said, 'Oh, this is a bore' is acceptable while 'Tom said that oh, this is a bore' is not. If his observations are correct they suggest that when we report another's speech in the indirect idiom we sieve out as irrelevant much stylistic and presentational idiosyncrasy. A rough summary of the trend of his remarks is that the interests served by indirect speech reports concern only the truth- and inference-related aspects of the reported remark. This idea is consistent with the uncontroversial observations about differences between direct and indirect speech which we considered in Section 8. But others have disputed some of Hand's claims. For example, Larson and Segal suggest that indirect discourse attributions may on some occasions be sensitive to such matters as how the person reported pronounces words. Adapting their example, they say we might agree with a report vocalised as 'Jason said that Harverd is a fine school' but not with one vocalised as

'Jason said that Harvahd is a fine school', depending on how Jason himself pronounces the name 'Harvard' (Larson and Segal 1995). We need not take a stand on these issues, since both views are compatible with the outline theory sketched here. All that follows if Larson and Segal are right is that the notion of 'proposition' covers an even wider range of more specific sortals than it would if Hand were right.

If it is correct that 'proposition', like 'tune', is a term for a family of kinds of thing, then we have an explanation of the many competing intuitions on propositional identity and on the truth of indirect speech reports exhibited in the literature. To take a very familiar example, some accept and some deny that one who says 'Hesperus is visible' may be correctly reported as having said that Phosphorus is visible. On the proposal of this essay each of the disputants is right in thinking that the kind of identity criteria for propositions which he or she favours are sometimes used. But both are wrong in thinking that the same criteria must be used on all occasions. (The same suggestion is made by Rumfitt [1993] and by Moore [1999].)

Many philosophers have wanted to find a formal compositional semantic account of indirect speech. It is surely true, in some sense, that we understand an indirect speech report on the basis of understanding the words in it, including the words of the complement. It seems to follow from this that there should be a way of setting out explicitly how an understanding of the words and construction yield a grasp of the truth conditions (and perhaps other semantic features) of the whole. The attempt to provide a theory of how this works has produced an immense and ingenious literature, including papers and books by Soames (1987), Salmon (1986), Richard (1990, 1993), Crimmins (1992a, 1992b), Forbes (1993), Larson and Ludlow (1993), Larson and Segal (1995) and many others.[3]

An implication of the view sketched in this essay is that the prospects for the kind of account they seek are not good. Let us change our example from tunes to colours to illustrate the principle at issue here. Suppose I say 'My curtains are this colour {a ripe tomato}'. Let us imagine that

---

3. Much of this literature is usefully summarised by Richard (1997). I should insert a warning at this point. Of the works cited in the text, those by Soames, Larson, Ludlow and Segal are all explicitly about indirect-speech reports, and Forbes claims to be addressing the problem of oblique or opacity-inducing contexts in general. However, other of the mentioned authors (e.g., Salmon, Richard and Crimmins) take as their explicit focus only the semantics of belief reports rather than that of the semantics of indirect discourse more generally. It is possible that these authors would reject the adaptation of their theories from belief to speech. If so, I apologise for my misappropriation of their views.

we have a formal theory of colour in the shape of a systematic canonical way of labelling how colour presentations may differ (for example, in hue, brightness and so forth). Let us suppose that we have also unpacked the concept of colour, in the sense that we have made explicit all the possible more specific sortals which can be taken as colour sortals. Thus we know (let us suppose) that the more specific sortals falling under colour are (*a*) colour as one of red, blue, green, etc. or (*b*) colour as hue or (*c*) colour as specific shade – where the last is individuated by combination of hue, degree of saturation and degree of brightness. In the light of this theory, together with specification in its terms of the colour properties of the ripe tomato which is used as the vehicle of the indexical predication, we can now work out that 'My curtains are this colour {a ripe tomato}' could have the truth condition (*a*) my curtains are red or (*b*) my curtains are of hue such and such or (*c*) my curtains are of specific shade so and so. ('Such and such' and 'so and so' stand in here for some description of hues and shades in the canonical vocabulary of the theory.) The most, then, which we can say about the type 'My curtains are this colour {a ripe tomato}' is that any token of it is such that it is either true iff (*a*) or true iff (*b*) or true iff (*c*).

Let us now suppose that we are equipped with a complete formal semantic theory for unembedded sentences. (Different philosophers will have very different ideas of what this formal theory might look like, since we are not agreed on how to do formal compositional semantics. But we may set all these disagreements on one side, as they are irrelevant to our concerns here.) Suppose also that we have a complete and explicit account of all the specific kinds of 'proposition' and how they are to be defined in terms of the semantic features which the formal theory illuminates for us. Consider now a sentence of the form 'X says that a is F'. The formal theory, together with our account of the variety of propositions, may enable us to offer a set of options as to what the truth conditions of a token of 'X says that a is F' could be. One option might reflect a notion of proposition where match of reference in subject and predicate is sufficient for two utterances of this form to be of the same proposition. Another might reflect a notion where matches in some but not all aspects of sense were required. Perhaps another requires also match in some words actually uttered. And so on. But if the proposal of this essay is right, there is no one equivalence of this kind which we can endorse as the sole correct account.

Something then is wrong in the very natural assumption that we can integrate sentences of the form 'X said that p' into one unified formal compositional semantic theory in a much simpler way, which (as far as statements about truth conditions is concerned) delivers us just one statement of the conditions under which 'X said that p' is true. It seems plausible to us that we should be able to effect this integration because, we think, we understand type sentences of this shape and we do so on the basis of the words, including those of the complement sentence. The error in this line of thought can be seen by looking again at 'My curtains are this colour {a ripe tomato}'. It is correct that we have a (schematic) understanding of this type sentence in the sense that we know what kind of thing could be said by a token of it. But it does not follow from this that we are in a position to set out 'the' truth conditions which are associated with the type. Several colours, of different kinds, lie waiting in the tomato to be picked out. And so which aspect of itself the tomato contributes to the truth conditions of a token awaits determination by context. Similarly, many different kinds of proposition lie waiting to be called on in the complement sentence of an indirect speech report.[4]

So the very best we are going to come out with from our imagined completed formal semantics is a long disjunctive story. ('Any token of the type "X says that p" is such that it is either true iff. . . or is true iff. . . or . . .') How likely is it that we might get even that? The kind of account envisaged will only be available if there is some given set of specific notions of 'proposition' which we can enumerate exhaustively. But, plausibly, there is no such given stock. As we think more about the world and become aware of more of the implications of our views, our stock of thoughts becomes more nuanced and varied, and hence also the stock of meanings (as differentiated by our inferential dispositions) which we can express in our utterances. And as the meanings and their differences become ever more varied, so will the ways in which utterances can match or fail to match in what they express, and so also correlatively will the variety of notions of 'proposition' we can find useful. Both music and language are expressive tools which we continue to develop and extend. It may be no more appropriate to seek a once-and-for-all list of types of proposition than it would be to attempt to fossilise music in the set of forms available at one particular moment in musical history. This is not a reason for

---

4. There are some proposals on the semantics of indirect discourse which are alert to the importance of context, for example, those of Crimmins and Richard. But they share the view of the other writers there cited that all tokens of a that-clause pick out the same item. And so Crimmins and Richard are led to accommodate the context sensitivity in different and more complicated ways than that proposed here.

refraining from trying to sort out what notions of proposition we do now call on. But it is a caution against hoping for a timeless completeness in any account.

I believe that the ideas outlined here might have interesting implications for some other topics, for example for seeing our way out of the tangles posed by iterated reports ('X says that Y says that Z says that p'), which have tripped up many a promising-seeming theory about indirect speech. It seems possible also that they might be extended to throw light on reports of propositional attitudes more generally. But these are topics for another occasion.

11

Lagadonian Kinds and Psychological Concepts

1. INTRODUCTION

The so-called simulation theory of how we arrive at (some) judgements about others' thoughts is taken by many to be plausible. (See the volumes edited by Davies and Stone [1995a and 1995b] and by Carruthers and Smith [1996] for an introduction to the literature.) Goldman has contributed notably to this debate and also to the discussion of related questions (Goldman 1995, 2000a, 2000b). Among such related questions are these: Can the ideas invoked in the simulation theory of the heuristics of psychological judgements throw any light on our possession of psychological concepts? And can they throw any light on the nature of the mental? Goldman has trenchantly criticised one version of the idea that simulationism can help us in these areas (Goldman 1995). It may be that one could begin to muster some response to some of his objections (see Section 3 below), but I shall not be attempting to revive the kind of view which he attacks, since I share his scepticism about it. The purpose of this essay is, however, to suggest that there is another, and very different, way in which 'simulationist' ideas can be deployed to illuminate at least some aspects of our possession of psychological concepts. Whether this alternative approach has anything to offer on the nature of the mental itself is more obscure. I believe that it may, but will have only a little to say on this topic here.

The key idea of the 'simulation' approach to the heuristics of psychological judgements is that we may arrive at such judgements not by employing some detailed body of 'know that' about thoughts – namely a theory of how thoughts arise or cause other thoughts – but rather by employing our own 'know how' or skills of thinking. We are able to think about states of affairs and projects hypothetically as well as categorically. Thinking about what would be the case if so and so obtained, or how such and such a possible goal could be achieved, employs the same concepts and the same reasoning abilities as making actual inferences and forming actual decisions. So even if one person does not share another's starting points, she may follow the other's thinking and to that extent see things from the other's point of view. This ability can be used to arrive at predictions of that other's thoughts or actions.

This heuristic approach to other minds can be and has been spelt out in a number of different ways. But how to elaborate the view and the strengths and weaknesses of its various versions are not our concern here. Instead our question is whether the root ideas it calls on can figure helpfully not only in a story about heuristics but also in an account of psychological concepts. So now we need to ask which root idea or ideas we have in mind.

The verb 'simulate', as it appears in claims of the form 'A [mentally] simulates B' is sometimes used of an activity and sometimes of a state. Let us remove this indeterminacy by coining the terms 'co-reasoning' and 'samethinking'. So A co-reasons with B when they use their powers of reflection on the same subject matter and consequently their thoughts follow a (roughly) isomorphic pattern of development. By contrast, A samethinks with B when they are in thought states with the same content and hence with the potential for development in isomorphic ways. So an example of samethinking would be that B believes that p and A imagines that p. It is clear that both co-reasoning and samethinking are important notions for the simulation approach, since co-reasoning is central to the proposed heuristic and co-reasoning presupposes samethinking.

The idea we shall pursue is not that co-reasoning should figure in an account of psychological concepts. (A proposal of this nature has been discussed and is the target of objections by Goldman and others.) Rather the suggestion to be developed here is that samethinking should figure in our account. Further, the suggestion will be, not that samethinking should appear as an element in the content of psychological concepts, but rather that it should figure as a constituent of the vehicle in which thoughts exercising those concepts are carried. I hope that what follows will make this obscure-sounding suggestion somewhat more intelligible.

Gordon has speculatively offered a view about the relation of simulation and psychological concepts (Gordon 1995). Some have found his proposal obscure. It may be that the ideas of this essay will provide a possible way

197

of articulating his proposal, a way which makes clear the structure and viability of something like what he suggests, even if it does not provide a way of showing its ultimate defensibility. This possibility is explored in Section 6.

Here is a sketch of the structure of the essay. Section 2 will outline the assumptions about concepts and concept possession which guide the discussion. Section 3 considers linking simulation theory with psychological concepts by invoking co-reasoning and agrees with Goldman that this line is not promising. Section 4 explores two key ideas we need for an alternative approach, namely those of an 'indexical predicate' and of a 'Lagadonian kind'.[1] Section 5 suggests that these ideas, together with that of samethinking, provide an interesting and plausible view of how we represent the content of others' mental states. Section 6 asks whether the proposal explored in Section 5 for content will also serve to illuminate our concepts of the attitudes and concludes that the prospects here are not so good. Sections 4, 5 and 6 are thus the heart of the essay, and the main focus in them is on psychological concepts and what it is to possess them.

In invoking samethinking rather than co-reasoning, the account outlined does not offer a place to what many would see as the central element in the 'simulation' theory, namely its distinctive heuristic story. Also, as just acknowledged, the account turns out not to have much to say directly about what has been many philosophers' prime interest in this area, namely the general concepts of the attitudes. So on one plausible reading, the question 'Do the ideas invoked in the simulation theory throw any light on our possession of psychological concepts?' means 'Does the co-cognitive heuristic need to be invoked in an account of the concepts of the propositional attitudes?' Taken this way our question here gets the answer 'no' or 'not directly'. The question to which I offer the answer 'yes' is, rather, 'Must samethinking be invoked in an account of what is involved in having the concepts of the detailed contents of thoughts?'

Section 7, however, raises the possibility that the account outlined in Sections 4, 5 and 6 may have further implications. Perhaps we can derive from it constraints on a viable account of concepts of the attitudes, and also

1. Some of the customs of Lagado, the capital of Balnibarbi, are described by Jonathan Swift in *Gulliver's Travels* (Swift 1726/1967: 230–231). One notable one is that the learned and wise carry with them what they propose to talk about. So 'if a man's business be very great and of various kinds, he must be obliged in proportion to carry a greater bundle of things upon his back'. My suggestion will be that we need to follow this practice, at least for some kinds of thing – although our reasons for doing so are different from the reasons of the Lagadonians.

important clues to the nature of the mental in general. And if we follow this clue it might become apparent why co-reasoning has the central heuristic role it does in our thought about the mental. So in the longer run it may be that there are important links to be teased out between co-reasoning and the concepts of the attitudes. But these issues are not explored in this essay.

2. CONCEPTS

A concept of something is that which, if possessed, enables a person to think about that thing. (I use 'thing' here very widely to cover particulars, kinds and other aspects of states of affairs.) But what actually goes on in a thinker, what does a thinker do, when a concept is exercised? To exercise a concept a thinker must do something with a distinctive and possibly complex nature, namely a nature which makes what she does a suitable vehicle for the content which that concept-exercise contributes to the thought as a whole. The aim of this essay will be to tease out a distinctive kind of complexity involved in the thinking of thoughts about psychological states. By doing this we throw light on the nature of our vehicles of thinking about the psychological, and thus on psychological concepts and their possession.[2]

A creature's thoughts explain its behaviour. And the more complex and delicately attuned to the world a creature's behaviour, the richer its cognitive powers and states. In what follows we shall take it that a creature's cognitive workings need to be of a sophistication and structure sufficient to sustain language use if we are to credit that creature with possession and use of concepts. Following tradition, I shall take ability to use a word or phrase for something to be the most obvious mark of possessing a concept of that thing. To say this is not to deny or downplay the importance for concept possession of ability to produce appropriate non-linguistic behaviour, since a requirement of understanding language is that linguistic utterances dovetail intelligibly with non-linguistic action. But a corollary of approaching thought through its linguistic expression is that the semantic and structural properties of components of sentences (i.e., words) will be mirrored in the semantic and structural properties of components of thoughts (i.e., concepts). At least this is so at the level of reflection about thoughts which we are focusing on. It may well be that we can also delve deeper into cognitive processing, or approach it

2. The view of concepts called on in this essay owes a good deal to Peacocke (1992).

199

from other angles, thereby discovering other levels, structures, contents and kinds of representation. But pursuit of those issues is not our project here.

One possible ambitious programme would be to account for possession of concepts in naturalistic and non-intentional terms. A different but still interesting project would be to throw non-reductive light on certain concepts by elucidating them in terms of their relations to other concepts or intentional capacities. Classic 'conceptual analyses' provide examples of this second strategy. The project of analysis assumes that all 'ideas' are either 'simple' or 'complex' and proposes to tell us which simple ideas go to compose a given complex one. So, schematically, an idea of C may be found to consist of ideas of D and E. If this is correct, when anyone thinks of C she does so by thinking of D and E. In other words, the vehicle of our thinking of C is thinking of D and E. When C, D and E are predicate notions, this cashes out as the claim that we think of Cs as things which are D and E.

When an analysis of a concept is available it enables us to secure (certain kinds of) clarification about the nature of the kind of thing conceptualised. Through analysis we make explicit to ourselves the content of what we are claiming when we say that something is C, for example that it is D and E. To get such an explicit grip is certainly one legitimate way (although clearly not the only way) of understanding what it is to 'get insight into the nature of Cs'. Are there other ways in which consideration of concepts could provide insights into the natures of things, even where what the consideration provides is not an analysis? We shall return briefly to this issue in Section 7.

The classic programme has faced criticisms, which suggest, first, that it needs substantial modifications, and second, that, even so, its style of approach is at best applicable to only some concepts (Margolis and Lawrence 1999). One familiar worry focuses on the analytic-synthetic distinction. Perhaps 'ideas' are not as clear-cut, nor are the connections between them always as fixed, as the classic programme assumes, and hence there is no saying definitely which ideas go to compose another. We shall not engage seriously with this problem here. For our purposes it is enough to note that there are connections between some ideas which are relatively a priori, deeply entrenched and knowledge of which is part of our usual understanding of the terms. We shall not deal with the question of the various kinds of status these links may have.

The classic story may also face attack for its assumption that all 'ideas' come at equal levels of explicitness. Even for the concepts where some classic analysis seems most defensible ('vixen', 'bachelor' and the like), making a conscious and explicit judgement that something is C often need not involve equally conscious and explicit judgement that it is D and E. A proper response to this worry might be to acknowledge different levels of representation. We could then replace the crude idea of containment of one concept by another with the idea of the explicit exercise of one concept involving implicit exercise of another. Or we could replace it by the related idea of the explicit exercise of one concept priming a thinker for an inferential move to explicit exercise of another. A further ramification of these ideas is the possibility of recognising circles of holistic interdependence between concepts, where grasp of E involves grasp of F and also vice versa.

Indexicality presents another sort of difficulty for the classic programme, since it shows that there are kinds of 'idea' which the classic programme does not address at all. Indexicality requires us to make a distinction between the 'character' of some conceptual element in a thought (i.e., the mode of presentation of the item thought about) and its 'content' (i.e., contribution to truth conditions which that element [together with context] makes). The classical conception is internalist and, for it, character and content cannot come apart. But with the externalist structure of indexicality they can. To think of a thing under an indexical mode of presentation, for example as 'that thing over there', is for the thought to have a certain character, which is crucially important for its role in reasoning, in sustaining action, in underpinning some forms of a priori knowledge and the like. But the truth conditions of the thought depend upon which item is in fact picked out by the exercise of the concept and not upon the mode of presentation under which it is identified (Kaplan 1989).

Another related and instructive externalist challenge comes from the Putnam–Kripke proposals on the semantics of natural-kind terms, suggesting that such terms are not susceptible to classic analysis. Rather, on the view they propose, grasping a natural-kind term is a complex matter in which ability to recognise stereotypes, ability to identify defining specimens and grip on the idea of match in inner constitution all play their part, but not a part like that played by D and E in the imagined classic analysis of C (Putnam 1975; Kripke 1980).

As far as the project of this essay is concerned, what is important is that recognising the need to refashion and extend the classic theory in the light of all these sorts of difficulties does not require us to repudiate the idea that some concepts are complex, in that they are built from or involve other concepts. What the difficulties do is force us to extend the range of kinds of component elements which may figure in concepts and the kinds of arrangements they may be found in.

So our questions are these: Can we illuminate what it is to think about psychological states by discerning some further conceptual structure in what goes on when a person exercises psychological concepts? Are there other concepts which a person (implicitly or explicitly) exercises when he or she exercises psychological concepts? If so, what are they and how do they build together to constitute the exercise of a psychological concept?

When we speak here of 'psychological concepts' what do we mean? We shall restrict ourselves to concepts of propositional attitudes. They are the concepts which are displayed in ability to understand sentences of the form 'X expects that the weather will improve', 'X intends that he shall be on the summit of Mount Kilimanjaro by noon', 'X remembers that she has an appointment at two o'clock', 'X is disappointed that his candidate secured only twenty votes' and so forth.

So far so good. But at this point an unclarity emerges. Are the psychological concepts we wish to illuminate the general ones expressed by the words 'expects', 'intends', 'remembers' and 'is disappointed', or are they the more specific ones expressed by the complex predicate expressions 'expects that the weather will improve', 'intends that he shall be on the summit of Mount Kilimanjaro by noon' and so forth? Understanding some specific detailed psychological claim requires understanding both what kind of state is specified and also what it is for a state to have the content indicated by the that–clause. So a full account of our grasp of the psychological should surely tell us both what it is to grasp the concepts of the various attitudes and also what it is to grasp that an attitude has this or that content. What we say about one topic will constrain what we say about the other, but it is not the case that insight into one topic automatically supplies full insight into the other.

3. A NON-STARTER?

How might we use simulationist ideas to illuminate concepts of the mental? One possible move is discussed by Goldman. (This proposal is also the target of other discussions by Fuller [1995], Peacocke [1992: 168ff.] and Stich and Nichols [1995]. And objections similar to those of Goldman's are advanced by these philosophers too.) Goldman writes:

What is the relation, it may be asked, between the simulation approach and what it is for mental ascriptions to be *correct*? The simulation theory purports to give an account of the procedure used in ascribing mental states to others. What light does this shed, however, on the conditions that are constitutive of mental state possession (especially possession of the attitudes)? The interpretation strategist hopes to extract from the interpretation procedure some criteria of correctness for mentalistic ascriptions. . . . But the simulation theory looks distinctly unpromising on this score. Since simulation is such a fallible procedure, there is little hope of treating 'M is ascribed (or ascribable) to S on the basis of simulation' as constitutive of 'S is in M'. Furthermore, simulation assumes a prior understanding of what state it is that the interpreter ascribes to S. This just re-raises the same question: what state is it that the interpreter is imputing to the agent when she ascribes state M? What does her understanding of the M-concept consist in? . . . One cannot extract criteria of mentalistic ascription from the practice of interpretation if that practice rests on a prior and independent understanding of mentalistic notions. (Goldman 1995: 93–94)

What Goldman is here contemplating is the equivalence:

(1) S is in M iff M is ascribed (or ascribable) to S on the basis of co-reasoning.

He is not, I think, imagining someone who presents this as an analysis in quite the classic mould, but it is recognisably some proposal in the same broad area which we are to consider. The equivalence is supposed to set out something a priori, which unpacks for us the criteria we apply in making psychological claims. It attempts to show us through this what we (implicitly) take to be constitutive of the truth of a given psychological claim.

In interpreting (1) we must read 'M' as a specific mental state, complete with content as well as attitude, if the proposal is to make sense, since it is such specific judgements which simulation, for the most part, delivers. So an instance of (1) will be, for example, 'S expects that the weather will improve iff expecting that the weather will improve is ascribed (or ascribable) to S on the basis of co-reasoning.' Taken as a generalisation, the proposal says, 'For any specific mental state, a subject is in that state iff it is ascribed (or ascribable) on the basis of co-reasoning.'

Goldman gives two reasons for finding the proposal unsatisfactory. The first objection is that co-reasoning as a heuristic is fallible. One might seek to deflect this by suggesting that we could non-question-beggingly identify some favoured class of heuristic co-reasonings which are guaranteed to be infallible and the deliverances of which could be regarded as constitutive. Admittedly the prospects for this do not look good, but reasons have not yet been given for ruling it out decisively.

The second objection is that co-reasoning requires prior grasp of mental concepts. The exact form of this worry is worth pausing over. Perhaps the thought is that co-reasoning is something consciously and deliberately undertaken in the light of information already possessed about the subject. So to set out to co-reason with S, who believes that p, one must already be able to judge that S believes that p. Or perhaps the thought is rather that what one does when setting out to co-reason with S, who believes that p, is to put oneself in a state of samethinking with S, a state describable as 'imagining believing that p' or 'pretending to believe that p'. If either of these thoughts is true, then Goldman is surely right that the idea of co-reasoning with someone who believes that p does not seem at all a suitable element to figure in a quasi-analysis of what it is to believe that p, since mention of 'believing that p' occurs within the specification of an element of the proposed analysis.

There are, however, moves one might make to deflect this circularity objection, on either way of spelling it out. One is to deny that the simulation heuristic requires deliberate co-reasoning. Perhaps non-deliberate co-reasoning, which is triggered by appropriate awareness of the other but is not preceded by any explicit judgement about the other's mental state, is our route to psychological judgements of others (Gordon 1995). Another move is to deny that the samethinking which starts the process is rightly characterised as 'imagining believing that p' or 'pretending to believe that p'; perhaps it is better characterised just as 'imagining that p' (Fuller 1995; Davies 1994).

A third response (more powerful than these two and available even if they do not work) would point out that the circularity objection, in either version, is mistargeted. The fact that it is so becomes apparent once we pay attention to the difference between general and specific psychological notions and to the fact that the proposal concerns specific notions. The objection focuses on the input of heuristic co-reasoning, what is required to initiate it, whereas it is the output of the co-reasoning which is supposed in (1) to be important in defining the truth conditions of psychological judgements. So we may agree with the objector that a co-reasoning process which starts from taking the other to believe that p, requires the co-reasoner to possess the concept of belief that p and so cannot be used to illuminate it. But, then, that was not the form of the proposal. The output of a co-reasoning which starts from the other believing that p will not be the judgement that the other believes that p, but some other psychological claim about her, for example that she believes that q or intends that r. And conversely the judgement that the other believes that p will be the output of a co-reasoning which starts from recognition of some yet other specific psychological states. Once this is recognised, the circularity objection does not bite so immediately. All we seem to have discovered is a kind of interdependence of psychological notions: the truth of one sort of judgement ('she intends that r') is bound up with its being delivered by a process of co-reasoning which requires grasp of some other sort of psychological notion ('she believes that p') to initiate it. Is this so obviously unacceptable?

Clearly there is a morass of issues here which could be investigated further. It may be that we cannot get as quick a knock-down of proposal (1) as initially seemed possible. Some fancy footwork, in the form of attention to the distinction between general and specific psychological notions, more detailed focus on better and worse varieties of co-reasoning and so forth, may enable us to spin out the debate for a while. But nevertheless I share Goldman's scepticism as to whether anything enlightening would be found in the end. The proposal (1) does not seem to have any strong intuitive arguments in its favour which make it worthwhile to tread out into the morass. Do we really want an account which has the existence of mental states in one person as constitutively bound up with the occurrence of actual or possible judgements about those states by others? All in all it seems more promising to look elsewhere for possible links between simulationist ideas and psychological concepts.

4. INDEXICAL PREDICATION AND LAGADONIAN KINDS

Philosophers have focused much attention on referring indexicals. But there is also another class of indexicals which deserves attention, namely predicative indexicals. (See Essay 9.) Consider, for example:

(2) My curtains are this colour

said when indicating an item which is red. This utterance, together with the specimen, provides a vehicle of communication by which the speaker can convey that his curtains are red. The remark has a different logical and epistemological role from the superficially similar

(3) My curtains are the same colour as this object

said while indicating a red object. This latter involves the familiar referring indexical; the former does not.

Another example would be

(4) She did this

followed by the speaker doing something distinctive, for example, stand-ing on one leg, slamming a door loudly, singing the tune of "Yankee Doodle" and so on. The 'this' here latches on to a kind of action, that is, the semantic correlate of a verb (together with its relevant object phrases, adverbs, etc.). Hence the whole, consisting of the utterance and the fol-lowing performance, makes the claim that she stood on one leg, slammed a door loudly, sang the tune of "Yankee Doodle" and so on.

A further case would be

(5) She sang thus

followed by the speaker playing "Yankee Doodle" on the violin. What this whole performance conveys is that the other sang that tune. Here the speaker need not herself sing in order to convey what the other did. That the other sang is conveyed by the word 'sang'. It is only a further feature of the singing, viz., the tune presented, which is conveyed by a feature of the violin playing.

What makes possible these ways of representing another's state or ac-tion is the possibility of what we might call 'samedoing', that is, one person's state or action resembling that of another, to a greater or lesser extent. If the person who utters (4) or (5) complements the words by a performance which actually is a samedoing with the person she speaks of (in the relevaant respect), then the whole is a correct representation of the other's state or action. If she complements the words with a performance but fails thereby to samedo with the one she speaks of, then what she says is false. What counts as 'samedoing', that is, how much resemblance there needs to be and in what respects, will vary from case to case, as deter-mined by the nature of the indexical, the interests of speaker and hearer, the knowledge each already has and so forth. In summary, the vehicle of a correct indexical representation of another person will be a samedoing with that person.

Let me stress here that to say this is not to say that one who employs such methods of representation needs to exercise the concept of samedoing. The person producing such an indexical representation needs only to be aware that what she says or does is a suitable vehicle for the content she wants to convey. Those who reflect theoretically on the representation (who may, of course, include the one who makes it) will see that if it is a vehicle of a correct representation then it will be a samedoing. But it does not follow from this that the one who produces it produces it as or under the description 'a samedoing'. So, for example, a person may accidentally or unconsciously make a distinctive gesture and may catch sight of herself in a mirror without recognising herself. In such a situation she can point to the person in the mirror (who is in fact herself) and use what she does to describe another by saying 'He did that'.

The predicate concepts exercised in the thoughts expressed in (2), (4) and (5) are indexical. One aspect of this is that the colour or action or manner of acting is presented to the person thinking the thought as 'this colour', 'doing this' or 'singing thus'. Another aspect of the indexicality is that if the whole thought is to be well-formed and have clear truth conditions there needs to be a colour, action or manner of acting in the context to be latched on to. We need not enter into controversies about 'de re' thought and about exactly what kind of deficiency in thinking exists if there is no colour, action or manner to be latched on to (whether, for example, the thought is then incomplete, or whether it is complete but lacks a truth value). What is clear is that the absence of the right sort of thing is a serious deficiency and that a properly functioning indexical predicate concept requires the presence of a specimen of the property which is indexically ascribed. (I speak of 'properties' here and in what follows as a shorthand for any kind of item which is the semantic correlate of a predicate or predicate component.)

Many of the predicate concepts philosophers have studied are (plausibly) entirely non-indexical. The mark of these concepts is that grasp of one of them is an intrinsic state of the thinker which he or she brings to a situation and which enables him or her to entertain thoughts there about the property the concept specifies, whether or not the situation itself contains a specimen of the property. 'Square' is such a concept. My grasp on it enables me to think while looking at some design, 'That patch would be better square', when neither the patch nor anything else in my environment is square. I can also exercise my grasp in working out what would need to be done to make the patch square, in comparing that option for improvement with others and so on.

Exercising such a non-indexical concept is being in a distinctive psychological state which is the vehicle of the relevant content. Being in this state involves only non-relational properties of the person, and these non-relational properties fix the truth conditions of a judgement in which the concept is exercised. A candidate for one such non-relational property is being primed for a distinctive recognitional response. For example, if I am exercising my concept 'square' in having the thought 'That patch would be better square', then I am disposed to think 'Right – like that!' if the patch becomes square but not if it becomes oblong or round. Another plausible non-relational property which contributes to fixing content is being disposed to make certain inferences, theoretical or practical, for example to think, 'If the patch is to become square then the left side needs to be longer'. The difference between thinking the patch would be better square and thinking that it would better round is (plausibly) a difference in how I am disposed, at the time of thinking, in these recognitional and inferential ways.

In talking above of entirely non-indexical concepts I mentioned two features of them: that they can be exercised in the absence of a specimen in the immediate context of thought, and that grasp of them is an intrinsic state of a thinker. These two properties may come apart. A consequence of this is that there are two ways in which a concept may fail to be entirely non-indexical. Memory enables us to recall particular episodes in our lives and also to build up a sense of the spatio-temporal shape of the world around us. So confrontation with a property on an occasion or number of occasions may, given memory, establish the possibility of thinking of it again later as, for example, 'that colour (viz., the one I saw in the fabric sample last week)' or as 'that stuff (viz., the one I saw specimens of in the desert)'. This kind of concept of a property is something we can bring to a new encounter where a specimen of the property is not present in the immediate environment. So it is unlike the concepts 'this colour' or 'sings thus' which we considered earlier. Yet grasp of such a concept is not an intrinsic property of the thinker. Rather, which concept the person is exercising, that is, the truth conditions of judgements exercising it, depend upon what colour or stuff it was which the person previously encountered.

So we may distinguish (at least) three kinds of concepts. Let us label them as follows: (i) 'narrowly indexical concepts' – these are the sort expressed by 'this colour', 'did thus', etc.; (ii) 'broadly indexical concepts' – these are expressed by 'that colour I saw last week' and related expressions; and (iii) 'non-indexical concepts' – these are ones like 'square', 'hard' etc. Natural-kind terms fit interestingly into this classification as an important sub-variety of broadly indexical concept. If the Putnam-Kripke account of them is on the right lines, then grasp of a natural-kind concept involves identifying and remembering some specimens as paradigms, and using these specimens, together with the notion of match in internal constitution, to fix the extension of the term. Burge points out the mistake of taking natural-kind terms to be narrowly indexical (Burge 1982). But the correct observations he makes should not blind us to the fact that such terms are nevertheless indexical in the broad sense – because the specimens used as standard setters, for example those encountered and baptised when the term is initially introduced, contribute to fixing extension.

We can and do have non-indexical, broadly indexical and narrowly indexical concepts of the very same item. So I may think of one person on various occasions as 'Arabella', or as 'that woman I met last week' or as 'this woman'. Indeed, our ability to make identity judgements linking such concepts ('This is Arabella!', 'This is the woman I met last week', etc.) is essential to our ability to act at the right place and time and with respect to the right particulars, since it is narrowly indexical ways of thinking of the world which we exercise in perception and which we need for action. The same is true of our cognitive and practical relations with kinds, properties, manners, and so on. For example, I may think of a shape both as 'square', as 'that shape I saw yesterday' and as 'this shape'. Often my ability to see that being square is being this shape, or that this shape is that shape, is what enables further appropriate thought and action.

The Putnam-Kripke line of thought about natural kinds has familiarised us with the idea that our central and usual way of thinking about natural kinds, the one manifested by most people's use of natural-kind terms like 'tiger', 'water' and so on, is by means of broadly indexical concepts. Of course this does not prevent the acquisition of further knowledge about such kinds. The ambition of scientific understanding is precisely to fill out place holders like 'same structure as that stuff' with some specification of the structure in question, given either in terms of other natural-kind concepts or, even better, in terms of non-indexical concepts. But this kind of understanding will not replace the broadly indexical concept as long as we need our term to remain anchored to the paradigm specimens. One reason for keeping it so anchored is that scientific speculations about structure may still be tentative. Another is that, even if experts are rightly convinced that they have correct non-indexical grasp of the nature of the kind in question, the theory they know cannot provide a way of thinking of the stuff in question for the non-expert. So the term in common use has to continue to be understood in the broadly indexical way.

We are now in a position to pose our crucial question. What of narrowly indexical concepts? Are there, in some roughly analogous way, kinds which we centrally and usually engage with by means of narrowly indexical concepts? There are certainly cases where a person's only cognitive engagement with a kind is in fact by use of a narrowly indexical concept. For example, I may only once encounter some complex shape, think of it indexically ('That's a funny shape!') and then never have occasion to think of it again. But our question is not about these uninteresting cases. It is rather about whether there are kinds which are encountered repeatedly but for which, nevertheless, the usual and useful representation is narrowly indexical, and is so for non-trivial reasons. These reasons might have to do with our cognitive capacities, with the sort of interest we have in the kinds in question or with the nature of the kind itself.

Finely discriminated shades of colour present a plausible example, at least for some of us. When subtly different shades of pinkish-red are presented, exhibiting minute variations in hue, saturation or brightness, we are able to discriminate among them, and also to make judgments about which best complements another colour and so forth. We may, while looking at these shades, coin labels for them, such as 'dusty rose', 'sunset blush' or the like. But no amount of practice with these labels or attempted analysis of the colours will enable us to hold the differences steady when the specimens are not there. Lacking a specimen of dusty rose we cannot tell of a newly encountered object whether it is of that exact shade or not, nor can we tell whether dusty rose paint is just the right colour to complement these green curtains. So no entirely non-indexical concept of the shade can be acquired. We may be able to develop a broadly indexical concept of it, by remembering particular encounters with it. We may also be able to build up some knowledge about it through experiment and memory. But it seems probable that there will continue to be many occasions on which a broadly indexical concept together with such acquired knowledge will not serve. If I want to judge match or aesthetic effect in a new case, memory of these old occasions is unlikely to supply what I need. If it does not, then to make the new judgement I require a specimen to look at so that I can revive my narrowly indexical way of engaging with the kind. In summary, a specimen actually to hand is an essential tool for doing central sorts of thinking about finely discriminated shades of colour.

Let us coin the term 'Lagadonian kind' for such kinds, that is, ones which, for non-trivial reasons, we centrally and usually think of by using narrowly indexical concepts.

A speculation I shall not follow up here is that it may be these kinds which philosophers have in mind, in some cases at least, when they talk about 'non-conceptual content'. If one's paradigm of a concept is an entirely non-indexical concept, then the idea that at least part of the content of a thought is carried in a Lagadonian way, for instance by sensory awareness of a colour, gives some motivation for labelling that content 'non-conceptual'.

Now we turn again to psychological concepts and to the question of what internal complexity may be detectable in judgements about the psychological states of others. The idea to be pursued is that some psychological kinds may be Lagadonian.

The possibility of samethinking, together with that of indexical predication, provides for ways of representing thoughts analogous to the ways of representing actions which we considered with (4) and (5) above. If we do centrally use such indexical vehicles of representation for psychological states, it would provide a linkage of the simulationist idea of samethinking to psychological concepts. This proposal, however, is entirely different from the proposal for linking simulation and psychological concepts discussed in Section 3. In particular, on the idea mooted here, the judger does not have to possess the concept of samethinking. She does not think, 'Now let me samethink with B'. Rather (as we saw in connection with samedoing in the last section), it is a corollary of the correctness of the judgement that A in fact samethinks with B. And on reflection A may realise this. But for the judgement to occur, neither samethinking nor thinking about samethinking is required, All that is needed for the judgement is that A in fact succeed in specifying the property which she aims to attribute to B through some thinking of her own. So, to repeat, the idea is not that the concept of samethinking figures in some quasi-analysis of the psychological. Rather it is that one who thinks about another's thoughts thereby does some first-order thinking of her own which, if the representation of the other is true, will in fact be samethinking. Let us spell out the proposal in more detail.

Suppose that B believes that the sun is hot and that A correctly judges that this is so by deploying the resources of indexical predication. Two possibilities present themselves as to how this could be done. The first is that A has a thought of the structure

(6) B is thus { ... }

where in the gap she herself judges that the sun is hot. On this story A exercises (at least) four concepts, viz., of B, of being or doing in the most general sense, of the sun and of being hot. The last two are exercised in the course of her having an occurrent belief that the sun is hot. In addition, crucially, there is an indexical conceptual element linking the thought of B's state with this occurrent belief that the sun is hot. In consequence, A's attitude of believing, taken towards the content that the sun is hot, is also a significant component of the whole. The whole is therefore analogous to the complex sketched in (4) with the singing of "Yankee Doodle". There the fact that the other sang, as well as what she sang, were all indexically conveyed by the subsequent performance. So in (6), in addition to the concepts of B, doing, the sun and heat, A is also exercising a narrowly indexical concept of believing that the sun is hot. The vehicle of the exercise of this concept is the exercise of other concepts (of the sun and being hot) in the belief that the sun is hot. The whole complex specified in (6) thus attributes to B belief that the sun is hot. (A fuller account would need to pay some attention to the difference between occurrent and dispositional belief. But I shall omit this complication here.) And since B actually does believe that the sun is hot then, as it turns out, A is samethinking with B.

The second possibility is that A has a thought of the structure:

(7) B believes thus { ... }

where in the gap she herself entertains the idea that the sun is hot. Here again A exercises (at least) four concepts, viz., of B, of belief, of the sun and of being hot. The last two are exercised (let us say) in imagining that the sun is hot. In addition there is an indexical element linking the thought of B's belief with the imagining of the sun being hot. So far all is as in (6). But the difference is that the nature of the indexical element (as defined by the context, the interests of the thinker, etc.) attaches it only to the content of what is imagined, and hence the attitude of imagining is not a significant component of the whole. So here A's imagining the sun's being hot fills the role which A's playing the violin played in the case of (5). There the speaker did not herself need to sing in order to convey that the other sang, and the violin playing conveyed only which tune was sung. Similarly with (7), she does not herself believe that the sun is hot and the imagining conveys only the content of B's belief. In upshot, then, the thought specified in (7) is one in which A exercises a narrowly indexical concept of the content that the sun is hot and the whole attributes to B belief that the sun is hot. And again, since B does have that belief, A samethinks with B, but in a more limited way than in the situation described in (6).

Suppose that the considerations advanced so far have persuaded us that such narrowly indexical representations of others' thoughts are possible; the pressing question is whether psychological kinds are Lagadonian kinds. Do we usually think of psychological kinds by using narrowly indexical concepts of them, and for principled reasons? This divides into two questions, namely whether we think of general psychological kinds this way and whether we think of contents this way. We shall postpone the discussion of general kinds until Section 7 and concentrate for now on content.

Arguably we do have both non-indexical and broadly indexical concepts of contents. For example, 'Pythagoras' Theorem' is a label for a content, and someone could be said to understand it and so to have a concept of Pythagoras' Theorem in virtue of grasping only that Pythagoras was a Greek mathematician and that some mathematical result is particularly associated with him. (This is the level of understanding which many of us have of 'Goldbach's Theorem' or 'Church's Thesis'.) Also, one may think of a content merely as 'that thought (i.e., the confusing one which I only half grasped in the discussion last night)'.

It seems clear, however, that these are not our usual ways of representing contents, nor are they ways which are helpful in answering most of the kinds of questions which interest us about thoughts in their content aspect. For example, when I know that someone else has a belief, one central matter of interest is whether it is true or not. But if all I know about her belief is that it is a belief in Pythagoras' Theorem, understood in the non-indexical way outlined above, then it is not immediately clear what to investigate if I am to find out whether it is true. What would be most useful in guiding such investigation is a representation of the world as it would need to be to make the belief true. To have this, what I need is a representation of the form 'That person takes the world to be a certain way, viz. {...}', where in the gap I myself think about the world. What we have arrived at here is a thought of the form suggested in (7), namely one where I exercise a concept of the other person and of belief and then myself think about the world.

Another question which interests us about others' thoughts is what further thoughts or actions they might lead to. If the simulation theory is right in proposing that a standard resource in answering such questions is co-reasoning, then what I need in order to pursue the question by this method is a representation in virtue of which I samethink with the person I seek to predict. So, again, it is thoughts of the form of (7) which we find we must call on.

The simulationist view about prediction is sometimes presented as if there were a sequence of, first, judging that another is in a certain psychological state and, second, getting oneself into a state of samethinking so as to initiate some co-reasoning. On this story, judging about another's psychological state is one thing, samethinking with it another. A parallel which may lead to this view of the structure of the case is that with the situation on which we first represent the shape and circumstances of an aircraft non-indexically and then build a model to test the design in a wind tunnel.

But this may be a misleading analogy. What is the non-indexical way of thinking about others' thoughts which, on this story, we first call upon in the psychological case? The central form of verbal expression of thought about another's thought ought to provide a clue to this, if there is such a thing. That form is, of course, the familiar 'A thinks that . . .' with a sentential complement. But it is clear that I do not understand such a sentence unless I understand the words in the that-clause. By far the simplest way of conceiving of this understanding is as requiring simply that I exercise the concepts which those words express. That is, I think about the world in the same way that I would if I heard those words in a non-oblique context, for example as the antecedent of a conditional. If this is so, then the psychological configuration expressed in the usual verbal report of a judgement about another's thought is precisely that described in (7) and not one which calls upon a non-indexical concept of content. And, conversely, if the proposal of this section is correct and the standard way of representing others' thoughts, at least in their content aspect, is by narrowly indexical concepts, then the natural verbal form for expressing such representations would be exactly what we find, namely utterances such as 'A thinks the sun is hot'.

There is a long philosophical tradition of theorising about the role of words in oblique contexts on the supposition that they do not function in their normal way but acquire some other role. Problems about non-extensionality, in the context of the demand for systematic semantic theories, motivate these proposals. The idea of indexical predication provides an alternative way of looking at these issues (one which endorses the recently mooted requirement for 'semantic innocence') and offers a simpler way of solving the problems. Clearly there are affinities between the suggestion floated here and Davidson's proposals about the logical form of indirect speech. But there are also important differences, since Davidson's proposals involve indexical reference whereas this one calls on indexical predication. We shall not explore these questions further here. (See Essay 10.)

The approach outlined does not require the idea that psychological states are the object of inner ostension or inner-directed quasi-perceptual attention. The approach does not rule out the existence of such awareness, but nothing said demands it. It might seem to do so if we assume all indexicality to be demonstrative and so to require the perceptual or quasi-perceptual awareness which demonstration presupposes. But this assumption would be false. 'Indexical', for all its etymological roots in ideas of index fingers and pointing, is now used philosophically merely to signal a particular kind of dependence of content on context. So in addition to demonstrative indexicals there are also what Kaplan calls 'pure indexicals' (Kaplan 1989: 523). For example, the rule for the use of the concept 'here' fixes that any token refers to the place where it is uttered. This rule operates independently of the thinker's perceptual state or capacities. A thinker can think of a place as 'here' even when blind and anaesthetised. Similarly, a token of 'I' refers to whoever produces it, whether or not the person is perceptually aware of him or herself. These rules for fixing reference are adequate by themselves and do not need supplementation by a demonstration, because a function from token to place of production or to producer delivers a unique result.

Similar non-demonstrative possibilities exist with predicate indexicals. In a well-formed thought of the overall shape of (7) there will be only one complex of concepts exercised in the appropriate relation to the concepts of B and of belief. The content of A's whole judgement (i.e., what thought A attributes to B) is then fixed by this complex without any requirement that A inwardly pick it out. There is no identificatory role which such picking out is needed to perform. To make a judgement just is to exercise concepts in the right configuration. A thinker does not, in order to think, need first to exercise concepts and then also, in order to get the concepts stuck together in the right way, to be aware of and form intentions about her performances. A basic unity and well-structuredness in our thoughts cannot be something which we as thinkers make happen by further cognitive efforts, on pain of infinite regress. Rather it is something which we as thinkers have to presuppose.

The upshot of these reflections is that there is a strong case for taking 'having the content that the sun is hot', 'having the content that the weather will improve' and the like to be Lagadonian kinds. We think of them standardly by employing (pure) narrowly indexical concepts – as I have just enabled you to do by providing the sentences 'the sun is hot' and 'the weather will improve', in understanding which you have brought into being in your own mind the crucial specimens, by calling on which you are, at this very minute, being enabled to think of the kinds in question.

How do we represent general propositional attitudes to ourselves? Do simulationist themes, in the form of indexical concepts and Lagadonian kinds, have a role to play here?

The possibility of the configuration described in (6) suggests that it is indeed possible to have indexical concepts of attitudes and to attribute attitudes in narrowly indexical predications. But the configuration (6) can only exist when A herself shares B's belief. So even if such a way of representing another is occasionally used, it does not seem likely that this way of thinking of others' mental states is standard or that reflection on it could throw light on our ordinary concepts of attitudes such as expectation, intention and the like. Surely, it seems, we shall have to look elsewhere to explain our grasp on them. This is implicitly what was being assumed in the discussion of the last section, where it was taken for granted that with (7) the representation of belief is non-indexical.

But could this assumption be a mistake? If it is, we could make the bold proposal that samethinking, of roughly the kind sketched in (6), is the usual vehicle of our correct representation of attitudes – and hence that the contrast between (6) and (7) which we assumed earlier may be illusory. This is one way of reading Gordon's suggestion that

(8) Smith believes that Dewey won the election

be seen as saying the same thing as

(9) Let's do a Smith simulation. Ready? *Dewey won the election.* (Gordon 1995: 68)

If we remove the perhaps misleading 'Let's do . . .' format (as Gordon's own later discussions suggest [Gordon 1995b, 1996]) this could be expressed:

(10) Smith is thus: *Dewey won the election.*

Here both the content and the attitude attributed to Smith are fixed by the nature of the performance staged after the 'thus' and we have arrived at something very close to (6).

The striking difference from (6) is that there we envisaged a real belief in the attributor to supply the content of the indexical predicate, whereas what is envisaged in (10) is that a simulated belief might do the job of supplying the content. Is this a feasible extension of the range of means by which indexical predication can be effected? Can models and simulacra play the role of supplying indexical predicate content? Let us for the sake of the argument allow that they can. (Interesting questions then arise about exactly how they function and what limitations there might be on their use. But we shall set these on one side.) The trouble is that even so the proposal in the particular case of psychological concepts is not a plausible one. Gordon himself supplies reasons for thinking this. He develops his view that simulation has an important role vis à vis psychological concepts partly through telling a developmental story. But the way the story ends suggests strongly that the fully fledged adult grasp of psychological concepts does not have the shape sketched.

The story on development runs (roughly) as follows. Infants have a tendency to 'catch' the psychological states of those who care for them, being frightened if they are frightened, attending to what they attend to and so on. Later these 'caught' states become segregated from the main control routes of the mind and so become mere models or simulations of the states they are caught from. The child also learns to relate these simulated states to the person from whom they are caught, by using co-reasonings based on these states to predict the other's behaviour. But none of this requires language, and hence the child does not yet have a grasp of psychological concepts, in the sense of 'concept' we are interested in.

Let us now add in the idea of an ascent routine, that is, a procedure in which a person, as a result of training, is able to produce a verbal formula such as 'I believe that p' as a spontaneous manifestation of the state of believing that p. A crucial element of such an utterance is that in it the word 'believe' figures merely as an expression of belief; it is not produced as a result of introspecting and labelling the state. Now let us suppose that the child is able to operate the ascent routine not only for voicing her own beliefs but also within the context of a simulation, and let us suppose further that she can be trained to substitute the name of the one simulated for 'I' in the resulting utterance so that what emerges is 'A believes that p'. The upshot of the joint exercise of all these various abilities ('catching' others' states, co-reasoning with them, using ascent routines, substituting a name for 'I') is the appearance of (what looks like) the ability to ascribe beliefs to others. But in the narrative we have not mentioned possession of a theory of the mind. Instead the essential elements invoked are these abilities, for example to simulate and to express via an ascent routine.

But is the child, at this point, really ascribing beliefs to others? Does she possess the concept of belief? Surely not. As Gordon himself stresses, so far we have only 'uncomprehending ascription'. The child does not yet appreciate such things as the facts that beliefs may be true or false, justified or unjustified, that beliefs are acquired by perception and retained in memory, that beliefs guide actions and so forth. Hence she lacks most of the normal ability to deploy the word 'belief'. So acquiring what we demand for full grasp on the concept must require further training in what licenses one to say 'A believes that p', in what inferences one can draw from it and so forth.

Let us imagine this further training undertaken. The crucial question is whether, at the end of it, the cognitive state now expressed in utterances such as 'A believes that p' still has the structure described in (10). The problem for the bold proposal that belief is a Lagadonian kind is that it is extremely plausible that gaining the requisite flexibility and sophistication in the use of 'belief' precisely enables comprehending utterance of the word 'belief' to float free of being expressive of, and so dependent on, the occurrence of some (simulated) belief in the speaker. To take just one case, consider general principles like 'Perception tends to give rise to belief' grasp on which is, arguably, the kind of thing which is required for understanding of the concept of belief. It is difficult to see how the use of 'belief' here could be given a narrowly indexical account.

The conclusion is that Gordon's story is, at best, a sketch of a possible developmental route to acquisition of general psychological concepts and is not an account which tells us much directly about what is constitutive of an adult grasp of the concepts of belief or other propositional attitudes. As to what that consists in we still do not have a full account.

A proposal of a different shape, with some affinities to the Lagadonian one, has been offered by Peacocke. His suggestion is that the concept of belief is somewhat like a natural-kind concept. To grasp such a concept it is sufficient to be able to identify the paradigm cases and to grasp that anything which falls under the concept does so in virtue of resembling the paradigms. Peacocke's suggestion about belief is that for each person his or her own beliefs provide the anchoring and standard-setting specimens, and another's having a belief is a matter of her being similar to the judger in relevant respects. Here is his account:

A relational concept R is the concept of belief only if
(F)   the thinker finds the first-person content that he stands in R to p primitively compelling whenever he has the conscious belief that p, and he finds it compelling because he has that conscious belief; and
(T)   in judging a thought of the third person form aRp, the thinker thereby incurs a commitment to a's being in a state that has the same content-dependent role in making a intelligible as the role of his own state of standing in R to p in making him intelligible, were he to be in that state. (1992: 163–164)

This account does not claim that belief is an indexical kind, in exactly the sense set out in Section 4, but it does present the concept of belief as a 'first-person concept', in the sense that what one ascribes to the other, in ascribing a belief, is fixed by how one thinks oneself (1992: 164–165). So the best route to finding out what one is committed to in judging 'A believes that p' is to do some believing (or simulated believing) oneself and investigate its upshots.

Peacocke recommends his account by pointing out that having a given belief is an extremely complex matter (1992: 149). He suggests that it is possible to give a theoretical account of what it is to believe, for example, that the Lincoln Plaza is square. He himself attempts to do this by sketching accounts of what it is to possess concepts like 'square' or 'Lincoln Plaza' in terms of recognitional and inferential dispositions. The account of judging 'the Lincoln Plaza is square' which results from putting these together is already complicated. And things get rapidly much worse with thoughts in which larger numbers of concepts are deployed in an intricate syntactic structure. There is therefore, Peacocke suggests, something implausible in the idea that when we think of others' thoughts we do so by calling on a version, whether explicit or tacit, of this theory.

Any simulationist will have a great deal of sympathy with this. But Peacocke's arguments in favour of the two-clause theory centre on the intricacies of content and not on anything specific to belief, as opposed to, say, desire, intention, perception, memory or any other attitude. The shape of account he offers, which presumably, if correct, ought to be mirrored for the other attitudes, tells us nothing about what is involved in understanding the differences between the attitudes. Indeed, a thinker who has only the competences specified in Peacocke's two clauses is curiously like Gordon's uncomprehending ascriber. She is someone who can say 'I believe that p' when she believes that p, and who knows that there is some role which this state plays in her and may play in others, but need know nothing else.

To be fair, Peacocke does not present his conditions as being sufficient for possession of the concept of belief, but only as being necessary, which suggests that he recognises there is more to be said. But when we see that the supposed reasons for favouring a two-clause account of belief have to do with content and not with the attitude itself, and when moreover we have the distinction between general and specific psychological concepts in focus, the conclusion is not that we need Peacocke's account of belief but rather that we need an account of content which is sensitive to the fact that we lack a theoretical grasp of its intricacies. The Lagadonian account of content provides exactly this. With it in hand, a two-clause account of the general notion of belief and the idea that it has some special first-person character are both unmotivated.

7. CODA – THE NATURE OF THE MENTAL

One reason we are interested in concepts of the mental, and what it is to possess them, is that we think that by clarifying them we may get light on the nature of the mental itself. Perhaps we shall come to see clearly that psychological properties can be functionally defined, and consequently we shall discover that what is involved in being a person, having mental states, is just being a creature with a certain intricate causal organisation. And, if so, it may then turn out that the brain sciences reveal to us what the occurrence of mental states actually consists in at the physical level. Or, alternatively, unpacking the concepts of the mental will perhaps reveal that the existence of minds and mental states requires more than natural science can offer, for example non-physical qualia. Or perhaps neither of these will turn out to be correct and some other view about what is involved in the existence of minds will be vindicated.

It may seem that, as far as these larger questions are concerned, we have made no progress. The proposals discussed in Section 6 both turned out unsatisfactory. So as far as understanding the nature of general psychological concepts is concerned, we are still where we were before. There are, of course, plenty of suggestive and plausible ideas in the existing literature. Some concern the different causal-explanatory roles of different kinds of state and the typical patterns of temporal sequence or co-existence they exhibit. Others bring out the contrasted semantic and normative features of different states, such as their different directions of fit. Yet others concentrate on different kinds of justificatory roles vis à vis other states or actions. Further views might stress differences in epistemic character, for example, whether or not some sort of first-person privilege in ascription seems to exist and typical routes of ascription to others. But it remains obscure and contested how these various strands (and others too) can be revealingly organised, and which of them, and how, should be incorporated in an account of the concepts. Relatedly, it remains obscure and contested what is involved in the concept of being a person, a creature to whom psychological predicates apply. We are, it seems, no further forward in seeing how to put the jigsaw together.

Indeed, as far as these larger questions are concerned, one may argue that the kind of approach to psychological concepts pursued in this essay could not possibly lead to progress. Even if the proposal of Section 6 had worked, it would not have moved us forward, and the plausibility of a Lagadonian account of content concepts could not provide any clues either. This negative conclusion is suggested by the fact that the idea we have been pursuing is that our concepts of the psychological are indexical and that the vehicles of our (correct) psychological judgements are samethinkings. Surely, one could argue, a central point about an indexical concept of something is exactly that it does not reveal the nature of the thing which it presents to us under its distinctive indexical mode. An indexical predicate concept of something is all very useful in its way, one may say, but it needs replacement or supplementation by a non-indexical conception if we are to suppose that our thoughts succeed in representing the real natures of the things in question.

All I want to remark here is that this move may not be valid. Certainly for many indexical concepts (for example, those of complicated shapes) we want and can build a non-indexical replacement. And for others where we cannot acquire such a replacement (finely discriminated shades of colour) this is, plausibly, due to limitations in our memories or cognitive functioning. In both these cases it seems likely that there are non-indexical concepts of the kinds in question and that we would make cognitive progress by acquiring them. But it does not follow that it makes sense, for every indexical predicate concept, to suppose that it could be replaced by a non-indexical one. For all we have seen, there are kinds which are essentially and not merely accidentally Lagadonian. Hence there may be kinds the nature of which is revealed to us precisely when we reflect on the Lagadonian nature of our representations of them and why it is essential.

To say that a kind is essentially Lagadonian is to say that relating to it by means of a narrowly indexical concept is the right way of relating to it, not just in the sense that it is most convenient (which might well be uncontroversial) but in the sense that it is the one which is most appropriate to its nature. To say that a kind is essentially Lagadonian is not an obscurantist claim, denying the possibility of accumulating information about the non-indexical features of the kind. As with any indexical kind, there is nothing to prevent us observing these and seeking to systematise them. But if a kind is essentially Lagadonian, then the hope of coming to an end of accumulating such information, of acquiring a complete non-indexical account of the kind, is a mistake. To think that one can relate to such a kind by subsuming it solely under non-indexical concepts is to think that one can put a closure on what needs to remain open. If we accepted the idea that content kinds are essentially Lagadonian, that would then have implications for the concepts of propositional attitudes, since those concepts would have to be shaped in such a way that they respect the essentially Lagadonian nature of their completing contents. And that in turn would have implications for the concept of persons, the subjects of the psychological states.

This may all look rather wild. And clearly nothing said here seriously substantiates the suggestion that any psychological kinds are essentially Lagadonian. But I hope that it is at least plausible that the suggestion connects with familiar and important themes in the philosophy of mind. One is the relation of prediction and decision as concerns determination of our own future thoughts and actions. The idea that prediction cannot replace decision is a close relative of the idea that thought contents are essentially Lagadonian kinds. Related themes are the contrast of observer and participant status, or of reactive and objective attitudes. Finally, but most obscurely and tantalisingly, we have the persistent but difficult to clarify idea that persons are essentially subjects and cannot be fully captured as objects. It seems possible that the idea of an essentially Lagadonian kind might provide a tool for thinking about these issues, whatever view of them we finally adopt.

Part Four

*Thinking of Minds and Interacting
with Persons*

12

What Are Psychological Concepts For?

1. INTRODUCTION

We may distinguish at least two forms of scepticism about the mind and psychological notions. The most familiar is other-minds scepticism. It presents us with a conception of the contrast between inner and outer, and a related conviction of the necessary privacy of the mental, which we find immensely gripping but which threatens to make facts about others' thoughts epistemically inaccessible to us. The outlook to which we are tempted is one on which we allow that other minds exist but suppose that they must remain unknown. Wittgenstein has a good deal to say about this form of scepticism, but these issues are not our concern here. Rather, what I hope to do is bring some Wittgensteinian techniques and ideas to bear on another form of sceptical thought about the mental, or at least one version of it. This form of sceptical thought is more akin to moral scepticism than the familiar other-minds scepticism. Its target is the very idea that there are or could be facts which are reported by sentences using psychological vocabulary.

Such 'eliminativism' comes in a variety of forms, some of which concentrate on supposed a posteriori difficulties for the existence of the mental and others of which invoke more a priori arguments.[1] The

1. The term 'eliminative materialism', later shortened to 'eliminativism', was introduced by Churchland in his provocative writings, and he is one of the prime exponents of an empirically based eliminativism (Churchland 1981). Discussion particularly relevant to his approach can be found in the collection edited by Greenwood (1991) and in a special issue of the journal *Mind and Language*, 1993. There is a recent lively discussion by Stich (1996), which also provides an introduction to the literature. Some think that Wittgenstein himself should be lined up with the eliminativists, although the eliminativism he is taken to expound is based on a priori considerations (Kripke 1982; Wright 1986, 1997). The assumption of this

225

particular line of thought which is our topic calls on both a priori and a posteriori considerations and starts from the assumption of a link between thought and rationality.[2] What it pursues are considerations in favour of eliminativism which are likely to seem compelling when we locate the idea of a link between thought and rationality in an intellectual context where we take it for granted that our psychological talk has a similar role in our lives to that of theoretical talk in natural science. Section 2 considers how this idea, if combined with a bold and simple definition of rationality, leads very directly to eliminativism. Section 3 explores ways of evading the conclusion by adjusting our account of rationality. Section 4 argues that even if this succeeds we shall find other considerations, even more deeply rooted in the context, which combine to make eliminativism attractive.

Section 5 will sketch an alternative conception of rationality of significantly different shape from that considered earlier. Section 6 examines the links of this concept to forms of interaction with others and occasions for the deployment of psychological concepts which were backgrounded or overlooked in the account given earlier. We might thus regard Section 6 as assembling reminders about actual occasions of use of psychological concepts, that is, about what some might call the 'nature of the language games' in which they are employed. Finally, Section 7 will return to the issue of eliminativism and make some suggestions on how the alternative conception of rationality may suggest ways of avoiding at least some eliminativist pressures.

It should be emphasized that this essay traces only one strand of reflection on the relation of psychological and physical. A fuller account would weave in the ideas suggested here with other lines of thought concerning, for example, the supervenience of psychological on physical or the issue of the possibly different explananda of physical and psychological explanations. It is also the case that this essay presupposes some sympathy with the idea that natural science should not overly dominate our conception of what it is for something to be a fact. Those who find this broadly

---

essay is that the reading of Wittgenstein as a meaning sceptic, or meaning eliminativist, is not accurate, but we shall not pursue the exegetical issue here. Many have attacked this reading of Wittgenstein, and I have outlined my doubts about it elsewhere (Heal 1989).

2. This line of thought takes off from ideas presented in the earlier writings of Dennett (1979, 1987a). Dennett would now repudiate the label 'eliminativist' and has consistently tried to distance himself from the instrumentalism, and hence eliminativism, which many have seen in his writings. He has written voluminously on these and related issues, and this essay is not presented as an adequate discussion of his views. Rather, it develops one line of thought which may be based on his reflections, and a possible response to that line.

Wittgensteinian idea congenial but would like some more suggestions on the different roles played in our lives by the psychological and the physical will find relevant considerations here. But a full-scale engagement with the rights, wrongs and temptations of reductive naturalism is well beyond the scope of what can be attempted in this essay.

2. RATIONALITY, PREDICTION AND ELIMINATIVISM

The line of thought we are to examine takes off from a frequently made assumption, which we shall not question, that there is some close link between the notions of thought and of rationality. An initial statement of the view says that any being to whom intentional states can be truly attributed must be rational. How we understand this will alter as we proceed, but this rough-and-ready formulation will do as a starting point.

Let us now focus on the version of this idea articulated by Dennett. He proposes that there are different 'stances' one might take up when attempting to predict the behaviour of some complex item, for example a machine or person. First there is the physical stance, where one predicts on the basis of knowledge of the material composition and structure of the item. Next there is the design stance, where one relies on information about what the item has been constructed to do. Finally there is the intentional stance, where one assumes that the item is a rational agent, attributes to it the goals and information it ought to have given its situation and predicts that it will act as it ought rationally to do given those goals and that information. The intentional stance is what we take when we use psychological concepts. We shall call upon different sets of concepts and make different kinds of moves, depending upon what stance we take up. There is thus some resemblance between the idea of a stance and the idea of a Wittgensteinian language game. One way of putting the central suggestion of this essay is that when we look more closely at what we actually do with psychological concepts we shall see that much of what is important to them is not captured by the idea of taking the intentional stance in order to generate predictions.

The Dennettian line of thought, however, is quite explicit in its claim that the purpose of taking the intentional stance is the same as the purpose of taking the physical stance, namely the generation of predictions. Ability to predict the behaviour of physical objects is important to us because it enables us to anticipate good happenings or to mitigate bad ones, and because it connects with our ability to control events, in those cases where we can ourselves influence the occurrence or non-occurrence of circumstances in which a given event is predicted to occur. Accepting all this does not commit us to a crudely pragmatic or technological view of the value of science. Of course, we can also allow that scientific understanding is worthwhile and fascinating for its own sake. But it is clear that the major practical import of natural science is in the area of prediction and control. To identify the intentional stance as an alternative to the physical stance – that is, to take it as a way of doing the same thing as could be done by taking the physical stance – is tacitly to assume that our relations to other human beings are of the same very broad kind as our relations to inanimate objects; it is to take it that both people and objects are things in our environment the behaviour of which may impinge on us pleasantly or unpleasantly, and which we therefore seek to anticipate and influence to our advantage.

The upshot of this complex of ideas is that a certain conception of how we use the rationality assumption is presented to us. It goes like this: we know such and such about others' current situation, centrally their beliefs and desires; we wish to generate predictions of their further thoughts or behaviour; our tool in doing so is a rationality assumption. Given the conception outlined here, the rationality assumption is conceived as analogous to a physical theory, where a physical theory is, for example, some set of equations governing the evolution of the physical magnitudes in a system, which can be used in conjunction with information about the current state of that system, to generate a prediction of its future states.

This view of the large-scale structure of our position vis-à-vis others then has further implications for how the rationality assumption itself is to be unpacked. The content of the assumption needs, like that of a physical theory, to be rich enough to generate determinate predictions, given a whole variety of different inputs about initial conditions. Also, like a physical theory, it needs to be general in that it applies to all beings to whom intentional states are attributed. The difference from physical theory is that it will not be based on empirical observation. Rather it will be normatively based, calling centrally upon the idea of what ought to be thought or done, given such and such initial beliefs and desires.

For an understanding of the content of the rationality assumption so conceived we turn naturally to those who study the normative aspects of reasoning, in logic, decision theory and the like. At this point in developing the line of thought matters become less clear. Certainly deductive logicians offer some definite normative demands. For example, they offer the ideal of consistency (believing no contradictions) and completeness (believing all the logical consequences of what one believes). But for non-deductive reasoning and practical reasoning matters are less agreed upon. There are unclarities (e.g., about the nature and defensibility of inference to the best explanation) and unresolved paradoxes (e.g., Newcomb's paradox).[3]

The fact that we do not have a complete agreed upon account of rationality may be read merely as parallel to the fact that we do not yet have a complete physics. The lack of a complete physics means only that taking the physical stance to an item is to be construed as assuming that it obeys the laws of physics, whatever they are. Insofar as I know some of them I can predict it, but where my knowledge runs out, so too does my ability to predict. Analogously, one might say, taking the intentional stance to an item is to be construed as assuming that it obeys the dictates of rationality, whatever they are. Again, insofar as I know them, I can predict it, and where I do not, I must give up.

This is not a satisfactory position in the long run. Significant divergences between the rational and the physical appear when we reflect further. Thus, if we do not know physical laws we can gain clues to them from observing actual behaviour. But we cannot similarly gain clues to unknown portions of the demands of rationality by observing our own behaviour. The position here, at least in some cases, appears to be the other way round, viz., when we do not know what rationality requires we do not conform to the demands of rationality, but when we do know, then we do conform. So thinking about what we ought to do can make a significant difference to what we in fact do. By contrast, we do not have any tendency to conform more accurately to the laws of physics in virtue of being aware of them. The story I shall tell later, from Section 5 onwards, easily accommodates these obvious but nevertheless interesting points. They are less easy to fit in on the approach we are now considering,

---

3. Newcomb's paradox concerns a situation where a person is faced with a choice between two boxes, one of which is open and can be seen to contain £100 and the other of which is closed. She is told that there is already either nothing or £1,000 in the closed box, and that she may take either both boxes or only the closed box. She is also told that her choice has been predicted by a super-predicter, which has similarly predicted those of many other people faced with the same choice, and that on all previous occasions when the person took both boxes the closed one proved to be empty, while when only the closed box was taken it proved to have £1,000 in it. There seem to be compelling arguments in favour of taking both boxes (after all, either the thousand pounds is already there or not, and £1,100 is better than £1,000, as £100 is better than nothing), and also in favour of taking only the closed box (previous persons who reasoned in the greedy way got only £100). For more about the paradox, and a way into the literature about it, see Nozick 1995.

since doing so would mean fine-tuning predictive strategies to differences in outlook about rationality in those predicted, thus dissolving the one unified 'intentional stance' into a multiplicity of different predictive strategies. But let us for the moment overlook all these complications which stem from our limited knowledge of what rationality requires and imagine that we have some package of demands of rationality, including at least consistency and completeness in belief together with some other suitable elements, which is agreed to spell out (at least a substantial part of) what rationality demands.

We should at this point note a verbal difficulty in specifying what rationality requires, given our assumption of a constitutive connection between rationality and intentional states. Stating conditions for rationality as having to do with relations between beliefs (e.g., 'a person is rational only if all her beliefs are consistent') seems to suggest the possibility of beliefs which are not consistent. A more guarded statement would say that when considering if a being is rational one needs to look at its candidate intentional states – that is, candidate beliefs and candidate intentions – where these are thought of as states with apparent content. I shall on occasion use this more verbose terminology where the argument requires clarity. If such candidate states fulfil the requirements of rationality, then they are admitted to be real intentional states. If however they fail the requirements of rationality, then, given the strong constitutive link, they have to be denied the status of real intentional states. This is indeed the route the eliminativist takes.

Thus far we have been pursuing claims supposedly available to us a priori, about the connection of thought and rationality and about the nature of rationality. Now we come to the a posteriori premises of the eliminativist argument. Observation shows, it is said, that the others we seek to predict fall short of the prescriptions of rationality. This is obviously so, independent of any worries about what exactly the requirements of rationality are. Let us consider just consistency and completeness. Satisfying the demand for consistency is, given the immense number of different (candidate) beliefs each of us possesses, an enormous task. We do not have the time or the resources to do the necessary cross-checking, and the chances are that all of us have at least some inconsistent (candidate) beliefs. Satisfying the demand for completeness is even worse. Although each of us has an immense number of (candidate) beliefs, there is still a gap between it and the number of beliefs (viz., infinitely many) which we would have if we were to deduce all the consequences of the beliefs we do have. (Consider, for example, all the truths of elementary arithmetic and geometry, to say nothing of the endless trivial empirical truths now deductively available to me, such as that I have more blue socks than there have been English kings called Henry.)

If we insist that satisfying the demands of rationality is necessary for being a believer, it follows from this shortfall that others do not really have the beliefs we credit them with. Certainly (we may say) people behave up to a point as if they were believers, and we find it useful predictively to treat them as if they satisfied the norms and so to infer some of their (candidate) beliefs and intentions from others; indeed, we have no other option because it is unmanageably complicated to take the physical or the design stance towards people. But (it seems natural to continue) using the thought attributions licensed by the intentional stance is just an instrumentally useful way of carrying on. It is not to be taken as description of fact.

3. AN AVENUE OF ESCAPE?

How might one seek to evade this unwelcome conclusion while retaining the central elements of the stance idea? One move would be to suggest that talk of rationality is like talk of frictionless slopes or rigid levers, namely a simplification and idealisation of the kind often found in science. Although no slope is ever entirely frictionless nor any lever entirely rigid, nevertheless some may be nearly frictionless or rigid; some slopes and levers have real properties to which the idealised versions are pretty close. Similarly, even if we are not perfectly rational, nevertheless we are nearly rational, and talk of our rationality (and relatedly of our beliefs) latches on to some reality which is not intolerably distorted by the representation.

But a move of this form is not defensible in the rationality case. Given the demandingness of rationality as currently conceived, there is not merely a slight looseness of fit between what it requires and what we are capable of: there is a vast gap. The fact is that we are not even nearly rational, in the highly demanding sense of 'rational'. Taking us to be rational in this sense is more like envisaging the heavenly bodies as attached to a collection of crystal spheres than it is like treating an iron bar as a rigid lever. The sphere idea is indeed useful for certain predictive purposes, but the gap between how things actually are and how things need to be for it to be strictly true is so wide that the only sensible thing to do is to take the idea instrumentally, and hence to be an eliminativist about crystal spheres.

Another move of a similar kind is explored by Dennett. To speak of rationality being manifested in some stretch of speech and behaviour is, he suggests, like speaking of a pattern as being present in some array of dots. We may allow that a certain pattern is 'really' present in an array even if the presence of some errors or distortions means that the array is not a perfect specimen of the pattern (Dennett 1991).

Again the size of the gap between what rationality requires and what we actually do makes this an unpersuasive position, if we are assuming the above-sketched demanding version of rationality. Suppose we have an array of dots which can be seen as a hand but it is placed in the midst of a random confusion of other dots. It would be stretching things exceedingly to say that a pattern representing a whole human body was, albeit in a patchy and imperfect way, present. Too much of the human-body pattern is missing for this to be a defensible move. Similarly, it may be that a few of our remarks and pieces of behaviour hang together in a way which suggests to the fully rational observer from Mars that we are similarly rational. Further investigation, however, will show so much to be missing, in the form of further claims we should make and further actions we should undertake were we really rational, that the observer would be sensible to abandon the idea, or to treat it where used as merely instrumental.

However, versions of these moves might work if we could combine them with cutting down the notion of rationality, to make it less demanding. (Dennett makes moves in this direction; 1987b: 94ff.) The rationality assumption will need still to have some rich, determinate and general content, otherwise it will not be analogous to physical theory and will not have the power to generate interesting predictions over the full range of cases. But if the notion of rationality invoked were less perfectionist, then there might be some hope of our (at least nearly) conforming to its norms and so being properly taken as the subjects of intentional states. A plausible way of cutting down starts from the fact that we have only finite resources of time and logical acumen. Hence only certain inferences, those which are fairly short and simple in structure, are psychologically feasible for us. Moreover, many of the inferences which are feasible concern subject matters which are not worth thinking about (e.g., relations between my socks and the kings of England), so that it would be silly for a finite creature to waste its resources on them.

Given these facts, we might propose an account of rationality along these lines: a person is rational if she makes a fair number of the feasible inferences available to her on matters of interest, and does not make too many mistakes. A detailed spelling out of the rationality assumption would then list the kinds of inference which are feasible for humans (e.g., use of the natural deduction rules of elementary logic, some simple moves in probability calculus, employment of basic arithmetic, simple induction . . .) and specify the kinds of lengths of chains of reasoning a rational person should be able to undertake. It would need also to lay out analogous things about the kinds of practical reasoning to be expected of a rational person, for example, how many different alternatives are to be weighed, what kinds of comparison made and so on. (This proposal is derived, with some modifications, from the excellent discussion by Cherniak [1986].)

The general account of rationality suggested here is interestingly vague. What it gestures towards is not one notion but rather a family of notions, defined by interpreting crucial terms such as 'fair number', 'not too many' or 'feasible' in different ways. There is, as we shall see later, something right about allowing this flexibility. We do indeed expect different standards of reasoning from people with different backgrounds and training. But it is an unwelcome complexity from the point of view we are exploring and brings a threat of ambiguity and loss of unity in psychological notions.

For example, we may construct two different ways of spelling out rationality in detail, one of which does and one of which does not include enough grip on probability to avoid falling for the gambler's fallacy. On the one hand, predicting a ten-year-old child with the package including sophisticated grip on probability is likely to produce the wrong results and would suggest that the child did not really believe that nine fair tosses of the fair coin had produced nine heads. ('If she really believed that, she would not now be giving greater probability to a tail next time.') On the other hand, predicting the professional gambler with the even more cut-down version would equally produce the wrong results. A third option would be to use different packages of demands for different people. But if we do this, and thus get the correct predictions for both child and gambler, then, prima facie, we have got two different senses of 'rational' in play. This then threatens the idea that we have one univocal notion of 'belief', since belief is defined by its link with rationality.

Thus the cutting-down strategy offers us the chance of crafting a conception of rationality which we might have some hope of (at least nearly) instantiating, and so it seems to offer the chance of avoiding eliminativism while retaining the 'intentional stance' idea. But the strategy also generates various questions. There are many different ways of cutting down. If we are to avoid 'belief' becoming ambiguous, we must, it seems, fix on just one revised package. But why should we favour one over another out of the multiplicity available? And if we do hit on one, how are we to explain what seems a plain fact that we do use different assumptions about reasoning when thinking about different individuals?

I do not say that these questions are unanswerable within the context of the approach we are exploring, merely that they pose problems for it. (We shall return to these issues later, and see how they can be naturally resolved in the context of a rethinking of the rationality assumption and its role for us.) But, for the moment, let us imagine them dealt with and thus imagine that arguments for eliminativism generated by the immense gap between actual performance and norms has also been dealt with. The next section will suggest that, even so, we are not free of the eliminativist threats.

4. ANOTHER ARGUMENT FOR ELIMINATIVISM

Here is another line of thought on which the sort of view we are considering pushes us in the direction of eliminativism. This line has plausibility whether we take rationality in the perfectionist way contemplated in Section 2 or in some cut-down version as suggested in Section 3.

It is sometimes proposed as a further element of the approach we are exploring that the usefulness of predictions generated by the rationality assumption is, by itself, sufficient for rationality and hence belief. All there is (it is said) to being a believer is being usefully predictable by taking the intentional stance. To be rational a being need only have its candidate intentional states conform to the patterns prescribed. The issue of how that conformity comes about is irrelevant. The attraction of this further assumption for many philosophers is that we can now give full recognition to the discoveries of natural science, in particular the workings of natural selection, in suggesting explanations of how the observed patterns of behaviour came to be shaped. We do not have to acknowledge any explanatory factors other than those operating in the inanimate natural world.

I would suggest, however, that this seeming strength of the proposal is also a source of weakness, viz., of the persisting sense that it is eliminativist. In fact our notion of rationality when unpacked also assigns a further, and as yet unmentioned, role to the norms of rationality, apart from that of prescribing patterns among candidate intentional states. It gives the norms an explanatory force in the generation of the beliefs or actions which constitute the patterns. Some familiar kinds of thought experiment will serve to make this claim plausible. Consider a being who, regarded externally, satisfies whatever version of rationality we have hit on, but only (as it turns out) because every possible individual apparently inferential move has been programmed in through an immense set of post-hypnotic suggestions. It seems unhappy to say that this being is rational. Her sets of candidate beliefs may indeed cause other candidate beliefs, but the driving force of the transitions is entirely unconnected with their normative status.

The conclusion from this thought experiment is that when we link intentional states and rationality, and attribute both of them to a creature, we commit ourselves to the propriety of some story invoking norms in explaining the behaviour of that creature. It is not just the surface contours of the behaviour which are important to us; the routes by which things come about are important as well. To be rational is not merely to conform to but to respond to the norms of rationality.

Now it would indeed be extremely odd to suppose that normative facts have some direct quasi-causal influence on movement of matter in space and time. We can avoid that particular sense of uneasiness by taking it that norms exert their influence only via the medium of a mind which can become aware of and responsive to them. So norms get a foothold in the spatio-temporal world by figuring as the content of spatio-temporally located states and happenings, namely the awarenesses and thinkings of persons. That, at first sight, looks more intelligible than the idea of norms exerting direct causal influence over matter. But even here, we still need to explain how norms impress themselves upon human beings.

If I am right that the assumption of rationality assigns an explanatory role to norms, then to avoid eliminativism we need to amend the account we have been giving to reflect this. But it is difficult to see how this can be done in the framework of the current approach. The current account says that the rationality assumption is a tool for achieving a goal, namely prediction of happenings, which could also be achieved by doing natural scientific theorising. So it cannot but seem appropriate to compare the rationality postulation (with its corollary of an explanatory role for norms) to the postulation of molecular mechanisms, genes or natural selection, with respect to how accurately each represents how things come about. In a confrontation conceived this way, the norm-free entities and forces of natural science win hands down. If we focus on human beings as suitable subjects for natural science and construe adoption of the intentional stance as an attempt at the very same predictive job as is done by natural science, we cannot but accept that it is the interactions at the molecular level which do the real causing, and so provide the real explanations and the more solid underpinning of the predictions. Other things can be allowed genuine explanatory roles only if they are constructs out of, or reducible to, physical complexes. Norms cannot be so regarded. Hence assigning an explanatory role to norms can only be instrumentally construed.

The difficulty can be illustrated by considering again Dennett's pattern analogy. We can imagine an imperfect version of a pattern appearing in an array of dots by a process in which a perfect version of the pattern is copied by an error-prone process. But there are other ways in which exactly the same array might emerge which assign no role at all to any perfect version of the pattern. Dennett is concerned to stress that his picture of the emergence of rationality patterns is the second and not the first. But if the intentional story is not to be merely instrumental, the norms of rationality need to get in on the act, as things which persons are aware of and strive (sometimes unsuccessfully) to conform to. Hence they need to play the role which the perfect version of the copied pattern might play. The possibility of their playing any such role has, however, been pre-empted by the molecular and evolutionary story. Contemplating giving an explanatory role to the set of norms which define rationality forces us into highly suspect metaphysics. We shall need to postulate 'top down' causation by non-material forces or immaterial souls capable of intuiting platonic realms. If we do not think like this, how are we to get the norms into an explanatory relation with the occurrences which are said to manifest a creature's rationality? There seems no respectable way to do so. The upshot is that an important element of our conception of thought and its link with rationality is not allowed for on this account of how we use the rationality assumption. The rationality is not really there in the sense of 'really there' which we would like.

The root of the trouble, on the diagnosis I am offering, is the idea that psychological thinking serves the same large-scale purpose as natural scientific thinking. This idea has two corollaries. One is that it forces us to construe rationality as the achievement of an actual performance of conforming to some determinate demands. If we do not construe it like this, then the rationality assumption is of no use for generating predictions. It follows from this that accommodating an explanatory role for norms must take the form of finding an explanatory role for these particular demands. The other corollary is that the approach leads us to locate the idea of norms playing an explanatory role in the same logical space as, and hence as a rival to, the idea of molecular linkages, natural selection and so on playing an explanatory role. The upshot of the two corollaries working together is that an explanatory role for norms gets envisaged as a kind of mysterious, non-natural top-down causation by a particular package of norms, and so has to be rejected. Eliminativism is the outcome.

5. A TWO-ELEMENT CONCEPTION OF RATIONALITY

Let us see if we can extricate ourselves from this unfortunate position. We shall first, in this section, sketch another kind of account of what it is to be rational. Section 6 will then explore its implications for the nature of psychological concepts and for the kinds of interactions with others in which they figure. In these two sections we shall ignore questions about the defensibility of the picture sketched. We shall return to this issue, and to the topic of eliminativism, in the final section.

The idea of rationality explored in the previous sections insists that a rational person actually achieves a specified standard in thought, in that his or her candidate intentional states do indeed exhibit certain patterns, which are exemplifications of a designated package of inferential moves. Let us consider instead an account which emphasises that a person's rationality is a capacity rather than a particular achievement. On this view, rationality cannot be captured in one list of fulfilled demands but rather consists, in any person, of two elements of very different logical kinds. The first is something which every rational person shares with every other rational person, namely a grasp on the high level and general notion of there being better and worse in inferential transitions between thoughts. The second element varies from person to person and from time to time, and is what we may call a particular 'inferential outlook'. A person's inferential outlook at a time is the assemblage of his or her views at that time about what transitions in thought are approvable and disapprovable.

Grasp of the high-level notion (in the sense I intend here) is shown by effective engagement in a certain practice, namely that of asking about and assessing inferences or reasoning. For example, a person may consider such questions as 'In the light of of so and so, would it be proper to think that such and such?' or 'Does so and so follow from such and such?' or 'Is this a reason for that?' And perhaps he or she may point out some transition in thought and then condemn or commend it. ('I used to think that a run of heads made a tail more likely on the next toss. But now I see that was wrong'.) The second element is shown in the actual inferential transitions which an individual makes, whether unreflectively or as mediated by formulated rules. It may also be shown in the examples of good and bad reasoning he or she would cite, and in whatever explicit theorising about reasoning he or she has engaged in. There is, of course, a close relation between the two elements. The second will develop and change over time, in response to teaching and through reflection and experience, as the person has occasions to exercise the first.

What is meant by 'effective' in the above mention of 'effective engagement in the practice of asking about and assessing inferences'? Effective engagement is not mere willingness to utter verbal formulae such as 'Is this a good reason for that?' but requires that actual progress be made, namely sensible answers be offered, or at least moves relevant to a sensible answer, when such questions are raised. It is not required however that all questions be answered correctly, still less that they be answered quickly and easily. But a person cannot be said to engage effectively in the practice, and hence to have grasp of the general and high-level notion, unless some progress is made on a good number of occasions.

A comparison of rationality with sight may be useful here. To credit someone with sight is to credit him or her with a capacity which, if exercised in not too unfavourable conditions, results in acquisition of information about the shapes, sizes and relative positions of objects in the world around. But to have sight a person does not require to be able to answer infallibly and easily all questions on these subject matters, still less already actually to possess complete knowledge of the spatial layout of the whole universe. Rather, to have sight he or she needs to understand what shape, size and position are, and to have the ability to set about getting answers to a good range of particular questions about them, by undertaking suitable kinds of looking. Actually achieving answers may be easy in some cases, where an enquirer just needs to take a quick glance, but extremely difficult in others, where she has to resort to examining a situation from many angles, to asking others who have better close or long-distance vision, to microscopes, telescopes and the like. Possession of sight is compatible with discovery that there are some areas of the spatial universe which it is impossible that one should ever see, for example those which are too distant or in some way blocked off, like the inside of black holes. Also, possession of sight does not require an individual to be free from liability to visual illusions. Nor does it require that a person be willing to put in the effort of looking and finding out about shapes, sizes and positions on all occasions when questions arise. He or she may be too lazy, preoccupied, prejudiced, drunk and so forth.

We may develop the parallel between rationality and possession of sight as follows. It is a presupposition of the whole debate we are conducting that there is a realm of norms. (It is not scepticism about norms we are considering but eliminativism about the intentional.) This realm contains,

238

for example, all the facts about what entails what, since these fill in the detailed requirements of the norm of thought that it is wrong to combine belief in a premise with belief in the negation of something entailed by that premise. It will also contain plenty of other norms as well, for example, about what intentions are justified by what considerations. Thus it will contain norms relevant to practical as well as to theoretical thought. Indeed, it is impossible for a finite creature to separate the two completely, since theoretical reflection is a resource-consuming activity, and so the values of truth detection and falsehood avoidance which it pursues will always need to be weighed against other values we could promote by use of the same resources. To credit someone with the first element in the two-element conception of rationality – that is, with ability to engage effectively in the practice of asking about and assessing reasons for forming beliefs and intentions – is in effect to credit that person with a capacity for coming to know at least something about this realm of norms. (It is at this point that an explanatory role for norms is built into the story we are telling. Section 7 will consider whether the story thereby becomes vulnerable to eliminativist pressure.)

Given this, we may transfer to the subject matter of norms everything we have said about sight. Thus some parts of the realm of norms we may discover to be very difficult or impossible of access. (For example, some kinds of proofs are so complex that we have great trouble in grasping them. Or perhaps there are certain kinds of proofs which, because infinitary in a particular way, we see that we can never master.) Further, to be rational we do not require to have already total grasp of all entailment relations, together with all the other facts about good and bad in reasoning. (This was what was imagined on the first, highly idealised, conception of rationality considered in Section 2. But from the perspective we are now developing, that earlier conception can be seen as the result of conflating possession of a capacity to acquire information of a certain kind with the state which would be the outcome of a total and perfect exercise of the capacity.) Moreover, we may be rational even if we are liable to some illusions about inferential connections. And we may be rational even if we are sometimes too lazy, prejudiced or drunk to exercise our capacity to assess reasoning.

What is involved in reflecting effectively on a question such as 'Does this follow from that?' It is worth unpacking this notion a little further. One model of such reflection is that it must be the application of a decision procedure. The account fits some cases tolerably well. For example, if I wonder whether it follows from the fact that I have 12 × 12 apples that I have fewer than 11×14 apples, then a systematic check through my stock of available clear-cut ways of settling questions will turn up procedures for calculating and comparing numbers which can be applied to derive an answer. But not all cases are like this. Sometimes a question arises from some doubt about how to apply an existing rule or from our finding ourselves in a situation to which no existing rule seems to apply. In such situations we are not always completely at a loss. Rather we are thrown back on a variety of less formal moves, such as looking for hitherto unrecognised analogies, seeking new distinctions, wondering if insertion of new variables might help and the like. The kinds of casting about we can engage in are open-ended and can interact with each other and with the material thought about in many complex ways. So what the casting about consists in, by what transformations of thought it leads to new insights (if it does), is something of which we can only give the above, hand-waving, sort of account. This is not surprising, since what we are talking about is precisely the skill of dealing with situations where explicitly formulated rules give out.

Persons may differ very substantially from each other in their actual inferential outlooks and in how much self-conscious and explicit grip they have on the norms of inference. But if a person is to reflect effectively on some particular question about reasoning, he or she must have already to hand at least some materials with which to think about the issue, for example, some already recognised specimens of good reasoning, some rules for assessment, some techniques of analysing, analogising or extrapolating. So grasp of the general notion of better and worse in inference cannot be had without actual applications of the notion being made. It does not follow, however, that there is one fixed set of specimens, rules or techniques which is always associated with grasp of the general notion. Nor does it follow that every question must be handled with the same set of tools or that there is only one set of starting materials for effectively tackling a given particular question. It is also true that if people are to discuss issues about good inference they need to share some common ground of particular judgements and techniques to start with. But again it does not follow that it is the same common ground on every occasion.

All of the moves mentioned towards the end of the last paragraph are examples of the familiar 'quantifier shift' fallacy where a correct claim of the weak 'for all X, there is some Y which, . . .' form are misconstrued as claims of the stronger 'there is some Y, such that for all X, it . . .' form. Were the quantifier shift move valid, there would be grounds for saying that the two-element view of rationality was not really all that different from the earlier view, since we would be able to suggest that one and the same package (e.g., one set of specimens, rules and techniques) was required to be present in every case of effective thinking about inferences and hence is definitive of rationality. Part of the interest of the two-element account is precisely that it need not be spelled out in this way and is open to the idea that effective thinking about reasons can be extremely various.

6. PREDICTION, DISCUSSION AND EXCUSE

Suppose that we think of ourselves and others as rational in the sense sketched in Section 5, what forms of interaction with others might we engage in? Would the assumption that others were rational, together with information about their beliefs and desires, enable us to predict their further thoughts and actions – and relatedly to control or manipulate them in some circumstances? The answer is that the mere claim of rationality, by itself, does little to help prediction or control. That claim says only that the rational person grasps the general notion of better and worse in inference and possesses also some or other current inferential outlook. To arrive at predictions we need knowledge of what this particular outlook is, which will vary considerably from person to person depending on upbringing, natural acuity, experience and so on. (We need also knowledge of such things as how willing the person is to exercise his or her capacity to reason at this time.) It is these specifics about the individual which do all the work, and not any supposed generally applicable prediction machinery, use of which is licensed by the attribution of rationality. Certainly we may use inductive evidence, as well as evidence derived from interaction with the individual, to arrive at views about an individual's likely inferential outlook. ('The average ten-year-old reasons like this: . . .' 'Most professors of logic are capable of . . .', etc.) So in practice the derivation of a prediction will proceed in some cases as if one were applying a standard package. But the underpinning of the proceeding is now quite differently envisaged.

In this view of how generation of specific predictions occur the first element in the two-element rationality conception plays no role. How then can its presence in our thinking be significant? The answer is that it underpins kinds of interaction between people which are overlooked, or insofar as noticed wrongly interpreted, on the earlier prediction-centred account.

Let us consider just two of these. The first is inviting and participating in joint consideration of some question about reasoning in which both of us are, or can be brought to be, interested. For a schematic example, imagine that you and I are in the grip of the gambler's fallacy, but that you are beginning to have doubts about whether it really does follow from the fact that there has been a run of heads in coin tossing that a tail is more likely to turn up next time. You invite me to reflect, saying: 'What do you think? It somehow seems obvious that a tail must be more likely, since long runs of heads are unlikely and one should not expect the unlikely. Yet surely there's something to be said on the other side too, since the coin is fair and that means that the chances of tails must be evens'. By your question I am induced to think about the issue and after some to-and-fro discussion (including, perhaps, consideration of whether 'likely' is an absolute or a relative characterisation, of how and when to apply the maxim 'don't expect the unlikely' and so forth) we see what our mistake was and reform our inferential outlooks accordingly.

You may initiate such a dialogue by asking me a question when you already know what my current inferential outlook is (I am prone to the gambler's fallacy) and are thus in an excellent position to make specific predictions about me and to manipulate my behaviour if you wish to do so. What makes it sensible to ask me is not this specific knowledge, but the fact that you think that I am capable of changing my outlook for the better by reflecting on it. You pose the question to me because you hope, from sharing any insights I may come up with, that we shall both end up with a better grip on the topic than we had before. The presupposition which makes your move sensible is your commitment to the presence in me of the first element of the two-element conception.

Discussions of such kinds are notable contexts for uses of psychological terms. ('What do you think?' 'I am inclined to suppose that . . .', 'I used to take it that . . . but now I am more doubtful, because . . .'; 'I'm quite certain that . . . but less certain that. . . .') It is notable that dialogues of somewhat similar import could occur in which there was no use of psychological terms. ('Is it the case that . . . ?' 'Perhaps not, because . . .', etc.) Nevertheless, the psychological terms are not otiose. They serve to make explicit that you and I are aware of each other as fellow thinkers and that it is precisely the sharing of your thinking on the matter which I invite.[4]

---

4. The matters touched on in this paragraph relate to familiar issues concerning the morals to be drawn from Moore's paradox and a whole related slew of questions concerning psychological concepts and first-person authority. For some discussion, see Essays 13 and 14.

The suggestion of the last three paragraphs is that psychological terms are centrally at home in dialogues such as the one about the gambler's fallacy and that it is the rationality conception outlined in Section 5 which best makes sense of them. But can the earlier account, the prediction-centred one, also make sense of such dialogues?

How does that earlier account explain asking another 'What do you think about . . . ?' There seem to be two sorts of occasion which it can easily accommodate. The first is occasions on which asking someone 'What do you think?' is like checking the oil in a car, namely a procedure designed to elicit information about a person which one will use in prediction of that person. I do not at all want to deny that questions about others' thoughts may have this role. But the gambler's fallacy dialogue is not of this kind; to ask the question you do not need to be planning to make use of my answer in working out what I am going to do.

The second is occasions when you may use another person like a calculator, asking, for example, 'What do you think is the product of 57 and 692?' because you know that the other is quicker and more accurate at doing sums than you are yourself. Here you are not interested in predicting the other's behaviour but in reading the arithmetical facts off from her answer. This is a particular example of the fact that of course we do not always use prediction-relevant facts about an item in predicting that item. We may instead use them to derive information about some other part of the world. So you may be interested in the temperature of the oil in your car not because of its effects on the car but because of its diagnostic role vis-à-vis some fact external to the car. Similarly, you may be interested in another's arithmetical opinions because you take it that you can read off from them to the arithmetical facts.

This second sort of enquiry after another's beliefs may seem to be more like our dialogue. Your question may be presented as designed to get me to evolve into an inner state, which I then express to you, where you can read off from that inner state whether or not a run of heads makes a tail more likely. Reflection suggests, however, that this construal of matters is seriously distorting. In the gambler's fallacy case, you indeed want my help in thinking and suppose that I may have something useful to say. But you do not know how I will tackle the question (ex hypothesi, the question is one in handling which we do not have well-recognised procedures) and you are not committed to accepting what I offer. Even if you have some inductive evidence from other occasions of my abilities in coming up with helpful reflections in puzzling cases, whether or not you do so here will depend upon whether my suggestions make sense to you.

Another kind of interaction underpinned by the first element in the two-element conception revolves around disagreement and excuse. The same gambler's fallacy case can be pressed into service again, in a slightly different format, to illustrate the idea. Suppose that I have fallen for the fallacy and say that a tail is more likely next time, whereas you, having always had at the forefront of your mind that the coin is a fair one, insist that the chances are even. How are we to respond to our difference?

One possibility is that we write each other off as confused or partially irrational and do not bother to look into possible explanations of what seems to each to be the other's mistake. But another possibility is that we investigate our difference with a view to testing the credentials of each view. And our investigation hopes to find a particular kind of account of whichever turns out to be in error, namely an account which shows that arriving at that error was, all the same, an exercise of rationality. The result of such a discussion is (perhaps) that we both come to appreciate that my mistake is the result of having an oversimple conception of 'the unlikely' and so of applying the rule 'Don't expect the unlikely' in an inappropriate way.

My having such an oversimple conception is an unfortunate feature of my earlier state of mind. But it is not one which shows that I do not satisfy the two-element conception of rationality. Given our limited cognitive resources, it is good policy to stick with simple concepts until one is forced to make matters more complicated. And that good policy is the one I was following. Certainly I learn something important from the discussion, namely that 'likelihood' is more complicated than I had assumed. But it may also be that you learn something. For example, you are made aware of the possibility of this simpler (and as it turns out inadequate) way of conceptualising matters. Also you come to see how my making the mistake is compatible with my being rational.

We can imagine also other cases of a different structure, where discussion of disagreement might result in both parties shifting their views, each recognising some merit in the other's concepts and contentions and so coming to an enriched understanding. For example, very schematically, we might have a case of disagreement about action, where in effect one person was applying a deontological and another a consequentialist mode of appraisal to the situation. Discussion might enable both parties to come to a more complex, if less easy and simple, appreciation of the costs and benefits of the various options available.

As we saw, in Sections 2 and 3, the earlier construals of rationality which we considered arose from assimilating what we do with psychological concepts to what we do with the concepts of natural science, namely formulate claims which will enable us to make predictions about items around us. In doing this we were implicitly assimilating our relations to other people to our relations with complex items in our environment such as plants and machines. The thrust of the remarks of this section could be put the following way.

We can, if we insist, describe the situations we have discussed in terms of prediction and manipulation. For example, it is your belief that I can think effectively about better and worse in inference, which licences you to predict that you may get some helpful remarks from me if you ask me to reflect on some question. It is because you desire this potential benefit from me that you prod me with your question. Similarly, asking me to explain myself may result in my saying things which will enable you to get a better grip on my particular inferential outlook. Both of these discoveries may contribute to your future ability to predict or guide my behaviour.

But forcing things thus into the prediction and control pattern is achieved largely by verbal shifts, for example, by weakening the content of predictions until they become extremely unspecific ('the other may say something helpful', 'the other may be able to explain her inferential outlook to me'). Moreover, if we insist on foregrounding this way of describing things then we overlook a more revealing account of what goes on. Other people are not devices which we try to operate, endeavouring to cause them to do this or that useful manoeuvre. Rather, they are fellow human beings with whom we talk, with whom we co-operate on shared projects, from whom we ask help when we are muddled and with whom we seek to forge a jointly created and growing understanding. Something went missing right at the beginning of that earlier train of thought, when we placed the physical stance and the intentional stance side by side as alternative ways of achieving the same goal.

7. ELIMINATIVISM AGAIN

What I have sketched in the previous two sections is an account of a kind of creature, one possessing certain distinctive capacities, and of a kind of interaction which creatures of this kind might undertake with each other. My hope is that it will be found plausible as a picture of how we actually think of ourselves and interact with each other, more plausible than the proposal that we take ourselves to be rational in the senses canvassed in the earlier Sections 2, 3 and 4. To repeat a crucial difference, in the conception of Sections 5 and 6 there is no one identifiable package, reasoning in accordance with which is definitive of rationality. The proposed conception shares with the perfectionist conception the view that there is a realm of norms which sets an ideal standard for us; this realm is something which, we acknowledge, it would be good to know about in its entirety. But the conception shares with the cut-down versions the recognition that our actual achievements must fall far short of that. Its two-element structure thus allows it to acknowledge some truth in each of these earlier ideas while accepting neither of them. What is central to it is the conception of rationality as an onward-moving capacity and not as a particular level of achievement. We now need to consider how this account of rationality removes at least some pressures to eliminativism.

The one-element conceptions of rationality make particular empirical demands which we can see to be falsified by discoveries about human finitude and evolution. On the perfectionist account, rationality demands completeness and consistency, which in turn require infinite complexity of behaviour of the kind which finite beings clearly cannot exhibit. On the cut-down account of rationality, which sees it as a finite but still definite package of norms enforcing conformity with itself, empirical problems arise because we can see no place to insert the definite package in the train of explanatory happenings. On the two-element conception both these sources of empirical tension disappear. The first disappears because we abandon perfectionist demands. The second disappears because there is no longer a particular place in the explanatory stream where any specific norm or package needs insertion, nor yet any definite package to be inserted.

But is there still some other source of incompatibility between the nature of the world as revealed by the empirical studies of the natural sciences and the nature of the world required if rationality in the two-element sense is to be truly attributable to us? We need to consider possible remaining sources of unease.

The second element of the two-element conception is uncontroversial. It says only that at any particular time a person will have a particular inferential outlook, in the sense of a particular complex disposition to behaviour and to transitions between candidate intentional states. No empirical investigations, whether at the level of neurophysiology, evolutionary biology or social psychology, could possibly falsify this claim. All that such investigations can do is fill in the details of the patterns to be discerned in the candidate intentional states. The fact that the patterns will often exhibit errors and limitations, at least from the point of view of some

246

demanding norms, is itself no threat to the two-element conception, since that conception explicitly allows that any individual's inferential outlook at a time will be imperfect, incomplete and idiosyncratic.

So if there is pressure to eliminativism it will be centred on the first element, the one which credits us with grasp of the general notion of better and worse in thinking. It is crucial to resisting eliminativism that we should be able to hold on to this first element. The postulated grasp of the general notion is, so to speak, the point of contact between us and the norms. If we do exercise real grasp of the general notion when we deal with particular questions (about what follows from what, whether this really justifies that, etc.), then we can each be seen as exercising real ability to become aware of the norms. Thus we can be seen as arriving, bit by bit, at some knowledge of what the norms require of us. It is thus this first element which, through allowing us this point of contact with the norms, makes it proper to take our candidate intentional states to be real intentional states, because it allows that their formation does manifest our responsiveness to norms. As already remarked, on the two-element view there is no definite package of norms to be inserted to play a role at some definite point in the explanatory story. Awareness of norms gradually dawns on us, as it were, but it may be a different set of norms, with dawning awareness spread out over time and in a different pattern, for each culture and each individual.

But could we be wrong in taking it that we grasp the general notion of better and worse in thinking, and that this grasp is exercised in moving from less good to better inferential outlooks? It is, I suggest, difficult to say 'no' on the basis of any clear-cut empirical argument, because the empirical commitment of this idea is so extremely thin. If we take a backward-looking perspective, the commitment is only to the possibility of reading at least part of the past histories of ourselves and other ordi-nary, adult human beings as manifesting grasp of the general notion of better and worse in thinking, as our responding to the force of reasons. More important is the forward-looking commitment, which is to its being sensible for us to carry on with the practice of discussing reasons. This forward-looking commitment is more important because, if it can be de-fended, then so can the backward-looking one. If, here and now, I can rightly treat you as someone who may engage effectively in the practice of debating about reasons, then there is a presumption in favour of taking you to have had the same capacity in the past and hence a presumption in favour of seeing your past history as manifesting (in some parts at least) growing awareness of some part of the realm of norms.

So let us concentrate on the forward-looking commitment. Could it be in error? In other words, could empirical discovery show that the practice of discussing issues of better and worse in thinking ought to be abandoned? We can certainly imagine science fiction scenarios in which one person discovers empirically that she cannot carry on the practice because some brain illness has reduced every human being except her to a state of automatism or idiocy. But this is not the interesting scenario. The interesting issue is whether, such disasters aside, empirical discoveries made in the neurosciences, evolutionary biology, social psychology or whatever might show to be foolish the practice of discussing with others issues of better and worse in reasoning. This, however, is an incoherent idea. All that such particular discoveries can do is provide more information about the detailed contours, current strengths or limitations, and neural underpinnings of our actual current inferential outlooks. They cannot discredit the whole practice of asking after reasons. Indeed, they themselves will emerge in a context in which the practice, in the form of discussions among scientists as to whether this or that theory is best supported, is being vigorously carried on.

It may seem, however, that natural science offers us a worldview which, taken as a whole, poses a threat to the practice of discussion of reasons, or rather to our ability to take at face value what we do when we engage in it. There is pressure to argue as follows. The general picture of the world already available to us as a result of the progress of science shows us that what we are is immensely elaborate neurophysiological assemblages, which have come into existence as the result of the workings of natural selection. Therefore none of us really satisfies the two-level conception. We may not be able to envisage any way of carrying on in which we abandon (what we describe as) the practice of discussing reasons with each other. But we cannot reflectively endorse the conception of those activities as our exercise of our capacity to discover more of the realm of norms. We must think of ourselves as packages of matter going through developments, the complete explanation of which lies at the molecular, genetic or theory of evolution level and therefore can have nothing to do with norms. The idea of ourselves as norm-responsive is an illusion, which may be practically unavoidable but is still to be, when we consider the real truth about things, repudiated.

This is not the place to discuss the general issues which this argument raises. It is clear that its force is bound up with the complex and controversial questions (about reductive naturalism, supervenience, kinds of explanations and explananda – and also about the notions of truth and fact)

248

which were mentioned in Section 1. But we should note that there are very general Wittgensteinian lines of thought which stand opposed to the conclusion the argument tries to enforce. The Wittgensteinian holds that we have a variety of practices of engaging with and talking about the world, both scientific and non-scientific, and that we may acknowledge that they are all, in their own way, practices in which we discover truths. This is not to say that the world is a mere mush upon which we impose a structure, since to think that way is to surrender to a quite unacceptable form of idealism. But respect for objectivity does not require us to conceive of the properties of the world as exhausted by those discovered in natural science. Perhaps the world has more aspects available for appreciation by beings who approach it with the right sensitivities. Perhaps we ourselves can rightly be seen both as complex, evolved neurophysiological organisms and also as creatures responsive to norms. And perhaps as our practices of enquiring after norms develop and change, we ourselves also develop and change and so transform ourselves into beings with further sensitivities to whom yet more of the realm of norms is accessible.[5]

Of course these possibilities have not here been given serious defence. What I do hope to have made plausible is the claim that, since the two-element conception of rationality is the right articulation of what we mean when we take ourselves to be rational, then it is with these possibilities that we must grapple in order to resolve the issues about eliminativism. There may seem to be quicker and less controversial ways of establishing eliminativism on the basis of a link of rationality with intentionality, namely the ways explored in the earlier sections of this essay. But they depend upon a misunderstanding of the role which psychological notions play in our lives and on the related one-level misconstruals of rationality to which those misunderstandings give rise.

---

5. There are links here with themes pursued by McDowell (1998). See, in particular, his essay 9, "Two Sorts of Naturalism". McDowell is there talking about ethics, but his issue and ours cannot be disentangled. We have so far been concentrating mainly on better and worse in thinking in connection with theoretical reasoning, and with issues such as what sort of grip we can credit ourselves with on what follows from what. But, as remarked earlier, theoretical reflection is a practical activity. It takes time and resources of energy and attention which, given that we have only finite supplies of them, might be better devoted to other activities. There is no considering good and bad in thinking without considering good and bad more generally, and it would be wrong to suppose that progress in thinking was always a matter of acquiring more insight of a narrowly logical character. But these points raise issues we cannot pursue here.

13

Moore's Paradox: A Wittgensteinian Approach

1. INTRODUCTION

'I believe that it is raining but it isn't'. It would be perfectly absurd, claimed Moore, to say this or its like (Moore 1942: 540–543; 1944: 204). But why? After all, it is clearly possible that I could believe that it is raining when it is not and that others should realise and remark on the error I make. Why should my doing so myself be somehow absurd?

My aim in this essay is to suggest that Wittgenstein's approach to this issue has much to recommend it, and that seeing its attraction might provide an entry point to understanding the nature of Wittgenstein's later philosophy of mind (Wittgenstein 1953: 190–192; 1980: 90–96). A proper account of that is clearly beyond the scope of this essay and moreover could not be given without treating those issues of meaning and metaphysics which Wittgenstein discusses in the early part of the *Investigations*, before he moves on to reflect on psychological concepts. So my object is to consider some features of the paradox in detail but only to gesture in the direction of the larger topics, in a way that may at least make it seem worthwhile to look into them further.[1]

The next section outlines the paradox slightly more fully and suggests two conditions that a satisfactory solution should meet. It sketches two possible approaches to the matter, the Wittgensteinian (which at this point will not look at all attractive) and the more familiar one initiated by Moore himself. Section 3 examines this second approach in more detail and suggests that it cannot meet the two conditions. Sections 4 and 5 consider

---

1. A related approach is explored by Linville and Ring (1991). Gombay offers much thought-provoking material (1988). Pears (1991) is also helpful. Baldwin (1990) has much of interest, although I disagree with him for reasons discussed later.

the question of how the paradox could be treated in the framework of a functionalist theory of belief. Section 4 argues that on certain particular versions of functionalism the oddness of the Moorean utterances disappears. We do not get an explanation of why they are absurd; rather we get a view on which there is no absurdity to be explained. Section 5 suggests that this disappearance of the paradox is likely to be a feature of all versions of functionalism and is, moreover, a serious defect in them. The upshot of this discussion is to put us in a better position to appreciate the attractions of the Wittgensteinian strategy, which is briefly outlined in the final Section 6.

2. TWO APPROACHES TO A SOLUTION

So what is Moore's paradox? An initial point to note is that there are really two paradoxes, one having to do with sentences of the form 'I believe that p but not p' and the other with sentences of the form 'I don't believe that p but p'. One of Moore's discussions of the issue deals with the first and the other with the second, but it looks as if he did not notice that there might be a significant difference. Wittgenstein also makes no explicit differentiation. His actual discussion is, however, mainly centred on the first. I shall endeavour to say something about both.

Moore himself describes what is paradoxical in terms of assertion. What is to be explained is why it would be so strange to (attempt to) make some public and informative statement with this sort of content. Why cannot I do so, given that others clearly can make such assertions (given appropriate changes of pronouns, etc.) and that I can state such things of myself in the past or future? However, this stress on assertion overlooks the fact that there is something equally strange about the idea that someone realises the sentences to be true of him or herself, that is, makes the sort of judgment which they express, whether overtly communicated to another or not.[2] We have just the same reasons as in the case of assertion – that others can have the thought of me, that I can think it of myself in the past or future – to suppose that it ought to be possible.

This yields the first condition on a solution, namely that it must be of adequate generality to explain the oddness of both thought and assertion.

---

2. The point is made by Linville and Ring, and by Baldwin. It is also emphasised by Sorensen in an interesting discussion which differs substantially in approach both from the Wittgensteinian one explored here and the Moorean one (Sorenson 1988). Sorensen's book also contains much useful material on earlier writing on the paradoxes.

So any proposal which calls essentially on features which are found only in communication and have no relevant analogue in thought will not fit the bill. A second condition is this: the solution must identify a contradiction, or something contradiction-like, in the Moorean claims. It will not do, for example, to show that they are odd merely in that they depict situations which we take to be empirically extremely unlikely. The oddness is conceptual: there is some kind of tension or incompatibility between the two parts of the claims, and it is this which needs to be elucidated.

Let us now sketch briefly the two possible lines of approach to a solution. Consider the first paradox, namely 'I believe that p but not p'. Here we have two potentially contradictory elements, namely 'p' and 'not p'. But the one is insulated from the other by the operator 'I believe that'. We could then try to generate a contradiction or tension by, somehow, neutralising or removing the 'I believe that'. This is Wittgenstein's line:

> One may say the following queer thing: 'I believe it is going to rain' means something like 'it is going to rain'. . . . Moore's paradox may be expressed like *this*: 'I believe p' says roughly the same as 'i-p' but 'Suppose I believe that p' does not say roughly the same as 'Suppose p'. (1980: 91–92)

How can this be? Is it that I have so much confidence in my own judgement that I can present, to others and to myself, the fact that I believe something as strong or conclusive evidence that it is so? Do I make the inference (and expect others to as well) 'I/she believe(s) that p; so p'? The solution has the virtue of satisfying our two conditions. This, however, is about all that can be said for it. The cost of adopting it is to represent the thinker (and his or her potential audience) as willing to overlook the very feature of belief – namely its acknowledged fallibility – which generated the paradox in the first place. The thought was 'Everybody knows that belief is a state of the person – a feeling, disposition to behave or what not – which is independent of how it is outside. Why therefore may a person not self-ascribe such a belief state to herself while acknowledging its falsehood?' The currently proposed 'solution' seems just to ignore the central point, the very one which generates the puzzle.

Another serious weakness of this solution is that it is difficult to apply to the second paradox. It is true that we sometimes use 'I do not believe that p' as a way of expressing disbelief. Where this is the case, then the second paradox is merely an alternative wording for the first. But where 'I do not believe that p' is taken as a self-ascription of ignorance as to whether p, then we do have a genuinely different conceptual structure. We could get some equivalence between 'I do not believe that p' and the claim that 'not p' only by imagining our thinker or speaker as considering him or herself to be omniscient. ('What I am not aware of, is not there to be thought of'.) This looks several degrees stranger than even a claim of infallibility.

So this whole approach looks very unattractive. I shall suggest in Section 6 that it is not in fact the only way of getting 'p' out of 'I believe that p' (for the first paradox). Wittgenstein discusses and implicitly criticises the particular solution just discussed (1980: 92), and it is distinct from the view he wishes to recommend. But for the moment we may find it difficult to see in what other way this skeletal first strategy could be fleshed out. So let us turn to the other and more familiar line. This is, of course, the reverse, namely to expand the 'not p' into an 'I do not believe that p' (for the first paradox) and the 'p' into 'I believe that p' (for the second), and so generate a tension at this level. Most discussions assume that this is the line we need to pursue for both paradoxes. But let us bear in mind that we might need one line for the first paradox and a different one for the second. For the moment, however, we shall consider attempts to apply the second strategy across the board.

3. MOORE'S ANSWER AND RELATIVES

It is clear that the contents 'p' or 'not p' alone will not suffice to do the job of generating the propositions 'I believe that p' or 'I do not believe that p'. Whatever it is which supplies us with these claims, in such a way that they can be in some kind of tension with the claims in the other halves of the Moorean judgements, the propositions by themselves cannot do it. Qua propositions, they carry only whatever the logical implications are of 'p' or 'not p', which do not in general include anything about people thinking or not thinking. So, it seems, it must be the occurrence of some event (or state) which has the proposition or not as content which brings with it the idea we need.

Many discussions, starting with Moore's own, take the event in question to be that of my (apparently sincerely) asserting that p or that not p. This event does the job by, somehow, implying that I do (or do not) believe that p. A number of different stories could be told about how the new proposition gets brought to our attention. We could say that it was merely a matter of inductive generalisation: those who assert that p (or not p) usually do believe that p (or do not believe that p): hence the new proposition enters the scene in virtue of hearers making such inductive inferences. This (very crudely) is Moore's own approach.

More subtly, one could say that it is a matter of how the speech act of assertion works. Thus Baldwin (calling on the sort of ideas about assertion offered by Grice) writes:

The implication [of belief or non-belief by assertion] must arise from the intention, constitutive of the speech act of assertion, of providing one's audience with information through their recognition that this is one's intention. For since one cannot be understood as intending to inform someone that p unless one is believed by them to believe that p, the intention to be thus understood includes the intention to be taken to believe what one asserts. (1990: 228)

Suppose that this is correct. Then when I say 'I don't believe that p but p' it seems that, by the first part of my utterance I intend to induce the belief that I do not believe that p (because that is the content of that bit of the assertion), while by the second part I intend to induce belief that I believe that p (in virtue of the principle stated in the last sentence of the quotation). So I intend to produce contradictory beliefs. Thus it looks as if, by this sort of unpacking, we could reveal some contradiction or contradiction-like phenomenon in the Moorean claim.

The above sort of story works best for the second paradox. In order to account for the oddness of the first Moorean claim (viz., 'I believe that p but not p') we have to go through more elaborate manoeuvres. That I say 'not p' somehow carries with it (in virtue of truths about the workings of assertion, or whatever) the idea that I believe that not p. This is the first step. But we can get from that to the idea that I do not believe that p only if we assume that I am rational and so do not have contradictory beliefs. So I, as a speaker, seem to be committed to inducing the (quite coherent) belief that I have contradictory beliefs. But I will be committed further to inducing contradictory beliefs in my hearer only if I assume that he or she will take me to be rational and I intend him or her to make the extra step.[3]

It is worth noting that more work needs to be done to make these arguments really cogent. For example, one difficulty is this. The original Gricean account, which seems to be invoked, says that in asserting that q I reveal to my audience my intention that she believe that q, and intend her to have this knowledge as her reason for believing that q. It is true that I cannot achieve my intended goal by this route (in normal circumstances) unless my audience also takes it that I intend her to have a true belief

---

3. Jones offers some more reflections on this and on how bringing in the conception of assertion as conveying knowledge might strengthen the account (Jones 1991).

and that I am myself well informed as to whether or not q. So, if all goes as planned, my audience will after the utterance be in possession of information from which she can infer that I believe that q. But we cannot, without calling on further principles of epistemic logic and the logic of intention, derive from this that I must intend my audience to believe that I believe that q. If, on the other hand, we take the later Gricean account (on which when I assert that q I intend my audience to believe that I believe that q) we run into other snags. I shall not pursue these matters in detail, since it is not part of my case that this general line of explication of the absurdity of the Moorean assertion does definitely work, although it seems plausible that something of this general sort can be made defensible. But if this is not so and the sort of account sketched above ultimately fails, because contradiction or some contradiction-like phenomenon can be derived only by calling on further invalid principles, then this strengthens the case for thinking that we should look elsewhere for a solution.[4]

Let us however concede, for the sake of the argument, that the above approach can be developed persuasively, and the act of uttering either of the Moorean sentences in an attempted sincere assertion can thus be shown to be bizarre and (in one case at least) to involve an attempt to induce contradictory beliefs. The question remains of whether these reflections say all there is to be said. And the central reason for thinking that they do not is that they fail to meet the first condition on a solution of the paradoxes. They tell us what would be odd about asserting a Moorean claim but say nothing about why it might be odd to think it. If there is no public and communicatively intended utterance, these strategies of solution can get no grip.

But can they be extended? Can we find some interior analogue? Baldwin (1990: 229–232) argues that we can. And he suggests further that reflection on the parallel will show us something of Wittgenstein's purposes in discussing the paradox, which, as Baldwin remarks, clearly have little to do with Gricean ideas about the structure of acts of assertion. Baldwin holds that a rational thinker will not consciously hold a Moorean belief 'for much the same reason that a rational speaker will not consciously assert a Moorean sentence'. Clearly, when I consciously make some judgment I do not put on some inner performance with the intention of convincing myself of something. But the fact that the belief is conscious (where a 'conscious' state is understood as one accompanied

---

4. For further helpful discussion of the pitfalls of employing epistemic logic in attempted solutions of the paradoxes, see Sorensen 1988: 19ff.

by awareness of itself) will do some similar work, in making the fact of my belief do double duty as also a sort of claim that it itself exists. So let us suppose that I consciously believe 'I believe that p but not p'. Now let us also take it that holding a conjunctive belief (whether consciously or otherwise) implies belief (whether consciously or otherwise) in each of the conjuncts. Then it follows that I consciously believe that I believe that p and I consciously believe that not p. So now, because of this second belief and in virtue of the consciousness, I believe that I believe not p. So I (consciously) believe that I believe p and I believe that I believe not p. If we are further allowed to take it that any two beliefs (even if one is conscious and the other not) yield a belief in the conjunction of their contents, then I believe that I believe p and that I believe not p. So I believe that I have a contradictory belief.

In the case of the second paradox, a suitably adapted chain of similar manoeuvres (which I shall not spell out in detail) can yield the conclusion that I believe of myself both that I do not believe that p and that also that I do believe that p. So here we get the outcome that I actually have a contradictory belief about myself if I consciously believe the second Moorean claim.

It is again important to note how much work is being done here by principles of epistemic logic. But let us waive this point. And let us grant also what Baldwin claims, namely that the two resultant beliefs can neither of them be held by a conscious rational thinker. The interesting question is what significance this has.

Wittgenstein concentrates on the first paradox (absurdity of self-attribution of particular error). What the paradoxicality of this shows, Baldwin claims, is that an individual cannot hold apart her conception of the world as it is and her conception of the world as she takes it to be. The subject of belief cannot appear in the world as the subject of belief. Baldwin (1990: 231) suggests that this is as far as Wittgenstein goes explicitly in his later discussions, but that what is implicit in it is a Tractarian view of the subject. 'Wittgenstein's view is that the way to come to terms with Moore's paradox is through a metaphysical conception of the subject. The reason that there are truths about me which I cannot believe is that because these are truths about me as a metaphysical subject, they cannot appear in my world.'

I would like to suggest that this is not a mandatory reading of the later Wittgenstein on this topic. One reason for uneasiness with it is that postulation of a metaphysical subject seems very likely to lead to solipsism, and thus to a strong form of first/third-person asymmetry in the meaning of psychological terms. But there seem to be many indications that these are views that Wittgenstein is struggling against in his later writings. Other people are in the world, as embodied fallible subjects, and so am I. Arguably this 'I' (the embodied, fallible, one among many) is the only sort of subject or person the later Wittgenstein wants us to recognise. If this is right, then his problem is to explain the phenomena – that is, Moore's paradoxes – in a way which precisely does not tempt us back to the Tractarian non-worldly 'limit' subject.

Another reason for worry is that further thought suggests that we have not, in the above reflections on conscious belief, fully satisfied the second condition on a solution for the first paradox; we have not yet found something contradiction-like in the thought 'I believe that p but not p'. Let us remind ourselves again of exactly what absurdity or tension enters the scene in the would-be Moorean thoughts. There is an important asymmetry here. In the case of the second paradox, what we would have without consciousness is a complex thought event, the occurrence of the second element of which (my believing that p) necessarily falsifies the content of the first (that I do not believe that p). The addition of consciousness gives me the further thought 'I believe that p'. So I end up believing a contradiction about my own psychological state. We can certainly agree with Baldwin that a rational thinker will not make this judgement, since doing so is itself a manifestation of irrationality. The contradictoriness is right there in the judgement which is made. Thus, as far as the second paradox goes, this line of solution seems satisfactory.

When we consider the first paradox, however, things are less clear. If I have the thought 'I believe that p but not p' without consciousness, there exists a complex thought event the second element in which (my believing that not p) can occur without falsifying the content of the first (that I believe that p), provided that I have contradictory beliefs. And, unfortunately, I can have such beliefs. It is this fact of our known liability to error and irrationality which prevents us from disentangling the first paradox by using the same sort of thoughts as we used to disentangle the second. When consciousness is added to the original thought, I come to be aware that I believe not p and so to be aware that, if I still believe that p as I take myself to do, then I have contradictory beliefs. But having this thought is not itself (in any obvious way) a manifestation of irrationality. Rather (one might say), it is a commendable recognition of fault. Originally I had one view about myself (that I had a certain belief) and I also had a view about the world which entailed the falsity of that belief. All that I am now doing, in the fully self-conscious judgement, about this complex

257

situation is, perfectly rationally and properly, recognising the nature and consequences of that original unfortunate complex state.

On this line of thought we must indeed acknowledge that I cannot truly make the Moorean judgement of myself unless I am irrational. I am irrational because my recognition of the error of a belief has failed to eradicate that belief in me. This is bad cognitive functioning in me. But if this is how things are (and we have no account yet which shows that it could not be so with me), how could it be irrational or contradictory to recognise that it is (unfortunately) so? On this representation of the structure of the thoughts, the recognition and persistence of the error and the consequent contradictoriness are all outside the conscious Moorean thought which I am now having. Hence the Moorean thought conceived this way is not itself irrational but is, rather, the sensible acknowledgement of irrationality.

But intuitively this is extremely unconvincing. 'I believe that p but not p' (as a conscious thought) seems to be in itself contradictory and tension-ridden, in at least as strong a way as 'I do not believe that p but p'. Someone who thinks it seems to be thinking contradictorily in that very judgement, not merely to be committed to recognising difficulty elsewhere. Our problem was to explain why it is absurd to think 'I believe that p but not p'. But all we have succeeded in doing is showing that if I were able to think it I would then be committed to recognising that my thoughts were contradictory. We have no explanation of why this should be something absurd for me to do.

We might try saying that it is conceptually impossible to think that p and that not p consciously at the same time. The Moorean claim would inherit this conceptual absurdity precisely because it seems to countenance such a possibility. But this move is unsatisfactory. It is acknowledged on all hands that a person may have contradictory beliefs. How does the addition of consciousness guarantee removal of our liability to such error? One may say that consciousness brings the two beliefs together and hence makes it extremely likely that rationality will operate in noticing the clash and removing one or both. But 'extremely likely' is not 'conceptually certain'. We may insist by fiat that it is necessary, but it would remain mysterious why we should be entitled to do so. Consciousness is being invoked as a deus ex machina, but the explanation we have of its nature (as involving second-order thought) does not show how it could have the postulated powers. If we admit that, however unlikely, it is nevertheless an empirical possibility that a person should (thoroughly irrationally of course) believe p and not p consciously at the same time, then we invite the response that if this happens to someone then the right thing for him to do is to acknowledge it in a Moorean judgement.

The object of this section has been to examine the second strategy for dealing with the paradoxes, namely that of expanding the 'p' or 'not p' into some claim about my beliefs and thus generating a contradiction. The suggestion I wish to make is that it may work for the second paradox but is far from satisfactory in dealing with the first, for the reasons just outlined. I also wish to suggest that, although Baldwin is quite right in emphasising that the contradictoriness of Moore's first paradoxical remark (if and when we do get it explained) connects closely with the impossibility of prising apart the conception of the world and the conception of what we believe the world to be, talk of a metaphysical conception of the subject may not be either the later Wittgenstein's reaction or the best reaction to the phenomenon.

4. FUNCTIONALISM AND THE PARADOX

It is natural at this point to think that we might get help with our problem by looking more closely into the meaning of the word 'believe'. If we set out in more detail what the state of belief is, then perhaps the nature and source of the Moorean oddity would become apparent to us. Let us therefore consider functionalism and its implications for our question. What I shall suggest is that, far from being helped to track the source of the contradiction, what we find is that the oddness of the Moorean claim seems to evaporate. (I have focused here on a functionalist account of belief because it is the most likely to seem plausible to a modern reader. But a line of argument similar to the one about to be developed could, I think, be produced if we had started instead with a Humean feeling-based account or a Cartesian inner-act view.)

We start from what is common to all versions of functionalism, broadly construed, namely this: to say that someone believes that p is to say roughly: 'He or she is in a state which, together with his or her desires, will normally cause behaviour which satisfies those desires only if p'. This general view is compatible with a whole variety of further detailed views, on how 'normal' is to be captured, on how desires are to be identified, on whether further conditions on normal causal origins should be imposed and so on. My aim is simply to gesture in the direction of those accounts of belief which are offered when, recoiling from Cartesian introspectionism, we insist that psychological notions have as their central role a causal/explanatory task vis-à-vis behaviour and we stress that

259

psychological states are attributed on the basis of observed patterns and dispositions in behaviour. Let us summarise these views by saying that they equate having a belief that p with being in a state apt to cause behaviour appropriate to its being the case that p.

It is very important to functionalism that the meaning of 'believe' is uniform and is given by some such account whether I attribute belief to myself or to another. The functionalist may admit that I do not observe my own patterns of behaviour in order to see what I believe. Perhaps, he will say, I have some internal, pre-consciously operating, self-scanning device which delivers to me usually true judgements about my beliefs. This operates in a way which enables me to shortcut any need for self-observation. All the same, the functionalist will insist, what I mean when I say 'I believe . . .' is fully captured by the mention of causes of behaviour and so on. There is, and could be, no more than this, namely the facts about truth conditions and the descriptive meaning of 'believe', to be said about the role of the word in the language.

Now consider the following case. We are familiar with the Mueller-Lyer illusion where the visual appearance of one item being longer than the other is not dissipated by the discovery that it is in reality equal or even shorter. Suppose such a case to involve some objects A and B, say sticks and not merely lines, and suppose that A looks, and continues to look, longer than B, while the reality is that B is very slightly longer than A. Suppose further that, in my particular case, it is not only visual impressions which fail to fall into line with increased information, but also a considerable part of my bodily behaviour. For example, if I want the longer of the two sticks then I find my hand reaching out towards A rather than B; if someone asks me to point to the longer, I point to A and so forth.

Is this quite absurd and unimaginable? It would be rash to rule it out on a priori grounds. Moreover, phenomena do exist which somewhat resemble what has been described and which give some hint of what it might be like to experience it. For example, when watching a film taken from a roller coaster people sway and clutch their seats. Despite their knowledge that they are not moving, the visual input carries such vivid messages of plunging and swooping that the appropriate bodily behaviour is difficult to restrain.

The account of belief sketched above mandates us to say in such an extended Mueller-Lyer case: 'I believe that A is longer than B, but B is longer than A'. That is, we can believe and assert of ourselves, with perfect intelligibility and propriety, the Moorean sentence. There is some state in me (viz., the illusion with its extended powers) which is causing me to behave in a way which will be successful in fulfilling my desires only if A is longer than B; but A is not longer than B, as I have realised and stated in the other part of my utterance. The question which set us off brooding on the paradox was this: to say 'I believe that p' is just to say that things are a certain way with me, without commitment to how it is with the rest of the world; so why can I not discover that things are that way with me while also remarking that in the world outside not p? What we have done with the thought experiment is to flesh this out with a particular account (the functionalist one) of what has to be the case with me when I believe. And we have discovered that when belief is so construed, the oddness vanishes.

Here is another case. I embark upon a certain course of action, entering a competitive examination for a job, exhibiting many signs of cheerfulness and confidence; I am jaunty and smiling; I say, 'I'm going to win this one'; I make no arrangements for alternative jobs. At the same time I do other things which are appropriate preparations for the treatment of a person who has received a horrible and unexpected (let me stress that) shock. For example, I collect herbs and brew a potion, the peculiar and sole virtue of which is to console for the frightful pangs associated with unanticipated misfortune. It is clear from when I brew the liquid and where I stow it that I am the intended recipient and that the day it is to be taken is the day of the announcement of the examination result. I am aware of what I am doing and say: 'I believe that I am going to fail and more, I believe that I believe falsely that I shall succeed. But of course I shall succeed!'

The case makes essentially the same point as the extended Mueller-Lyer. Both seem to licence the straightforward making of the Moorean claim. The second case, however, shows additionally that (assuming functionalism) we can also licence on the basis of non-linguistic behaviour ascription of the belief 'I believe falsely that p'.

What should we conclude from these cases? One move would be to take them at their face value and, accepting functionalism, to say that they show that there is no paradox; there is really no oddness in Moorean claims, hence no problem in explaining why there should be oddness; we have been led into the mistaken idea that there was some oddness simply by lack of imagination and by the rareness of the cases; Moorean claims are not conceptually quasi-contradictory but merely extremely unlikely to be true.

A way of avoiding this somewhat unwelcome and implausible collapse of our whole problem would be to say that there are faults in the so far rather vague functionalist story we have been telling. It is clear, it might be said, that not all my behaviour, in the extended Mueller-Lyer, is appropriate to A's being longer than B. After all, I intentionally produce, in the second part of the utterance, a verbal account of how things are. This action is under the control of some other representation of the world than the one which is directing the movement of my limbs. Similar remarks are clearly appropriate in the examination case. Perhaps we should so formulate our functionalist account that a belief can be attributed only if all behaviour is unified under the control of one consistent set of representations.

But this is clearly too strong a demand. People do have contradictory beliefs, and each of such a pair will manifest itself in a different area of behaviour. In general, when we become aware of such contradictions after reflection one belief or the other or both disappear. What is undoubtedly unusual about the cases imagined is that the person has contradictory beliefs, and knows it, but that both persist, one controlling one part of behaviour, for example limb movement, and the other some different part, for example vocalisation. This is doubtless all very unfortunate for the person who is its subject and (in some sense) irrational. But to acknowledge that it is regrettable and irrational is very different from supposing that it could not happen or could not be quite straightforwardly described if it did happen. Nothing in the functionalist story seems to entitle us to rule out the persistence of contradictory beliefs in the imagined cases, even when the subject is aware of them as contradictory. So we seem driven back to the conjecture that the whole idea of a paradox was a mistake. Is this acceptable?

In setting up these cases I have helped myself to the whole normal background of human life, behaviour and speech. I have helped myself to the idea that the Moorean utterance as a whole (if made sincerely) expresses a belief of mine, and consequently that its second part expresses my belief that not p. It is clearly presupposed in setting up the paradox that the 'I' spoken of in the explicit self-description is the same as the person whose belief is expressed in the utterance as a whole, and also that the 'belief' explicitly spoken of is the same as the belief expressed, viz., belief in the ordinary sense. (If 'I' meant 'this rabbit' and 'believe that p' meant 'eats grass' of course there would be no paradox.) In toying with the idea that there is really no paradox we have assumed these presuppositions to be fulfilled – namely that the 'I' spoken of and the 'I' who speaks are the same, and that the functional account of belief is the one and only one, which captures not only the sense of the explicit self-description but also what could be said of me about my relation to the whole proposition expressed by the Moorean sentence.

Are these assumptions right? One fact to note is that it is extremely natural to fall into some kind of contrastive emphasis and/or verbal elaboration in reporting the imagined cases. For example, one might well be tempted to say 'This body believes that p but not p' or (bringing out the fact that the second part expresses a belief) 'This body believes that p but I believe that not p'. Another formulation might also seem apt: 'I believe in a bodily way that p but not p' or 'I believe *in a bodily way* that p, but I really believe that not p'. The impulse to produce this kind of contrastive description suggests that there may be something wrong in the assumptions that the sense of belief and/or the postulated subject of belief are uniform. The impulse behind the reformulations is to allow me to distance myself from the explicitly ascribed belief, either by assigning it to another subject or by denying that it is full belief. But if it is right to do either of these things then we will be wrong to think that we have discovered the non-existence of the paradox. If the subject of belief or the sense of 'believe' are not the same, we may find when we bring them into line again that the paradox has reappeared.

Which of the two sorts of reformulation, if either, is likely to be the more defensible? Distinguishing between 'me' and 'this body' is plausible at the level of sense or mode of presentation but highly controversial at the level of reference. It would seem rash to embark on a defence of dualism. The alternative, distinguishing kinds of belief, has no such obvious drawbacks and does seem to provide a way of expressing something which needs saying, namely that my relations to the proposition that p and to the proposition that not p are importantly different in the imagined case. For example, as far as conversation and further personal interaction with me is concerned (debating what is really the case, making plans for the future, sharing a joke, being outraged at my flippancy, blaming me, encouraging me, condoling with me, etc.), you will treat me as one who believes not p; it is on the basis of this that all your moves will be premised. This is part of what we understand in grasping that normal human life is proceeding as the background to the strange events. The regrettable fact that in certain respects I carry on as if I believed that p, namely that my limbs from time to time execute various manoeuvres, is something that you and I will plan to change or circumvent.

Let us, then, use 'believe' in the clear understanding that we are speaking of a particular relation to a proposition, namely the one I have when I 'really' believe it. Now suppose I say 'I believe not p – as our conversations, plans, etc. rightly assume – but in fact p'? The paradox has reappeared, since this utterance is extremely odd, as is equally the idea that I should make this judgement about myself. All the old flavour of contradictoriness is detectable.

What we found earlier was that we had a worrying disappearance of the paradox on our original functionalist account of belief. We first considered avoiding this by reformulating functionalism to rule out contradictory beliefs and found that unsatisfactory. Can we now explain the reappearance of the paradox by pointing to some further modified and enriched functionalist account of belief? If so, we can preserve both functionalism and our intuition that the paradox is central to the nature of belief. This would seem to be rather a satisfactory outcome. So perhaps we should try something like this, as an elucidation of the sense of 'believe' I have been gesturing at with this talk of conversation and normal human life: 'A believes that p' means 'A behaves, including behaviour in deliberation and vocalisation, in a way which will be desire-fulfilling if and only if p'. (Making this move might also satisfy the impulse to insist that what has gone wrong so far is that we have not considered specifically conscious belief. On the account suggested earlier, conscious belief is belief accompanied by belief in itself. And this latter will on the current approach consist in dispositions to behaviour appropriate to the first-level belief, e.g., among other things in explicit deliberative and vocal behaviour.)

This formulation does not, however, provide the stable resting place we might hope. Instead it invites the imagination of further bizarre cases. Suppose, for example, that under the influence of certain drugs or tiredness the extended Mueller-Lyer case extends itself even further, so that I find not merely my bodily behaviour but also some chains of images and representation and some vocalisations taking off under the control of the belief that A is longer than B. In other words, I find that I cannot stop ideas of what would be the case if A were longer than B coming into my mind, and when they get there they exert the same control over bodily behaviour as the original erroneous belief; and I find myself uttering these new conclusions, even though, in some sense, I wish to repudiate them. I still, however, have enough control of my voice, when I try, to say 'I believe that A is longer than B but B is longer than A'.

It is clear that if this happens to me I am in an even worse case than when my limbs alone are carrying on bizarrely. But, to reiterate the earlier point, to remark that something would be a grave misfortune to a person is quite a different thing from supposing that it cannot happen or be recognised and described by him or her when it does happen. On the current hypothesis about the meaning of 'believe', an entirely straight-forward form of words is instantly available, to be used quite literally and unparadoxically, to describe my unfortunate state, viz., 'I believe that p but not p'. So we have again mislaid the strange nature of the Moorean claim, and the revised functionalist story does not, after all, quite capture that apparent sense of 'believe' we meant to gesture at when we talked of normal human life and conversation.

5. WHY FUNCTIONALISM CANNOT RECOGNISE THE PARADOX

What conclusions should we draw from the discussion of the last section? I wish now to suggest that there are general reasons for thinking that any functionalist approach must encounter the same troubles as the versions we have examined and so must fail to account for the idea that there is something contradictory about the Moorean claim. I shall further urge that this is a serious problem for functionalism.

The first point to note is that functionalism is formulated within a (nat-ural and attractive) metaphysical view. On this view, the world contains a variety of phenomena which people may come across and of which they may form some conception (Wittgenstein 1953: 190). Among these are states of themselves, including beliefs. They come across these either by introspection (although this idea would more naturally go with a Humean or Cartesian view than with a functionalist one) or in seeking to ex-plain, in proto-scientific folk psychology, the behaviour of themselves and those around them. The linguistic behaviour of the word 'believe' is to be explained by unpacking the truth conditions of claims about beliefs; these in turn are explained by pointing to the conception people have of the phenomenon they have come across, a conception which will more or less accurately capture the nature of the pre-existing phenomenon. (Lurking behind this commonsensical-seeming account are further pic-tures, e.g., of the world as already sliced by nature at the joints and awaiting only labelling from us, of empiricism as the right account of concept acquisition and of the correspondence theory of truth.)

The second point to remark is the particular content of the conception of belief with which functionalism fills out this general schema. Belief is something which goes on within a person (and has the kind of properties such internal or intrinsic states could have, e.g., experiential character or causal power vis-à-vis bodily behaviour) but is independent of how things are outside him or her. What we 'come across' when we come across belief is something which has a representational character, but where what is represented may either exist or not.

Given this general conception, it is difficult to see how any functionalist account could discover contradiction in a Moorean claim. By its second element, functionalism has been set up to give maximum force to the thoughts that make it appear that the Moorean claim should not be absurd. But also, by its first element, it has deprived itself of any materials from metaphysics or theory of meaning which it could use to extract itself from this difficulty. The second element says that when I ascribe a belief to myself, I say that I am in such and such an inner state, which is independent of how things are in the world. The first element says that we must talk only of truth conditions in explaining semantic features of sentences. (Thus talk of language games or deep 'grammatical' first/third-person asymmetries or any such waffly stuff is ruled out.) So if there is a contradiction it must come from the truth conditions. But the truth conditions have been set up precisely to rule out the possibility of such contradiction.

This is not a tight proof that something recognisably functionalist cannot deliver the goods, and we may if we choose try yet more elaborate versions of the kinds of accounts examined in the last section. But I would suggest that there are good reasons to be sceptical of success in exhibiting any contradictoriness in the Moorean claim by this route. Suppose this scepticism is well founded. Should we nevertheless stay with the idea that some functionalist story (such as the more elaborate one considered at the end of the last section) does give the right account of belief? And should we in consequence say that there is no contradiction in the Moorean claim? Philosophers, in thinking that there is, have perhaps merely over-reacted to the fact that the claim describes a very unusual situation, or to the fact that there is some kind of pragmatic oddity in the Moorean utterance, or to the fact that there is contradictory belief somewhere in the psyche of the person who makes the Moorean claim.

There is a problem of principle with this proposal, which provides some backing for the feeling that we should not just dismiss the apparent contradictory character of Moorean claims as a mass delusion among philosophers. When we consider the unfortunate people enmeshed in the extended Mueller-Lyer situations, it is clear that the particular functionalist account of the end of Section 4 does not capture the ordinary sense of 'believe'. We may agree that the use of the word 'believe' is not totally inappropriate. Someone who found him or herself in such a situation might well say, 'It is as if I believed that p'. But such a person would not say straightforwardly, 'I believe that p' – as the functionalist story demands. What is true of this version of functionalism will (I suggest) be true of any other version which fails to deliver a contradiction in the Moorean utterance, for the following reason. If there is no contradiction, then the subject may coherently acknowledge the supposed belief that p while at the same time affirming that in reality not p. And if the subject does thus affirm that not p (while coherently acknowledging also the continuance of the supposed functionalist belief that p), we will surely want to say that this affirmation is what expresses his or her 'real' belief and hence that whatever was captured by the functionalist story is not (contrary to hypothesis) real belief. In summary, if functionalism does not deliver a contradiction, we can have the subject acknowledging the supposed 'belief' but also disowning it; and then the functionalist story has not captured the ordinary sense of 'believe'. My challenge to the functionalist, in brief, is to show how what happened to the definitions proposed in Section 4 could be avoided by any other proposed definition which satisfies the functionalist overall demands. Putting these thoughts together in sequence we have this: a deep-seated metaphysical picture motivates functionalism; but functionalism cannot deliver a contradiction; in failing to deliver a contradiction it undermines its claim to capture the normal sense of 'believe'.

The thrust of the argument is to suggest that the source of the muddle we find ourselves in is the metaphysical picture which dictates the shape of the functionalist account. The next section pursues that thought. Other options are available at this point. I do not claim to have conclusive proof that no version of functionalism can reveal the Moorean claim as contradictory. Nor have we proof that we must retain the idea of the contradictoriness. The considerations urged on both these issues were suggestive rather than fully cogent. Hence two options at least are to look to further versions of functionalism or to the defensibility of abandoning the paradoxes. A third quite different possibility would be to suggest that we should look to the epistemology of belief to find a solution. It has been suggested (following Wittgenstein) that usually when a person self-ascribes the belief that p, he or she does so on grounds which are the same as his or her grounds for judging that p. Thus, if I am asked 'Do you believe that p?' I do not think about myself. Rather I ask 'p'? And if the answer is 'yes' then I say 'I believe that p'. If this is the standard route to self-ascriptions of belief then perhaps some contradictory character appears in 'I believe that p but not p' when said in circumstances where the presumption is of the normal epistemology. (I shall not examine the details of what contradiction would emerge or exactly how.) On this scenario it is not the metaphysics behind functionalism nor yet its particular account of the meaning of 'believe' which leads to our inability to elucidate the paradox, but rather our blindness about the distinctive epistemology of 'believe'. Investigation of this proposal would require more space than we have here. So I simply note it and turn to ask how things might go if we did not like the look of any of these options and chose instead to question functionalism and its framework.

6. A WITTGENSTEINIAN ACCOUNT AGAIN

What alternative could there be to using the word 'believe' as a label for some phenomenon, some internal state of people, which people come across in themselves or others? A possible answer is that it is a phenomenon which comes into existence together with certain practices of ascribing it. The full phenomenon of belief, the kind of belief which people have, only exists when creatures like ourselves engage in practices of belief ascription – where those practices do not have the shape which the metaphysical picture underlying functionalism demands. Someone being trained to use the word 'believe' in his or her first language is not simply being taught to connect the word with a pre-existing something of which he or she is aware; rather, such a learner is being educated into being a believer. Let me try to make this less schematic by outlining what I suggest to be a Wittgensteinian account of belief ascription, together with how it accounts for the contradictoriness of Moorean claims.

The proposal may be put like this. We have a practice with the word 'believe' which combines a number of features. The first, (A), is that beliefs are often attributed to people on the basis of observed patterns in behaviour. So the sort of third-personal criteria which the functionalist emphasises are indeed connected to the concept. It is no mistake to think they are. But there is much more to be said than this. A second feature, (B), is that a person learning the language is also trained to say 'I believe that p' sometimes as a substitute for the plain assertion 'p'. This training, of its very nature, makes the trained person's utterance of 'I believe that p' very often occur without his or her checking any criteria. In particular, the trained person does not check up on his or her behaviour. If any evidence is looked at, it is evidence as to whether p. But often, of course, if a person has already settled that p, then he or she does not check anything before saying 'p', and in these cases he or she would likewise not check anything before saying 'I believe that p'. (Here the practice which is the basis for the distinctive epistemology alluded to at the end of the last section appears, but placed as an element in an overall account of a non-functionalist character. There is clearly a parallel between what is suggested here about 'believe' and Wittgenstein's views about how 'It hurts' or 'I am in pain' are introduced as replacements for non-linguistic pain behaviour. It seems highly probable that it was the possibility of linking Moore's paradox with these strands of his thought which aroused the enthusiasm Wittgenstein expressed in his 1944 letter to Moore, quoted by Gombay [1988: 192].)

If we stopped at this point and considered only (B) we would have an extremely direct solution to Moore's problem. 'I believe that p' is merely (as far as [B] alone goes) an alternative way of saying 'p'. So of course one who says 'I believe that p but not p' contradicts him- or herself; in effect, what has been said is 'p but not p'. This is, in essence, the solution we shall continue to defend. All the same, we cannot stop at this point, for this would leave the two uses of 'believe' (the third-person behaviour-based one and the first-person present-tense one just described) unconnected with each other. However, there is a third feature, (C), of the practice with 'believe' which knits them together. It is that these first-person utterances – produced criterionlessly as sketched above – are taken as self-descriptions in which the speaker presents him- or herself as satisfying the behavioural conditions for belief mentioned in (A). Not only are such utterances taken as self-descriptions; they are also taken as authoritative, provided they are sincere. So the non-existence of appropriate behaviour is ground for questioning the truth of a self-ascription of belief and at the same time ground for questioning its sincerity.

Suppose we want to hold that these three features are all elements of the one unified concept of belief, and we want to say that the notion thus defined, in virtue of feature (B), helps to show why Moorean utterances are paradoxical; then we are faced with a problem. How can we retain the rough equation of 'I believe that p' with 'p' when (C) becomes part of the package? Isn't it much more sensible at this point to say that the lack of explicit attention to one's own behaviour (which everyone acknowledges to be a feature of self-ascription of belief) is the result of our having some unconsciously operating self-scanning mechanism? Should we not at the same time play down the idea that a subject is really authoritative about his or her own beliefs? Perhaps all that is involved in our uneasiness in attributing error to the sincere self-ascriber is our having got used to relying on what people say about themselves because it is generally true.

This way lies a return to the familiar functionalist story, and thus loss of the equation hinted at by (B) and loss of ability to explain the paradox.

Let us try another tack. There is a way to hold on both to the rough equation (of 'I believe that p' with 'p' suggested by [B]) and also to the authoritativeness of (C). It is to shift from thinking of this authority as epistemological to thinking of it as constitutive – to put matters in another idiom, judging that one believes that p has a sort of performative character. I do not mean by this that any element of choice is in question. A person does not choose his or her beliefs. Relatedly, the proposal is not that saying 'I believe that p' (which is a voluntary action) constitutes belief that p. The authoritativeness built into our practices with 'believe' is authoritativeness only for sincere first-person pronouncements; we build into the practice that questioning truth must also be questioning sincerity. The constitutive link which we can then see the practice as embodying is one which ties thinking that I believe that p (i.e., what the sincerity of my remark consists in) to believing that p. So the proposal is of 'performativeness' only in the sense that the abstract feature we are familiar with from consideration of performatives is present in this case too, namely that the occurrence of a representation of a state of affairs is itself what constitutes that state of affairs. The representation we are here speaking of is my thinking that I believe that p. In summary, I am entitled to pronounce on my beliefs, not because I have some privileged epistemological access to an independent state, but because when I come to think that I believe that p then I do, in virtue of that very thought, believe that p. It is, however, important to remember that, as with any performative, certain background conditions must be present which render the claim 'happy', in Austin's terms (Austin 1962). Thus we do not give the subject carte blanche to pronounce on his or her beliefs if she is tired, deranged, under stress, under the influence of drugs and so on.

If we are prepared to make this radical move, then we can hang on to something like the simple solution of the paradox. Suppose I say sincerely 'I believe that p' and thereby express my belief that I believe that p. This belief, namely that I believe that p, itself constitutes in me a belief that p. So my utterance 'I believe that p' also expresses belief that p. In doing this it is, from one perspective, just an alternative form of assertion that p. So if I now add 'but not p' then I have contradicted myself.

Thus we have in 'I believe that p' an utterance which is, at one and the same time, a member of two different classes. On the one hand, it is a self-description of me as a believer and as such has all the possibilities of grammatical transformation, entry into inference and possibility of incompatibility with behavioural evidence which that involves. On the other hand, it is an expression of belief that p, an alternative way of voicing out what could also be voiced out as 'p'. When we sense the contradiction in the Moorean utterance, we hear 'I believe that p' in this second role. When we become puzzled about why the utterance is contradictory, we hear it in the first role.

The remarks of the last paragraph bear on the oddness of the overt Moorean assertion. But what of the Moorean thought? Clearly a closely analogous solution can be offered. As we have already stressed, what is central to the proposal is not that the utterance 'I believe that p' constitutes belief, but that its sincerity does so. If our concept of belief does indeed work like this, then the same dual character to be found in the utterance 'I believe that p' will also be found in the thought with that content. When we contemplate someone having this thought, we take him or her to have a representation which is at the same time about the self and about the world. It is both a belief that he or she believes that p and a belief that p. One and the same state enters into two sets of inferential, evidence-responsive, and so on, relations. We have the troublesome sense that the Moorean thought is both coherent and incoherent as we concentrate now on one and now on another of the patterns in which its first element sits.

Functionalism is not entirely wrong. The third-personal behavioural criteria which it stresses are genuinely part of the notion of belief. But, to put things metaphorically, it captures only one dimension of a notion which has a type of complexity or depth not envisaged within the meta-physical and linguistic picture of which functionalism is a part. The real shape of the concept is one in which criterionless first–person ascription and behaviourally based third-person ascription are inseparably linked.

Even in the hypothesis the pattern is not what you think. When you say 'Suppose I believe' you are presupposing the whole grammar of the word 'to believe', the ordinary use, of which you are master. (Wittgenstein 1980: 192)

So in ascribing belief to another one may make the ascription on the basis of behaviour but will take for granted the ability of the subject to make criterionless self-ascription. In self-ascribing criterionlessly one will take for granted appropriate behaviour. If psychological notions did not have this complexity of shape then our normal human interactions with each other would be impossible.

We are strongly inclined to say that one utterance – 'I believe that p' – cannot be univocal and also combine the two roles of which I have spoken. Relatedly, we shall protest that a supposedly descriptive concept defined by the joint presence of features (A), (B) and (C) is misbegotten and impossible. There will perhaps be pressure to divide usage up into a proper descriptive element (behavioural criteria again) and something else (i.e., the aberrant first-person present-tense use) which is given an expressive or speech act account. But what entitles us to do this or necessitates it? Can't we have concepts of whatever shape we like, governed by whatever patterns of ascription rules we like, if they do good work for us? Clearly we could not set up the practice I have just sketched, and operate the notion of 'belief' which it defines, unless various contingencies obtained, most strikingly that people's sincere criterionless self-ascriptions do, almost invariably, pass the test of acceptability by behavioural criteria. The practice with the word 'believe' is erected on a substructure of facts about our social nature, ability to respond to certain training, brain workings and so forth. But is this any criticism of the concept or proof that it does not have the nature described? To answer this question would involve tackling large issues to do with concepts, meaning, truth and fact, and would take us beyond the scope of this essay.[5]

5. I discuss further why willingness to introduce considerations about the presuppositions of concepts and to talk of the 'language games' they are linked with need not undermine ideas of truth and realism in another place (Heal 1989).

14

On First-Person Authority

1. INTRODUCTION

What people say, in the first person and present tense, about their own thoughts is treated as authoritative. This is not to say that such remarks (avowals) are unquestionable. A person's claims about her beliefs, intentions, feelings, sensations and so on can be challenged. But the doubt usually centres on the speaker's sincerity or command of language rather than on the idea of her being in plain honest error. About some subject matters, for example the properties of objects in the material world or others' thoughts, one can easily be in plain honest error, and in ways which bring no criticism upon one. For example, the error may come about because the world has coincidentally piled up misleading evidence or because others have conspired to deceive one. About one's own thoughts, however, one cannot, in this everyday manner, just be mistaken. This is not to deny that there are cases where a sincere avowal seems so much at odds with other evidence that we cannot endorse it. But in such cases we find that the rejected avowal still retains a kind of shadowy credence. We are inclined to say that the person 'sort of' believes or intends as she insists she does. But at the same time we do not think her fault-free. Instead notions like self-deception and failure of rationality get a grip. And if a wide and persistent gap opens up between apparent sincere self-ascriptions and what other evidence suggests to be the case, then serious questions arise about the stability and continued existence of the person who apparently speaks to us.

It is also the case that when a person is asked about what she thinks, intends, feels and so forth she is very often able to answer straight off and without any reflection or assembling of evidence. And if she does need to reflect or pause before answering, what goes on then is very different from what goes on when she reflects with a view to answering similar questions about another. In the case of another, centrally important evidence is provided by that other's behaviour; in one's own case, one does not attend to one's own behaviour.

These are the familiar broad outlines of the phenomenon of first-person authority. A full picture would reveal much more complexity. There are many nuances, exceptions and phenomenological subtleties to be added. Different psychological concepts exhibit characteristic differences in the kinds of mistake they allow for and in their usual modes of self- and other-ascription. But I shall not attempt to fill in these details.[1] Rather, we shall look at the salient features of the phenomenon and explore some ramifications of a particular approach to it.

Central to the approach is the idea that first-person authority should be understood as 'constitutive', in some sense of that term. Section 2 reminds us very briefly of the difficulties of some familiar proposals and of the advantages of a constitutive account, if it can be made to work. Section 3 examines the case of promising, noting how similar difficulties may be encountered in explaining authority; and Section 4 considers how a constitutive account solves the problems here. Section 5 suggests how analogous ideas might apply to at least some psychological concepts and remarks on some corollaries of the approach.

2. THE CONUNDRUM OF FIRST-PERSON AUTHORITY

It would be good to have an account of the nature of the psychological which allowed us to combine all three of the following prima facie plausible claims:

(1) People's first-person present-tense self-ascriptions of their psychological states are authoritative, while second- and third-person ascriptions are not authoritative.[2]
(2) Psychological predicates have the same meaning and role in first-, second- and third-person uses.
(3) Persons and their psychological states are among the public and effect-producing occupants of the universe. Hence we operate exactly as we should

---

1. Helpful recent discussions which bring out some of the complexities of the phenomenon can be found in a recent collection edited by Wright, Smith and Macdonald (1998), in particular in the papers by Fricker, Martin, Peacocke and Wright.
2. And what about first-person ascriptions about the past or the future? A very interesting question, which raises problems we cannot deal with here.

when we attribute psychological states from a third-person point of view by observing, and seeking to account for, others' behaviour.

Claim (1) records the difference between first-person and other-person uses of psychological predicates which is our starting point. Claim (2) represents our sense that, all the same, we must not push this difference so far that our psychological talk fragments into two unrelated halves. Claim (3) summarises our aspiration to an account of the psychological which is 'realist' but does not involve us in suspect forms of dualism.

One of the most familiar facts about philosophy of mind is the difficulty we have in reconciling these three claims. (By 'we' I mean analytically minded philosophers of the last few decades.) Consider briefly some familiar approaches, with their strengths and weaknesses. Dualism seeks to accommodate (1) and (2) by postulating a special kind of fact, to which only the subject can have access. The cost of this is loss of (3). Analytic functionalism does admirably by (2) and (3) and is, moreover, very congenial to us because of its promise of a straightforward reconciliation of realism about the psychological with the naturalism of the natural sciences. This leads to familiar difficulties in dealing with (1). Both of these views endorse the commonsense idea embodied in (2), viz., that avowals are assertions and so expressions of second-level beliefs about the first-level states the speaker self-ascribes. Expressivism jettisons (2), maintaining that avowals express not second-level beliefs but rather the first-level states they seem to describe. Its claim is that it can thereby give proper weight to (1) and (3). None of these views, however, can satisfy all three desiderata.

Could a 'constitutive' account of matters provide a way out of the puzzlements? The idea distinctive of this approach is that the existence of a second-level belief about a first-level psychological state is itself what makes it true that the first-level state exists. Some advantages of the proposal are evident. A sincere expression of a second-level belief is, by definition, one which springs from that belief. And if a constitutive story is right, then this second-level belief brings with it the first-level state it is about. Hence the existence of first-person authority is explained.

Moreover, it is explained in a radically different way from that pictured in dualism. Dualism arises when we start from the idea that authority is the upshot of some cognitive faculty operating over against an independent item, which it nevertheless cannot but represent accurately. It is this 'privileged confrontation' picture of authority which forces its defenders in the unwelcome direction of strange metaphysics, since we cannot see how public, effect-producing spatio-temporal items could be either the subject or the object of such privileged cognition. An account of authority which does not build in this pressure to dualism is attractive.

But a constitutive story is, at first sight, not obviously less metaphysically problematic than dualism. What must beliefs and the people who have them be like if the constitutive story is to be correct? Can it be developed in a way which is not metaphysically bizarre and which respects the other two desiderata? These are the questions we must tackle.

Before we do that we need to clarify the logical shape of the proposal. One development of the root constitutive idea says that the occurrence of a second-level belief is in itself sufficient for the occurrence of the relevant first-level state. This claim is defensible in a few cases. For example (as noted by Burge [1996]), 'I am entertaining the proposition that p' is a thought the having of which guarantees that the person is indeed entertaining the proposition that p. But the view looks seriously implausible as a general account, as it gives us infallibility about our own thoughts rather than the more complex position sketched earlier, in which self-deception is allowed for.[3]

So a preferable development of the approach says that the occurrence of the second-level belief contributes a necessary element to a set of conditions which are jointly sufficient for the first-level state. (The first story is subsumed in this one, since a second-level belief by itself may be sufficient in cases where the set of extra conditions is empty.) This proposal opens the possibility of defending the claim that these other conditions are ones which we are entitled to assume are normally in place. Our assuming this would then explain the respect we accord to a sincere comprehending self-ascription because, given these other conditions, it shows the existence of the one missing piece (viz., second-order belief) which secures the existence of the first-order state. But the proposal also allows that the other conditions may, exceptionally, be thought to fail. And where this is so we can acknowledge the existence of an inaccurate but still sincere and comprehending self-ascription.

So much, then, in bald formal outline of the constitutive idea and its merits. The problem is that it remains extremely mysterious how it could possibly be correct. The next two sections will try to remove some of that mystery by considering another case – that of promising. My

---

3. Stoneham (1998) defends an infallibilist position of this kind. The two assumptions which enable him to do so are that we may unpack 'A believes that p' as 'A ought to act as if p', and that the obligation to act as if one ought to act as if p generates the same requirements as the obligation to act as if p. Although these premises have their attractions, they are also controversial.

hope is that by coming at the issues from this slightly unfamiliar angle we shall be enabled to gain a new perspective on the psychological and to see what is needed to make a constitutive account work. We find in the case of promising a first/third-person asymmetry of authority, and also analogues to the unsatisfactory dualist and functionalist moves for the psychological. Further, we can see how an expressivist option is here particularly attractive and why it fails. But what is also helpful about the promising case, I shall suggest, is that it allows us to see how an overly narrow view of what is required by desideratum (3) may block our route to a satisfactory position.

3. PROMISING AND AUTHORITY

Suppose that I am a keen gardener and I say, 'My marrows promise to be large this year'. What do I mean? The truth conditions of my claim seem to be that my marrows exhibit some observable feature (e.g., being already sizeable for their age and healthy) which shows that they have a real tendency to grow large and so entitles an observer to expect that they will be large. Many other uses of 'promise' clearly work on this model. My niece Sandra may promise to be a fine mathematician because she has mastered algebra at a strikingly young age. Were she self-aware and boastful, she might even say of herself on that basis, 'I promise to be a fine mathematician'.

It is clear that what young Sandra does is not to issue a promise, in the sense of 'promise' which has received most philosophical attention. To distinguish cases, let us call the familiar case 'personal promising' and what occurs with the marrows and Sandra 'natural promising'. Generalising the account, we say: A naturally promises to Φ iff A does something which shows a real tendency to Φ and so entitles an observer to expect that A will Φ. (I shall ignore here, as irrelevant to our concerns, complexities to do with the difference between threat and promise, whether what is promised must be taken to be desirable and the like.)

Consider now a philosopher who is aware of cases of natural promising and the use of 'promise' to label them, and who then meets with our practice of making personal promises by uttering such things as 'I promise to return the money next Friday'. Let us also suppose that this philosopher is blinkered, in that he cannot conceive of any way of construing our giving of personal promises except as self-ascriptions of natural promising, on the model of young Sandra's boastful remark. (It may seem a waste of time to pursue the blinkered philosopher's possible moves, since it is obvious that something has already gone wrong. But I suggest that it could be illuminating, as it may point us in the direction of a similar but much less obvious mistake we have made about the psychological.) How will things go? As in the case of the psychological, there are three facts to be accounted for, viz., there is an asymmetry of authority, the word 'promise' seems univocal in first-, second- and third-person uses, and promising is a public occurrence which has distinctive upshots. So can the blinkered philosopher make headway?

What may be surprising is how well his approach answers to start with. The account effectively captures some salient features of the situation. The information that the speaker is likely to do the act mentioned is clearly something the hearer derives from the utterance. We can see this because we see that the hearer goes away and makes plans which depend upon the speaker's doing what she promised to do. It is also clear that the speaker intends the hearer to acquire this information and to act in this sort of way.

Where the approach comes a cropper, however, is in its inability to account for the element of first-person authority in promising. Someone who says 'I promise' must be taken as promising (barring some unusual circumstances, which will be mentioned below). But if things are as supposed by our blinkered philosopher, this is seriously strange. It seems plain that I could make a mistake about whether or not I naturally promise to Φ. Hence it seems that I cannot be authoritative on the matter.

One response might be to suggest that the issuer of the promise is reporting on some special kind of fact to which only she has direct and infallible access. But (like dualism) this is unattractive, since it abandons the connection between my promising to Φ and the fact that a hearer is justified in expecting me to Φ. It thus loses sight of the fact that promising is an event in the public world with public consequences for behaviour. Another response is to say that experience has shown us that people are extremely reliable about whether or not they exhibit signs of being about to Φ, and hence we have a practice of treating their sincere self-ascriptions of promising with great respect. But this (like the parallel invocation in functionalism of some reliable mechanism for producing second-level belief) is no good because it fails to account for the conceptual nature of the authority.

As we have noted, a third move which is made in the case of the psychological is the 'expressivist' one. The idea is that a self-ascriptive token of (for example) 'I believe that p' does not have the meaning or the role which at first sight it seems to have. It looks as if it has truth conditions, viz., that I believe that p. And it also looks as if in uttering it I assert that I have that belief and so express a second-level belief. But some or all of these appearances are misleading, says the expressivist. Rather, the utterance is an expression of the first-level psychological state it seems to describe. Let us consider in more detail how this is supposed to work for the psychological and whether an analogous move would help in explaining the authority of promising.

A crude and strong version of expressivism denies all the appearances, including the appearance that an avowal such as 'I believe that p' has the truth conditions that I believe that p. If this can be sustained, then our problem – viz., of explaining how I can be authoritative in saying those truth conditions obtain – just evaporates. But this solution is unattractive because it runs up against all the facts which make (2) so plausible, for example that avowals, such as 'I believe that p', are from an inferential point of view, smoothly bound in with related utterances such as 'Everyone who believes that p is a fool' or 'You believe that p' or 'I believed that p', which are agreed on all hands to have truth conditions.

Perhaps a subtler version of expressivism will do the job? (Such an account is elegantly set out and defended by Jacobsen [1996].) This theory agrees that 'I believe that p' has the meaning and the truth conditions it seems to have but denies that it has the full role it seems to have, viz., of an assertion (and hence expression of belief) about my psychological state. Rather, it says, the role of the utterance is just to be an expression of the state the existence of which it seems to assert. And, it adds, if an expression is sincere, then what it expresses exists and hence a sincere utterance of 'I believe that p' is bound to be true. So (says expressivism) we explain the authority we give to sincere avowals.

If this strategy accounts for the authority of avowals, presumably it ought to work for the authority of promising as well. The strong version of expressivism, applied to promises, denies that they have truth conditions at all. This is implausible for all the reasons which apply to psychological avowals, and arguments against it have been offered by many philosophers, among them Heal (1975), Lemmon (1962), Searle (1989) and Sinnott-Armstrong (1994). We shall therefore set the idea on one side, despite its venerable pedigree as the original Austinian orthodoxy about performatives.

But what of the subtler version? Applied to promising it comes out like this. We acknowledge that 'I promise to Φ' has truth conditions but, we say, it is not an assertion to the effect that they hold; rather it is a happening of some other kind, viz., an expression or additional manifestation of the fact that they hold. If this is to work it must be possible that training can set up in me a disposition to utter spontaneously, 'I promise to Φ' when I do promise to Φ (in the natural sense). This looks somewhat bizarre – but certainly not unimaginable. And we need not labour this difficulty since the major problem with the proposal does not lie here. Let us suppose the training undertaken and the disposition in place. So now I utter, sincerely, 'I promise to Φ'. Does it follow that my utterance has authority in that we must allow that I do indeed promise to Φ?

This depends on what is meant by 'sincere', in which a crucial ambiguity now becomes apparent. If an utterance is sincere only if it arises from the fact of my promising, then indeed it does follow. But if an utterance is sincere provided merely that it is produced spontaneously and in good faith, then it does not follow. The possible contrast arises because nothing we have said about the training shows that it must be so effective that no putative expression ever occurs spontaneously and in good faith but in the absence of the state which the training designs it to manifest. For all we know, there will be a fair number of false positives. Consider a parallel. Perhaps people could be trained to 'express' their blood pressure by uttering 'My blood pressure is such and such', but if so we would not treat their utterances as authoritative. Nothing we have said shows that the promising case could be any different. So the authority supposedly secured by the expressivist account has slipped through our fingers.

And looking again at the expressivist story in the psychological case, we see that it has the same flaw – at least it does if the functionalist account of truth conditions of belief claims is the one we are assuming. This is because the same crucial ambiguity of 'sincere' has to be confronted and the same potential gap opens up, namely between utterances which actually arise from the relevant first-order state and ones which are merely spontaneous and in good faith. The upshot is that expressivism cannot help us to an account of authority, either for promising or for the psychological, if it is combined with the natural concept of promising or with the functionalist concept of the psychological. So even at the price of giving up (2), expressivism cannot deliver (1) and (3).

Before we carry on let us ask whether the denial of (2) proposed in the subtle version of expressivism is, in any case, defensible. The claim is that avowals are not assertions and so do not express second-level beliefs. Expressivism thinks it has to say this because it sees an incompatibility between allowing that they express second-level beliefs and saying that they are expressions of the first-level states they seem to be about (Jacobsen 1996: 24–25).

But is it right to deny that 'I believe that p' or 'I promise to Φ' are assertions about the subject matter they seem to talk of? In a sense the question is verbal. We all acknowledge that the aetiology of these utterances and the focus of interest of the speaker will nearly always be different from that of many paradigm assertions. The speaker does not check on the existence of the state of affairs seemingly reported on before speaking, nor is her interest consciously focused on getting across information about it. So if these are what is needed to make something an assertion, then the utterances are not assertive.

But other important features are present, which might well be thought of equal significance to these, namely recognition by the speaker of commitments undertaken and of potential grounds for criticism and withdrawal. This is very obvious in the case of psychological avowals such as 'I believe that p'. Hence the idea that they are not assertions has always seemed a paradoxical view. But the same is also true in the case of promising. To see this it will help to consider cases where the authority of a promise giver might be challenged. For example, a person with impairment of long-term memory might say, 'I promise to Φ tomorrow', but if we know that the memory of this will disappear in ten minutes can we allow that a promise has been made? Or what of the case where Φ-ing is impossible and hence there can be no such thing as a tendency to do it? In these circumstances there is real doubt as to whether the speaker does promise (although we might agree that she 'sort of' promises), precisely because she does not show a tendency to Φ or entitle an observer to expect her to Φ. Also these are all cases where earnestness and a certain kind of sincerity may not be in doubt, and it is thus entirely natural to say that the person really thinks she promises. These observations point in the direction of allowing 'I promise to Φ' to be an assertion that one promises and an expression of belief that one does so. (Does this mean that expressivism is wrong throughout? Is there not plausibility also in the idea that 'I believe that p' expresses the belief that p? Indeed there is. And, as we shall see, a constitutive account can acknowledge that the utterance expresses this belief as well as the belief that I believe that p.)

In summary, we have tried and failed to account for the authority of 'I promise to Φ' from the blinkered philosopher's perspective. We have tried dualist, reliabilist and expressivist accounts, and none works. The moral, which has indeed been staring us in the face for a long time, is that we need to think again about the content of 'I promise to Φ'. Something is wrong with what the blinkered philosopher takes it to mean. But what?

The blinkered philosopher thinks that A promises to Φ iff A does something which shows a real tendency to Φ and so entitles an observer to expect that A will Φ. Where does that fail as an account of personal promising? What I would like to suggest is that it does not fail, at least as a schematic outline! Rather, the trouble arises from the blinkered philosopher's limited imagination in envisaging ways in which the outline can be filled in. Crucially, he assumes that it must be some prior existing performance which provides the truth maker for the claim. But if we widen our view by removing this limitation, another possibility becomes apparent. It is that uttering 'I promise to Φ' is itself the requisite doing. So making the statement that one fulfils the conditions for promising is itself what makes that statement true.

If saying 'I promise' is itself what makes it true that one promises, then uttering 'I promise' cannot be the upshot of inspection to see whether the truth conditions of the utterance hold, since there will be no such conditions to check on until the utterance is made. The utterance must then have a different aetiology. And indeed it does. What a person reflects on before making a promise is whether she should promise, that is, do something which shows in her a real tendency to Φ and so entitles an observer to expect that she will Φ. If the upshot of the deliberation is positive, then she utters 'I promise to Φ' to carry out her decision.

What this suggestion amounts to is that we have a practice with the word 'promise' which has the following shape:

(a) We determine that the descriptive phrase 'promises to Φ' shall be correctly applied to an item which does something that shows a real tendency to Φ and so entitles an observer to expect that it will Φ.

(b) We train people to debate on whether they should promise and, if the outcome is positive, to issue what look like first-person present-tense descriptions of themselves as promisors – but they are licensed to do so without paying any attention to whether or not they satisfy the criteria set out in (a).

(c) We tell those to whom such utterances are addressed to treat them as authoritative.

For many concepts a practice of this shape would be a recipe for disaster. If people were encouraged to pursue a resolution to be wealthy by saying 'I am wealthy' without paying any attention to their bank balances, and others were encouraged to believe them implicitly, we should be in for both inefficacy and muddle. An utterance made on these grounds is not likely either to forward the project of being wealthy or to inform

282

hearers accurately as to the speaker's financial position. But the envisaged practice with 'promise' does not have analogous problems, provided that the participants have enough psychological integrity to carry out resolutions they have made. To resolve to have a real tendency to Φ is (in effect) to resolve to Φ. So coming to have the state of mind which results from the deliberation (if its outcome is positive), together with its manifestation in the utterance 'I promise to Φ', is the right kind of performance to make it true that one satisfies the condition specified in (*a*), that is, promises to Φ.

Only certain kinds of beings can apply the term to themselves and others in the way licensed by these rules. The practice requires creatures who are capable of posing to themselves the question 'Should I promise?' and of carrying out the intention formed in answer to the question. Inanimate beings, or beings who are animate but unreflective, cannot do these things. Hence the only kind of promising they are capable of is the natural kind. But given reflective creatures who can operate the practice, what comes into existence as they engage in it is personal promising.

The existence of personal promising brings with it a host of corollaries. Whether or not to promise is a matter for decision and not a thing which merely happens to one. So reasons for promising can be presented to a person, by the potential recipient and others. As a result we are into the area of such things as pleading, generosity and meanness. Those who promise do usually carry through with their intentions, but sometimes they do not. As a result we are into the area of reliability and gratitude, or letdown and need for compensation. And because the practice may be abused, we are into the realm of dishonesty and trust. The blinkered philosopher's account of matters, we now see, is inadequate not only because it cannot deal with first-person authority in promising but because it overlooks large parts of the human significance of the action.

Personal promising is different from natural promising precisely in exhibiting a first/third-person asymmetry in ascription. At the same time, the occurrence so labelled is something observable from a third-person point of view, having real effects in the public world. The authority arises because promising is a happening which is both an action and a representation of that action. It is an action inasmuch as its aetiology and consequences are those of an action. But it is also a claim that the action occurs, inasmuch as its form is that of a statement and it carries commitments and consequences appropriate to this claim. So a person promises by saying that she promises.

The performative account we have here ended up with is not controversial, at least given the assumption that 'I promise to Φ' is an assertion. But what may be of use in helping us with the psychological is the route by which we have arrived at it, in particular the detour via natural promising. The suggestion which that detour is designed to make plausible is that there may exist an outline notion with two contrasted realisations, as in the case of natural and personal promising, and that grasping this may help to free up our thinking about the psychological.

One realisation of the outline notion comes from filling it in with concepts from natural science, for example, disposition, force and law. The other realisation is supplied by the practice specified in conditions (a)–(c). This second realisation is possible only because what comes into being under the procedure licensed by (b) is in fact something which satisfies the condition laid down in (a), despite the fact that the deliberation required in (b) is not focused on whether or not that condition holds. This coincidence means that the event which is the upshot of the deliberation has a dual nature. In virtue of its aetiology under (b) it is an action, but in virtue of its form and the inferential links which (a) and (c) attach to it, it is a statement. And what underpins the possibility of such a dual-natured item are in turn facts about the nature of the creatures engaging in the practice – in this particular case, their responsiveness to the needs and pleas of others and their psychological stability. Hence the second realisation of the outline notion presupposes the existence of such creatures and calls upon the concepts – for example, ability, value and reason – appropriate to describe them and their capacities. If, however, we approach personal promising with only the concepts of natural science in hand, then the viability of the practice, with all that it makes possible in terms of authoritative speech and other human interactions, will escape us, and we shall be locked into the unsatisfying perspective of the blinkered philosopher.

5. AVOWALS AND AUTHORITY

How might these ideas be applied to the psychological? The suggestion is that our struggles with first-person authority here also stem from our being locked in to a blinkered view. Many psychological notions have, like 'promise', (at least) two related senses, each of which represents a different realisation of one underlying schematic notion. And one of these realisations invites a constitutive account of authority.

Let us take belief as an example. The schematic notion is of a state of an organism which may be responsive to the world in perception and which guides behaviour towards desire satisfaction. (It is part of the picture I am sketching that 'desire' and 'perception' similarly have [at least] two related senses, and also other key terms like 'reason' and 'language'.) On one filling-out we arrive at the familiar account in functional/causal terms. In the resultant sense of 'belief', which we may call 'natural' belief, beliefs must be allowed to unreflective animals, and perhaps even to machines of some kinds. And we ourselves also have beliefs of this kind, ones which attract labels like 'tacit', 'non-conscious' or 'unconscious'. About our natural beliefs we are not authoritative, just as we are not authoritative about whether we promise in the natural sense. But there is also another filling-out of the schematic notion to yield what we may call personal belief, and this is the one which the blinkers prevent us from recognising. For this a constitutive account is appropriate, and consequently these beliefs are things about which we are authoritative.

The model of performatives must, however, be used with extreme circumspection in spelling out this proposal. The general category to which promising belongs is that of performance. Hence uttering 'I promise to Φ', being itself a performance, is of the right category to be a promise. But many of the psychological items on which we want light are persisting states. It would therefore be logically inappropriate to identify uttering, say, 'I believe that p' with believing that p. Moreover, this identification does not capture the fact that such an utterance often reports on the existence of a state which predates the utterance. Rather, the identification appropriate to a constitutive account is between what is expressed by the utterance if sincere, viz., belief that one is in the state in question, and the state itself.

Before turning to ask whether this idea can be defended, it is worth pausing to note the difference between it and another 'constitutive' proposal canvassed by Wright and statable in much the same words, viz., that second-level belief may constitute a first-level state (Wright 1989a, 1989b). On his approach, this thought is located in the context of a dichotomy between extension-determining and extension-reflecting judgements, and the suggestion is that self-ascriptions belong in the extension-determining class. The practice of respecting or challenging others' claims as we do 'enters primitively into the conditions of identification of what a subject believes, hopes and intends' (1989a: 632).

It is not part of Wright's proposal that first-level belief is always partly constituted by second-level belief, since he allows that behaviour by itself may sometimes licence belief attribution. The idea is rather that if behaviour alone neither mandates nor rules out belief attribution and second-level belief occurs, then the first-level belief must be allowed to exist (1989b: 253). In such cases, if a subject conceives herself to possess a belief, then, says Wright, there will be nothing else – that is, nothing over and above this self-conception and its coherence with her other behaviour – which makes it true that she does indeed have the belief. This is what it means to say that the judgement is extension-determining. So on these occasions we have a mental state which is, so to speak, defined into existence merely by its putative subject thinking that it exists. No cognitive achievement is involved in such first-person authority, as there is no separate state for the person's self-conception to be faithful to.

This view secures the benefits of a constitutive approach outlined in Section 2, namely avoiding the privileged confrontation picture of authority and so the pressures to dualism. There is, however, a price to be paid, and it is loss of adherence to desideratum (3), viz., acknowledgement of the reality and power of mental states. How can a mental state, conceived as constituted merely by the opinion that one has it, have any real efficacy? By contrast, on the constitutive view proposed in this essay, it is not the case that there is nothing over and above one's view that one believes which makes it true that one believes – any more than it is the case that when one gives a personal promise there is nothing over and above one's saying that one promises which makes it true that one does. In the case of the promising, there is the fact that one has done something which shows a real tendency to perform a certain action and so has entitled someone else to think that one will. In the case of belief, there is the fact that one is in a state which will (probably) lead to certain further inferences, actions and so forth. It is true in both cases that the vehicles of these further facts are the first-person ascriptions. But the rhetoric of 'nothing more than' is quite out of place, precisely because the self-ascriptions do have further powerful aspects. In short, Wright's story has a distinctly idealist tinge, whereas the one which is told here has no such implications.

But is this story defensible? There seem to be at least some uses of 'belief' where it fits quite well. Consider the case where a person is asked 'Do you believe that p?' and has no ready answer to give, having as yet no view on the matter. To answer the question she needs to make up her mind, that is, to decide what to believe. It is plausible that this practical question about what she is to believe is transparent to, namely must be answered via answering, the theoretical question about how things are in the world. (I owe this useful way of putting things to Moran [1999].)

So this kind of case is one where Evans' Wittgenstein-inspired account of how one self-ascribes a belief, viz., by attending to the world, is at its most convincing (Evans 1982: 225–226). So there is a use of 'I believe that p' to express the making up of one's mind.

At this point the earlier considerations, invoked in connection with expressivism, can be called upon again to show that this 'I believe that p' is to be taken as an assertion that one believes that p. Hence this part of our practice with the word 'belief' has interesting similarities to the practice with 'promise' outlined earlier. There we had an action which was both a promise and an assertion. Here we have a judgement which is both the judgement 'p' (since it results from deliberation on that issue and has those consequences) and the judgement 'I believe that p' (since it has that form and those consequences too). So it is a judgement which represents the world as being a certain way in representing the self as being a certain way.

Against such a constitutive account it has been urged that we can distinguish between 'What should I believe?' and 'What do I believe?' Only the former, it is said, is transparent to 'What is so?' while the latter is a theoretical question, enquiring only about a current state of the self (Moran 1988). An implication of the last paragraph is that this is too quick. It is true that 'What do I believe?' may have a theoretical and solely self-directed reading, for example if I am concerned with my natural beliefs. But that is not the only way of taking it. The event of judgement expressed in 'I believe that p' has long-term consequences. In a mind which is stable and retentive, it will be the onset of a continuing state which has the same two aspects as the judgement and which can later express itself equally in 'p' and 'I believe that p'. This continuing state, surely one of the things which we call 'belief', is both an apprehension of the self and at the same time an apprehension of the world. It follows that the constitutive account of first-person authority is appropriate for it.

The constitutive account can be extended to other cases also. We credit people with belief in those propositions to which they would assent without hesitation because the answer is implicit in things to which they are already explicitly committed. For example, five minutes ago (if this is your first reading of this essay) you believed (in this extended sense) that there are no orchids on the moon. Did you then also believe that you believed that there are no orchids on the moon? We should agree that you did, since your answer to 'Do you think that there are orchids on the moon?' would have come just as readily and unhesitatingly as your answer to 'Are there orchids on the moon?'.

287

It looks extremely plausible also that a similar story can be told about our authority in reporting on our own intentions. Here too there is a use of 'I intend to Φ' which expresses a decision but should also be taken as a self-description. And in this case, too, the event may mark the onset of a continuing state which has the dual aspects of being an intention and a belief about that intention. The upshot is that the constitutive account of authority seems to fit with at least some of the ways in which belief and intention figure in our lives. But of course there is much more to be said, about these and also about other psychological concepts.

In Section 2 we asked whether a constitutive account could be had without bizarre metaphysics. The metaphysical assumption of the account turns out to be this: that there exist beings capable of successfully operating the practices described (for making promises or ascribing beliefs and intentions) and whose actions and states can therefore rightly be described by 'promise', 'belief' or 'intention' in the personal sense. The practices described have in common the characteristic that operating them requires a subject to announce as fact what she has seen reason to think ought to be so. Hence the practices require beings who are capable of becoming aware of and responding appropriately to values both epistemic and non-epistemic. There is therefore a dualism of a sort implicit in the picture – not a dualism of public and private, but rather a dualism of value-free and value-infused. And there is, of course, also much more to be said about whether or not that is a bizarre metaphysics and how it might interrelate with the metaphysics of natural science.[4]

---

4. Some interesting recent discussions, by Shoemaker (1996a, 1996b), Burge (1996, 1998) and Moran (1988, 1999), explore links between reflective rationality and authority. It may be that the proposal here would dovetail conveniently with their ideas.

References

Altham, J. E. J. 1979. Indirect Reflexives and Indirect Speech. In C. Diamond and J. Teichman, eds., *Intention and Intentionality*, 25–37. Ithaca, N.Y.: Cornell University Press.

Anscombe, E. 1957. *Intention*. Oxford: Basil Blackwell.

Austin, J. L. 1962. *How to Do Things with Words*. Oxford: Oxford University Press.

Bach, K. 1982. De re Belief and Methodological Solipsism. In A. Woodfield, ed., *Thought and Object*, 121–151. Oxford: Clarendon Press.

Baldwin, T. 1990. *G. E. Moore*. London and New York: Routledge.

Berlin, I. 1976. *Vico and Herder*. London: Hogarth Press.

Bigelow, J. 1975. Contexts and Quotations I. *Linguistische Berichte* 38:1–22; Contexts and Quotations II. *Linguistische Berichte* 39:1–22.

Blackburn, S. 1975. The Identity of Propositions. In *Meaning, Reference and Necessity*, ed. S. Blackburn. Cambridge: Cambridge University Press.

—— 1995. Theory, Observation and Drama. In M. Davies and T. Stone, eds., *Folk Psychology: The Theory of Mind Debate*, 274–90. Oxford: Basil Blackwell.

Block, N., ed. 1980. *Readings in the Philosophy of Psychology*. Vol. 1. Cambridge, Mass.: Harvard University Press.

Boden, M. 1990. *The Philosophy of Artificial Intelligence*. Oxford: Oxford University Press.

Brandom, R. B. 1994. *Making It Explicit*. Cambridge, Mass.: Harvard University Press.

Burge, T. 1982. Other Bodies. In A. Woodfield, ed., *Thought and Object*, 97–120. Oxford: Clarendon Press.

—— 1996. Our Entitlement to Self-Knowledge. *Proceedings of the Aristotelian Society* 96:96–116.

—— 1998. Reason and the First Person. In C. Wright, B. Smith and C. Macdonald, eds., *Knowing Our Own Minds*, 243–70. Oxford: Oxford University Press.

Carruthers, P., and Smith, P. K., eds. 1996. *Theories of Theories of Mind*. Cambridge: Cambridge University Press.

Cherniak. C. 1986. *Minimal Rationality*. Cambridge, Mass.: MIT Press.

Churchland, P. 1981. Eliminative Materialism and the Propositional Attitudes. *Journal of Philosophy* 78:67–90. Reprinted in W. G. Lycan, ed., *Mind and Cognition*. Oxford: Basil Blackwell, 1990.

Clark, H. H., and Gerrig, R. J. 1991. Quotations as Demonstrations. *Language* 66:764–805.

Cohen, J. 1999. Holism: Some Reasons for Buyer's Remorse. *Analysis* 59:63–71.

Cohen, L. J. 1980. The Individuation of Proper Names. In Zak van Straaten, ed., *Philosophical Subjects: Essays Presented to P. F. Strawson*, 140–63. Oxford: Oxford University Press.

Collingwood, R. G. 1946. *The Idea of History*. Oxford: Oxford University Press.

Crimmins, M. 1992a. Context in the Attitudes. *Linguistics and Philosophy* 15:185–198.

1992b. *Talk about Beliefs*. Cambridge, Mass.: MIT Press.

Davidson, D. 1979. Quotation. *Theory and Decision* 11:27–40

1980a. *Essays on Actions and Events*. Oxford: Oxford University Press.

1980b. Mental Events. In his *Essays on Actions and Events*, 207–228. Oxford: Oxford University Press.

1984. *Inquiries into Truth and Interpretation*. Oxford: Oxford University Press.

1968. On Saying That. *Synthese* 19:130–146. Reprinted in his *Inquiries into Truth and Interpretation*, 93–108. Oxford: Oxford University Press, 1984.

Davies, M. 1994. The Mental Simulation Debate. In C. Peacocke, ed., *Objectivity, Simulation and the Unity of Consciousness*, 99–127. Oxford: Oxford University Press.

Davies, M., and Stone, T. 1996. The Mental Simulation Debate: A Progress Report. In Carruthers and Smith 1996 (eds.) *Theories of Theories of Mind*, 119–137. Cambridge: Cambridge University Press.

2002. Mental Simulation, Tacit Theory, and the Threat of Collapse. In C. Hill and H. Kornblith, eds., *Philosophical Topics* (forthcoming).

Davies, M., and Stone, T., eds. 1995a. *Folk Psychology: The Theory of Mind Debate*. Oxford: Basil Blackwell.

1995b. *Mental Simulation: Evaluations and Applications*. Oxford: Basil Blackwell.

Dennett, D. 1979. Intentional Systems. In his *Brainstorms*, 3–22. Brighton: Harvester Press.

1982. Making Sense of Ourselves. In J. I. Biro and R. W. Shahan, eds., *Mind, Brain and Function*, 63–81. Brighton: Harvester Press. Reprinted with an appendix in his *The Intentional Stance*, 83–116. Cambridge, Mass.: MIT Press, 1987.

1984. Cognitive Wheels: The Frame Problem of AI. In M. Boden, ed., *The Philosophy of Artificial Intelligence*. Oxford: Oxford University Press.

1987a. *The Intentional Stance*. Cambridge, Mass.: MIT Press.

1987b. True Believers. In his *The Intentional Stance*, 13–35. Cambridge, Mass.: MIT Press.

1991. Real Patterns. *Journal of Philosophy* 88:27–51.

de Sousa, R. 1987. *The Rationality of Emotion*. Cambridge, Mass.: MIT Press.

Dilthey, W. 1976. *Selected Writings*, ed. H. P. Rickman. Cambridge: Cambridge University Press.

Dreyfus, H. L., and Dreyfus, S. 1986. *Mind over Machine*. New York: Free Press, Macmillan.

Dummett, M. 1975. What Is a Theory of Meaning? In S. Guttenplan, ed., *Mind and Language*. Oxford University Press.

Evans, G. 1982. *The Varieties of Reference*. Oxford: Oxford University Press.

———. 1985. Pronouns, Quantifiers and Relative Clauses (I). In his *Collected Papers*, 76–152. Oxford: Oxford University Press.

Field, H. 1977. Logic, Meaning and Conceptual Role. *The Journal of Philosophy* 74:379–409.

———. 1978. Mental Representation. *Erkenntnis* 13:9–61.

Fodor, J. A. 1980. Methodological Solipsism Considered as a Research Strategy in Cognitive Psychology. *The Behavioral and Brain Sciences* 3:63–73.

———. 1987. *Psychosemantics*. Cambridge, Mass.: MIT Press.

Fodor, J., and Lepore, E. 1992. *Holism: A Shopper's Guide*. Oxford: Basil Blackwell.

Forbes, G. 1993. Solving the Iteration Problem. *Linguistics and Philosophy* 16: 311–330.

Fricker, E. 1998. Self-Knowledge: Special Access versus Artefact of Grammar – A Dichotomy Rejected. In C. Wright, B. Smith and C. Macdonald, eds., *Knowing Our Own Minds*, 155–206. Oxford: Oxford University Press.

Fuller, G. 1995. Simulation and Psychological Concepts. In M. Davies and T. Stone, eds., *Mental Simulation: Evaluations and Applications*, 19–32. Oxford: Basil Blackwell.

Givon, T. 1980. The Binding Hierarchy and the Typology of Complements. *Studies in Language* 4:333–377.

Goldman, A. 1995a. Interpretation Psychologised. In M. Davies and T. Stone, eds., *Folk Psychology: The Theory of Mind Debate*, 74–99. Oxford: Basil Blackwell.

———. 1995b: In Defence of the Simulation Theory. In M. Davies and T. Stone, eds., *Folk Psychology: The Theory of Mind Debate*, 191–206. Oxford: Basil Blackwell.

———. 2000a. Folk Psychology and Mental Concepts. *Protosociology* 14:4–25.

———. 2000b. The Mentalizing Folk. In D. Sperber, ed., *Metarepresentation*. Vancouver Studies in Cognitive Science. Oxford: Oxford University Press.

Gombay, A. 1988. Some Paradoxes of Counterprivacy. *Philosophy* 63:191–210.

Gordon, R. 1995a. Folk Psychology as Simulation. In M. Davies and T. Stone, eds., *Folk Psychology: The Theory of Mind Debate*, 60–73. Oxford: Basil Blackwell.

———. 1995b. Simulation without Introspection or Inference from Me to You. In M. Davies and T. Stone, eds., *Mental Simulation: Evaluations and Applications*, 53–67. Oxford: Basil Blackwell.

———. 1995c. Reply to Stich and Nichols. In M. Davies and T. Stone, eds., *Folk Psychology: The Theory of Mind Debate*, 174–184. Oxford: Basil Blackwell.

———. 1996. 'Radical' Simulationism. In P. Carruthers and P. K. Smith, eds., *Theories of Theories of Mind*, 11–21. Cambridge: Cambridge University Press.

Greenwood, John D., ed. 1991. *The Future of Folk Psychology*. Cambridge: Cambridge University Press.

Grover, D.; Camp, I. L.; and Belnap, N. D. 1975. A Prosentential Theory of Truth. *Philosophical Studies* 27:73–125.

Guest, A. H. 1984. *Dance Notation*. London: Dance Books.

Hand, M. 1991. On Saying That Again. *Linguistics and Philosophy* 14:349–365.

Harman, G. 1973. *Thought*. Princeton, N.J.: Princeton University Press.

Harris, P. L. 1995. From Simulation to Folk Psychology: The Case for Development. In M. Davies and T. Stone, eds., *Folk Psychology: The Theory of Mind Debate*, 207–231. Oxford: Basil Blackwell.

Heal, J. 1974. Explicit Performative Utterances and Statements. *Philosophical Quarterly* 24:106–121.

———. 1989. *Fact and Meaning.* Oxford: Basil Blackwell.

———. 1994. Simulation vs. Theory Theory: What Is at Issue? In C. Peacocke, ed., *Objectivity, Simulation and the Unity of Consciousness*, 129–44. Oxford: Oxford University Press.

———. 1995. How to Think about Thinking. In M. Davies and T. Stone, eds., *Mental Simulation: Evaluations and Applications*, 33–52. Oxford: Basil Blackwell.

———. 1999. Thoughts and Holism: Reply to Cohen. *Analysis* 59:71–78.

Higginbotham, J. 1986. Linguistic Theory and Davidson's Programme in Semantics. In E. Lepore, ed., *Truth and Interpretation*, 29–48. Oxford: Basil Blackwell.

Hornsby, J. 1977. Saying Of. *Analysis* 37:77–185.

Hursthouse, R. 1991. Arational Actions. *Journal of Philosophy* 88:57–68.

Jacobsen, R. 1996. Wittgenstein on Self-Knowledge and Self-Expression. *Philosophical Quarterly* 46:12–30.

Jespersen, O. 1933. *Essentials of English Grammar.* London: Allen and Unwin.

Jones, O. R. 1991. Moore's Paradox, Assertion and Knowledge. *Analysis* 51:183–186.

Kant, I. 1953. *Critique of Pure Reason*, trans. Norman Kemp Smith. London: Macmillan.

Kaplan, D. 1989. Demonstratives. In J. Almog, J. Perry and H. Wettstein, eds., *Themes from Kaplan*, 481–563. Oxford: Oxford University Press.

Kenny, A. 1963. *Action, Emotion and Will.* London: Routledge and Kegan Paul.

Kripke, S. 1980. *Naming and Necessity.* Oxford: Basil Blackwell.

———. 1982. *Wittgenstein on Rules and Private Language.* Oxford: Basil Blackwell.

Kuhberger, A.; Perner, J.; Schulte, M.; and Leingruber, R. 1995. Choice or No Choice: Is the Langer Effect Evidence against Simulation? *Mind and Language* 10: 423–436.

Larson, R., and Ludlow, P. 1993. Interpreted Logical Forms. *Synthese* 95:305–355.

Larson, R., and Segal, G. 1995. *Knowledge of Meaning.* Cambridge, Mass.: MIT Press.

Lemmon, E. J. 1962. On Sentences Verifiable by Their Use. *Analysis* 22:86–89.

Lepore, E., and Loewer B. 1989. You Can Say *That* Again. *Midwest Studies in Philosophy* 14:338–355.

Leslie, A., and German, T. 1995. Knowledge and Ability in 'Theory of Mind': One-eyed Overview of a Debate. In M. Davies and T. Stone, eds., *Mental Simulation: Evaluations and Applications*, 123–150. Oxford: Basil Blackwell.

Lewis, D. 1972. Psychological and Theoretical Identifications. *Australasian Journal of Philosophy* 50:249–258.

———. 1983. *Philosophical Papers, Vol. 2.* Oxford: Oxford University Press.

Linville, K., and Ring, M. 1991. Moore's Paradox Revisited. *Synthese* 87:295–309.

Margolis E., and Laurence S., eds. 1999. *Concepts: Core Readings.* Cambridge, Mass.: MIT Press.

Martin, M. 1998. An Eye Directed Outward. In C. Wright, B. Smith and C. Macdonald, eds., *Knowing Our Own Minds*, 99–122. Oxford: Oxford University Press.

McDowell, J. 1980. Quotation and Saying That. In M. Platts, ed., *Reference, Truth and Reality*, 206–237. London: Routledge.

——— 1982. Criteria, Defeasibility and Knowledge. *Proceedings of the British Academy* 68:455–479.

——— 1994. *Mind and World*. Cambridge, Mass.: Harvard University Press.

——— 1995. *Mind, Value and Reality*. Cambridge, Mass.: Harvard University Press.

McFetridge, I. 1976. Propositions and Davidson's Account of Indirect Discourse. *Proceedings of the Aristotelian Society* 76:131–145.

McGinn, C. 1982. The Structure of Content. In A. Woodfield, ed., *Thought and Object*, 207–258. Oxford: Clarendon Press.

Mellor, D. H. 1991. I and Now. In his *Matters of Metaphysics*, 17–29. Cambridge: Cambridge University Press.

Moore, G. E. 1942. Reply to My Critics. In P. Schilpp, ed., *The Philosophy of G. E. Moore*. La Salle, Ill.: Open Court.

——— 1944. Russell's Theory of Descriptions. In P. Schilpp, ed., *The Philosophy of Bertrand Russell*. La Salle, Ill.: Open Court.

Moore, J. F. 1999. Propositions, Numbers and the Problem of Arbitrary Identification. *Synthese* 120:229–263.

Moore, J. G. 1999. Propositions without Identity. *Nous* 33:1–29.

Moran, R. 1994. Interpretation Theory and the First Person. *Philosophical Quarterly* 44:154–173.

——— 1988. Making Up Your Mind: Self-Interpretation and Self-Constitution. *Ratio* (new series) 1:135–151.

——— 1999. The Authority of Self-Consciousness. *Philosophical Topics* 26:179–200.

Nichols, S.; Stich, S.; and Leslie, A. 1995. Choice Effects and the Ineffectiveness of Simulation. *Mind and Language* 10:437–445.

Nichols, S.; Stich, S.; Leslie, A.; and Klein, D. 1996. Varieties of Off-Line Simulation. In P. Carruthers and P. K. Smith, (eds.), *Theories of Theories of Mind*, 39–74. Cambridge: Cambridge University Press.

Nozick, R. 1995. *The Nature of Rationality*. Princeton, N.J.: Princeton University Press.

Oliver, A. 1996. The Metaphysics of Properties. *Mind* 105:1–80.

Peacocke, C. 1992. *A Study of Concepts*. Cambridge, Mass.: MIT Press.

——— 1996. Entitlement, Self-Knowledge and Conceptual Redeployment. *Proceedings of the Aristotelian Society* 96:117–158.

——— 1998. Conscious Attitudes, Attention, and Self-Knowledge. In C. Wright, B. Smith and C. Macdonald, eds., *Knowing Our Own Minds*, 63–98. Oxford: Oxford University Press.

——— 1999. *Being Known*. Oxford: Oxford University Press.

Pears, D. 1991. Wittgenstein's Account of Rule Following. *Synthese* 87:273–283.

Perner, J. 1994. The Necessity and Impossibility of Simulation. *Proceedings of the British Academy* 83:129–144.

Perry, J. 1979. The Problem of the Essential Indexical. *Nous* 13:3–21.

Putnam, H., 1975a. The Meaning of 'Meaning'. In his *Mind, Language and Reality: Philosophical Papers*, Vol. II, 215–271. New York: Cambridge University Press.

——— 1975b. The Nature of Mental States. In his *Mind, Language and Reality: Philosophical Papers*, Vol. II, 429–440. New York: Cambridge University Press.

293

Pylyshyn, Z. 1980. Computation and Cognition: Issues in the Foundations of Cognitive Science. *Behavioural and Brain Sciences* 3:111–32.

Quine, W. V. O. 1953. Two Dogmas of Empiricism. In W. V. O. Quine, *From a Logical Point of View*, 20–46. Cambridge, Mass.: Harvard University Press.

1960. *Word and Object.* Cambridge, Mass.: MIT Press.

1969. *Ontological Relativity and Other Essays.* New York: Columbia University Press.

Recanati, F. 2000. *Oratio Obliqua, Oratio Recta.* Cambridge, Mass.: MIT Press.

Richard, M. 1990. *Propositional Attitudes.* New York: Cambridge University Press.

1993. Attitudes and Context. *Linguistics and Philosophy* 16:123–148.

1997. Propositional Attitudes. In B. Hale and C. Wright, eds., *A Companion to the Philosophy of Language*, 197–226. Oxford: Basil Blackwell.

Robins, M. H. 1986. Intention and Control. *Theoria* 52:41–56.

Rumfitt, I. 1993. Content and Context: The Paratactic Theory Revisited and Revised. *Mind* 102:429–445.

Sainsbury, M. 1991. *Logical Forms.* Oxford: Basil Blackwell.

1997. Reporting Indexicals. In M. Sainsbury, ed., *Thought and Ontology*, 161–172. Milan: Franco Angeli.

Salmon, N. 1986. Reflexivity. *Notre Dame Journal of Formal Logic* 27:401–429.

Schiffer, S. 1987. *Remnants of Meaning.* Cambridge, Mass.: MIT Press.

Searle, J. 1989. How Performatives Work. *Linguistics and Philosophy* 12:535–558.

Sellars, W. 1963. *Science Perception and Reality.* London: Routledge.

Shoemaker, S. 1996a. On Knowing One's Own Mind. In *The First-Person Perspective and Other Essays*, 25–49. New York: Cambridge University Press.

1996b. Self-Knowledge and "Inner Sense" Lecture II; The Broad Perceptual Model. In his *The First-Person Perspective and Other Essays*, 224–245. New York: Cambridge University Press.

Sinnot-Armstrong, W. 1994. The Truth of Performatives. *International Journal of Philosophical Studies* 2:99–107.

Smith, M. 1994. *The Moral Problem.* Oxford: Basil Blackwell.

Soames, S. 1987. Direct Reference, Propositional Attitudes and Semantic Content. *Philosophical Topics* 15:47–88.

Sorensen, R. 1988. *Blindspots.* Oxford: Oxford University Press.

Stein, E. 1996. *Without Good Reason.* Oxford: Oxford University Press.

Stich, S. 1982a. On the Ascription of Content. In A. Woodfield, ed., *Thought and Object*, 153–206. Oxford: Clarendon Press.

1982b. Dennett on Intentional Systems. In J. I. Biro and R. W. Shahan, eds., *Mind, Brain and Function*, 39–62. Brighton: Harvester Press.

1990. *The Fragmentation of Reason.* Cambridge, Mass.: MIT Press.

1993. *The Fragmentation of Reason.* Cambridge, Mass.: MIT Press.

1996. *Deconstructing the Mind.* Oxford: Oxford University Press.

Stich, S., and Nichols, S. 1995a. Folk Psychology: Simulation or Tacit Theory? In M. Davies and T. Stone, eds., *Folk Psychology: The Theory of Mind Debate*, 123–158. Oxford: Basil Blackwell.

1995b: Second Thoughts on Simulation. In M. Davies and T. Stone, eds., *Mental Simulation: Evaluations and Applications*, 87–108. Oxford: Basil Blackwell.

1997. Cognitive Penetrability, Rationality and Restricted Simulation. *Mind and Language* 12:297–326.

Stone, T., and Davies, M. 1996. The Mental Simulation Debate: A Progress Report. In P. Carruthers and P. K. Smith, eds., *Theories of Theories of Mind*, 119–137. Cambridge: Cambridge University Press.

Stoneham, T. 1998. On Believing That I Am Thinking. *Proceedings of the Aristotelian Society* 98:125–144.

Swift, J. 1726/1963. *Gulliver's Travels*. London: Penguin Classics.

Taylor, C. 1985. *Human Agency and Human Language, Philosophical Papers*. Vol. 1. Cambridge: Cambridge University Press.

Travis, C. 1989. *The Uses of Sense*. Oxford: Oxford University Press.

Unger, P. 1984. *Philosophical Relativity*. Oxford: Basil Blackwell.

Wellman, H. M. 1990. *The Child's Theory of Mind*. Cambridge, Mass.: MIT Press.

Wiggins, D. 1984. A Running Repair to Frege's Doctrine and a Plea for the Copula. In C. Wright, ed., *Frege: Tradition and Influence*, 126–143. Oxford: Basil Blackwell.

1986. Verbs and Adverbs and Some Other Modes of Grammatical Combination. *Proceedings of the Aristotelian Society* 86:273–304.

Wittgenstein, L. 1953. *Philosophical Investigations*. Oxford: Basil Blackwell.

1969. *On Certainty*. Oxford: Basil Blackwell.

1980. *Remarks on the Philosophy of Psychology*. Vol. 1. Oxford: Basil Blackwell.

Index

Forbes, G., 192, 192n
Frame Problem, 3, 54, 55–9
Fricker, E., 274n
Fuller, G., 202, 204
functionalism as a theory of mind,
    28–29
    implausibilities of, 3, 13, 49
    inability to explain Moore's paradox,
        265–268
    and Moore's paradox, 259–265
    see also theory theory

gambler's fallacy, 148, 233, 242, 243,
    244
German, T., 67
Gerrig, R. J., 185
Givon, T., 187
Goldman, A., ix, 46, 64, 77, 85, 132
    on links of simulation with
        psychological concepts, 196, 197,
        202, 203
golfers, varying skills of, 123 ff.
Gombay, A., 250n, 269
good bad reasoning, 147 ff., 244
Gordon, R., ix, 83, 85, 107, 136, 137,
    197, 204
    on the concept of belief, 216–219
Greenwood, J. D., 225n
Grice's account of meaning, and
    Moore's paradox, 254–255
Grover, D., 161
Guest, A., 177

Hand, M., 191
Harman, G., 12
Harris, P., 64, 76, 83, 85
Heal, J., 35, 64, 76, 108, 113, 115n,
    116n, 119, 226n, 272n, 279
Higginbotham, J., 186, 187, 188
Hill, C., ix
holism
    epistemic holism, 20–21, 51–53
    holism of the mental, 12–13, 20–21
    semantic holism, 53, 115 ff.
holistic property, 118
Hornsby, J., ix, 189n
Hursthouse, R., 79

imaginative identification with another,
    137–138
imagining, 3, 6
    'faint copy' theory of, 60–62, 77–78
    see also co-cognition and simulation
indexical predication, 7
    applications of, 171–173
    and indirect discourse, 174–195
    and psychological concepts,
        205–222
    what it is, 153–170
indirect discourse, 8, 174 ff.
intentions, that they have a belief-like
    aspect, 126

Jacobsen, R., 279, 280
Jesperson, O., 162n
Jones, O. R., 254n

Kant, I., 2, 29, 35
Kaplan, D., 24, 160n, 171, 201, 215
Kenny, A., 80
Klein, D., 63
Kripke, S., 201, 208, 209, 225n
Kuhberger, A., 85, 86

Lagadonian kind
    defined, 210
    essentially Lagadonian kinds, 221
    link with non-conceptual content,
        172n, 210
    psychological kinds as, 212 ff.
Lagoda, capital of Balnibarbi, 198n
Larson, R., 191, 192, 192n
Lawrence, S., 200
Lemmon, E. J., 279
Lepore, E., 115, 118, 119, 120, 121,
    122, 125, 183
Leslie, A., 63, 67, 83, 87
Lewis, D., 12, 155, 157, 158n
Loewer, B., 119, 183
logical form, 163 ff.
Lottery Ticket Buy-back, 84
Ludlow, P., 192, 192n

Macdonald, C., 274n
Margolis, E., 200

rationality
    as central to thought, 7, 8, 18, 20, 41,
        102, 122, 125, 225
    comparison with sight, 238
    how and how not to define, 21, 27,
        78–79, 142 ff., 228 ff.
    individual variations in manifestation
        of, 149, 237–241
    two-element conception of,
        237 ff.
relevance, difficulty in defining, 55
replicative strategy, 11 ff.
    see also simulation theory and
        co-cognition
Richard, M., 192, 192n, 194
Robins, M. H., 127
Rumfitt, I., 174, 189n, 192

Sainsbury, M., 164n, 186
Salmon, N., 192, 192n
samedoing, 206
samethinking, 197
scepticism, eliminative and
        epistemological, 225
Schiffer, S., 183
Searle, J. R., 279
Segal, G., 191, 192, 192n
Sellars, W., 174n
semantic direct reports, 185
semantic holism, see holism
semantic innocence, 189, 214
Shoemaker, S., 288n
Shopping Mall Questionnaire, 83
simulation theory, 4–7,
        29–30
    alternative articulations of,
        33–36
    ambiguities of, 93, 112, 197
    as an a priori claim, 36–40
    definitions of, 46, 92
    domain of, 75 ff.
    as an empirical hypothesis,
        33–35
    relation to imagining, 60–62
    unfortunate associations of the term,
        107

what states can and cannot be
        simulated, 80, 146–147
    see also co-cognition and replicative
        strategy
'sincere', ambiguity of, 280
Sinnott-Armstrong, W., 279
Smith, B., x, 274n
Smith, M., 80
Smith, P. K., 196
Soames, S., 192, 192n
Sorenson, R., 255n
Spinoza, 48
Stein, E., 42, 142
Stich, S., x, 12, 16, 46, 47, 142, 202,
        225n
    on alternative understandings of
        simulation, 91–113 passim
    on simulation and cognitive
        penetration, 63–88 passim
Stone, T., 64, 76, 196
Stoneham, T., 276n
subject matters of thought, 37, 94–96
subject
    living creatures as our paradigms of,
        129
    as a unified locus of cognitive virtues,
        122 ff.
    why I think of myself as one, 125 ff.
Swift, J., 198

theory theory, 2–3, 28, 64, 111
    contrasted understandings of, 47–48,
        66–67, 92, 100
    implausibility of, 50–59
Travis, C., 155, 158
tune, context-relativity of identity, 178,
        190

understanding from the inside,
        28 ff. 35
    attraction of the idiom, 40–41
Unger, P., 155

vegetables and photographs, 95 ff.
Verstehen, 2, 3, 7, 29, 77
Vico, 2, 29

Weber, M., 2
Wellman, H., 49
whisky, predicting the effects of, 75, 76
Wiggins, D., 158n
Williamson, T., x, 147
wise woman, 47

Wittgenstein, L., 94, 127, 225, 226n, 227, 249, 256, 257, 259, 265
  on Moore's paradox, 252, 253, 268 ff.
Woodfield, A., 19
Wright, C., 225n, 274n
  on 'constitutive' account of first-person authority, 285–286